PRAISE FOR MARY KOLE

"*Writing Interiority* is for all writers ready to level up. Once again, Mary Kole has delivered an entire master class within one volume. I was fortunate enough to work under Mary's tutelage a couple of years ago in the Story Mastermind writing program (aka the best thing I ever did for my craft), and this book is a close second. It digs into the ins and outs of developing your character's inner monologue—something many writers struggle with. Mary touches upon the concept within *Writing Irresistible Kidlit*, and this book picks up where that left off. I highly recommend *Writing Interiority* for your next craft book."

ZANE RÉ-BLOOM

"*Writing Interiority* is crafted for guaranteed learning. Awesome reference tool to assist your writing endeavors. The craft and techniques contained within the lines are a goldmine for those wishing to find joy and new directions in their writing. The book is written to spark maximum reading and retention so writers can unlock their full potential, understand and demystify important concepts. Mary Kole is amazing in writing talent and full mastery ... only someone with understanding can make this look so simple. A very rewarding read, so stick with it, give it time, [and it will] supercharge your writing."

JANIS SMITH

"The craft world needed *Writing Interiority*! Such a difficult concept to do right if it doesn't come naturally. This book will give me better tools to improve my skills. It was broken up so clearly and logically."

"*Writing Interiority* explains step-by-step how to create and convey character thoughts, feelings, reactions and interpretations, expectations, and inner struggles on the page. With examples from more than fifty books, it is a masterclass on the topic and I'm sure I will reference it for years to come. I've recommended it to all my writing friends as a must-read book on the topic of creating engaging characters that readers are compelled to read about. Thank you Mary for writing such an invaluable resource."

"Mary truly is amazing! Thanks to her, I have learned so much about writing. She made me laugh. She made me cry. She made me a better writer!"

"I've read many books on the craft of writing, and *Writing Irresistible Kidlit* is among the best. I've never been so excited to get to the keyboard."

"The advice is wonderful, thoughtful, and so clearly written that no writer could read *Writing Irresistible Kidlit* and not walk away with something gained from it."

"Mary Kole brings years of solid experience and insight to the art of writing literature for younger audiences."

"From now on, if I see a writing craft book with Mary Kole's name on it, I will hit the 'one click purchase' button without a second thought. She respects writers. She feels for writers. She understands writers. She knows exactly what insights writers need as they work. *Writing Irresistible Kidlit* is possibly the very best book on writing craft I have read in twenty-five years."

"Mary Kole made me feel a renewed enthusiasm toward my writing goals."

"*Writing Irresistible Kidlit* is quite simply, the best 'how to' book on novel writing that I've ever read and probably ever will read in my life."

"Mary Kole helped me to find my way. Her suggestions on my query letter are just what I needed to begin fearlessly searching for a place to call my own. I now consider Mary Kole my secret weapon."

"Writing Irresistible Kidlit is the perfect blend of technical 'how to' guidance mixed with a healthy dose of encouragement. If anything I write in the future ever sells, I feel I may owe Ms. Kole a royalty for her shaping input from this book."

A. GABLE

"Mary Kole knows all that a story needs to be to be successful in today's market."

R. TATE

"I'm a big fan of everything Mary Kole does and this book was no exception. I learned so much reading Mary's feedback on the various components of each query letter in *Irresistible Query Letters.*"

JAMIE L.

"Kole is clearly passionate about her work and the world of kidlit, and that passion spills over the pages of *Writing Irresistible Kidlit.*"

ASHLEY B.

WRITING IRRESISTIBLE FIRST PAGES

HOW TO CRAFT COMPELLING STORY OPENINGS THAT WILL HOOK GATEKEEPERS AND READERS

MARY KOLE

GOOD
STORY
PUBLISHING

"Writing Irresistible First Pages: How to Craft Compelling Story Openings That Hook Gatekeepers and Readers"
By Mary Kole

1. Reference / Writing, Research, and Publishing Guides / Writing

FIRST EDITION
Print ISBN: 978-1-939162-19-9

Cover Design: Jenna Van Rooy
Editing: Amy Wilson
Author Photo: Joe Ferrucci
Printed in the United States of America

ABOUT THE AUTHOR

A former literary agent, Mary Kole knows the ins and outs of the publishing industry. She founded Mary Kole Editorial in 2013 to provide consulting and developmental editing services to writers across all categories and genres. She started Good Story Company in 2019 to create valuable content like the Good Story Podcast, Good Story YouTube channel, and the Writing Craft Workshop membership community. Her Story Mastermind small group workshop intensives help writers level up their craft, and she offers done-for-you revision and ghostwriting with Manuscript Studio.

She also develops unique and commercial intellectual property for middle grade, young adult, and adult readers with Bittersweet Books, alongside literary agent John Cusick and #1 *New York Times* best-selling author Julie Murphy.

Mary has appeared at regional, national, and international writing conferences for the SCBWI, Writer's Digest, Penn Writers, Writer's League of Texas, San Francisco Writers Conference, WIFYR, Writing Day, NINC, and many others. Her guest lectures have taken her to Harvard, the Ringling College of Art and Design, the Highlights Foundation, and more. Mary's recorded video classes can be found online at Writing Mastery Academy, Writing Blueprints, Udemy, and LinkedIn Learning.

Mary holds an MFA in Creative Writing and began her publishing career with a literary agency internship and the Kidlit blog, which she started in 2009. She has worked at Chronicle Books, the Andrea Brown Literary Agency, and Movable Type Management. Her books are *Writing Irresistible Kidlit: The Ultimate Guide to Crafting Fiction for Young Adult and Middle Grade Readers* from Writer's Digest Books/Penguin Random House, and *Irresistible Query Letters, Writing Irresistible Picture Books, How to Write a Book Now, Writing Interiority: Crafting Irresistible Characters*, and several companion workbooks, all from Good Story Publishing.

Originally from the San Francisco Bay Area, she lives with her three children, husband, two pugs, and a cat, in Minneapolis, MN.

MARY KOLE

"Receiving Mary's feedback on my novel has been one of the best things that has happened to my writing in recent years. Thanks to her, I see the possibilities in my book and also feel like a fire has been lit under me to continue. I know the work is not yet done, but today—*today*—I feel like it's possible."

ANONYMOUS

facebook.com/goodstoryco

x.com/goodstoryco

instagram.com/goodstorycompany

linkedin.com/company/goodstorycompany

pinterest.com/goodstorycompany

tiktok.com/@goodstoryco

youtube.com/goodstory

bsky.app/profile/goodstory.bsky.social

To Amy Wilson, the wind beneath my wings.

COMPANION BOOK

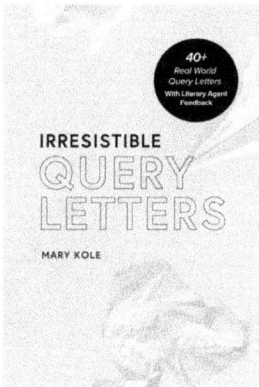

While this writing guide to story openings stands alone, it pairs very well with my book, *Irresistible Query Letters: 40+ Real World Query Letters With Literary Agent Feedback*, which is all about query letters, synopses, and submission strategy. It features comprehensive editorial notes on over 40 query letters from real-world writers, across all genres and target audiences.

AI TRANSPARENCY STATEMENT

1. No original text in this book has been *generated* using AI, such as automatic drafting based on an LLM's understanding of existing text.
2. No original text in this book has been *suggested* using AI. This might include asking ChatGPT for an outline.
3. No original text in this book has been *improved* using AI. An example is a system like Grammarly, which offers suggestions to reorder sentences or words to increase a clarity score. The author improved this text the hard way, through human feedback and revision.
4. Original text in this book has been *corrected* using AI (Microsoft Word's standard spelling and grammar check), but suggestions for spelling and grammar have been reviewed, then accepted or rejected, based on the author's human discretion.

Special Circumstances:

This book features published quotes and writer-submitted samples. Excerpts are clearly identified, and the author cannot make the above warranties for any text that is not original to this guide.

This AI Transparency Statement text is adapted from one Kester Brewin developed and published in *The Guardian*.[1]

---

1. Brewin, Kester. "Why I wrote an AI transparency statement for my book, and think other authors should too." *The Guardian*, April 4, 2024. https://www.theguardian.com/books/2024/apr/04/why-i-wrote-an-ai-transparency-statement-for-my-book-and-think-other-authors-should-too.

CONTENTS

THEORY

CRAFT CONCEPTS

MOVING FORWARD

WORKSHOP

MIDDLE GRADE FIRST PAGES

ACTION

CONTENT WARNING

This writing guide features published first lines and writing samples from aspiring writers. The stories referenced or excerpted deal with a number of potentially difficult topics, as novels and memoirs often reflect and even amplify the most dramatic events life has to offer. These topics include historical human slavery, the slaughter of indigenous people, racial tension, colonialism, sex and sexuality, war, domestic and familial violence, suicide, and mental health crisis. Go easy on yourself as you read if you find any of these subjects triggering, and make sure you have support. This is a writing guide, and I would hate for the subject matter in certain excerpts to overshadow their intended educational purpose.

There are also some swear words (theirs and mine—sorry Mom!).

INTRODUCTION

Forget "Don't judge a book by its cover." Readers, literary agents, and acquisitions editors at publishing houses absolutely make snap decisions about manuscripts and, later, published works. First impressions matter.

When you're published, you have the benefit of cover art, marketing copy, and even merchandising—where and how prominently a book is displayed online or in a brick-and-mortar store—which all help shape a potential customer's impression of a work.

But before you have all of those additional signals at your disposal, you can only use a query letter[1] and sample manuscript pages to hook a gatekeeper, especially if you're hoping for traditional publication.[2]

---

1. For comprehensive discussion of query letters, including over 40 examples from writers like you in all genres and categories, check out my book, *Irresistible Query Letters: 40+ Real World Query Letters With Literary Agent Feedback.*
2. If you want to publish independently, you *will* have a cover, marketing copy, keywords, genres and categories at your disposal, but your readers might still be browsing for their next book by physically or digitally flipping to your first pages and evaluating whether your project appeals to them. All of the story opening principles in this guide still apply.

The actual content of your manuscript becomes crucial in the submission pile, as agents will always check the craft itself. They know, probably better than anyone, that query-writing and prose-craft are two completely different skill sets. If a query rocks, that's great, but I never once offered representation based on a query letter alone when I was an agent. A great pitch simply made me more excited to read the pages, which, in most cases and with most submission guidelines, were enclosed after the cover letter. (That's right—a query is just a glorified cover document!)

Conversely, a lousy query could certainly cool my enthusiasm, but I would always at least skim the pages, unless there was a bigger issue which made the whole project ineligible (I'll offer some examples of those scenarios a bit later).

Long story short: A query letter can't singlehandedly make or break a submission, but the story's opening pages can. And do. Often. Hence my excitement to tackle this topic.

But first, I'm going to share a behind-the-scenes peek into the workflow of scouting the slush pile. This isn't done to demoralize you, but to offer a reality check, and maybe even raise your competitive hackles. For this thought exercise, I'll take you into the mindset of a literary agent logging into the slush pile, whether it lives in a dedicated inbox or a submission tracker portal dashboard. Most agents separate their submissions from their regular correspondence because they either a) can't stand the sight of that unread counter creeping up, up, up between slush sessions, or b) don't want to be distracted from their work.

You read correctly. An agent's actual job is to service the clients they have. (Unless they're new to agenting and don't have their own authors and/or illustrators, but most agents who get their agency's blessing to start building their lists will already have a few clients who have been passed on from other agents, or will be co-servicing clients with a more experienced mentor agent).

The primary role of a literary agent is to secure rights deals for the projects and creators on their lists, which include publishing contracts in their primary market (the U.S., Canada, the U.K., etc.), as well as foreign rights deals with publishers abroad, digital agreements (in those very rare cases where a publisher didn't buy ebook rights), audio deals (also, in those rare instances where the publisher didn't retain audio), film options from producers and studios, and other fun things like the occasional licensing deal or merchandizing contract.

Agents also negotiate these rights sales on a client's (or estate's) behalf and step into situations for their authors and illustrators: discussions about option books; opinions about editorial notes; or controversies about a cover design. They offer advice on marketing in the run-up to a release; consult on potential future projects; and navigate any number of other issues that make up the day-to-day life of a book creator.

As an agent performs all of these functions, the process of soliciting and evaluating potential new clients falls to the bottom of the list, along with reading for pleasure, self-care, mental health, speaking at the occasional conference to drum up even more business, etc., etc., etc. Relatively new agents have more bandwidth for these growth-oriented activities; established agents who rely mostly on referrals and are closed to queries obviously have less.

I hope this overview answers the first question many writers have: *Why don't they just read their slush pile already? Why does it take weeks or months or even years?*

Gatekeepers aren't in there every day. (The same can be said of acquisitions editors on the receiving end of literary agent pitches.) Some are so busy during business hours that they might only find time to read submissions on weekends.

I don't know about all agents, though this seems pretty standard among my former peers, but a gatekeeper can't just dip in and read one or two submissions at a time, either. Most people budget a few hours and really take a deep dive. It's not an exact science, but when you're in the slush, it's like getting ready to play paintball for the afternoon.[3] You'll need to put on a new outfit to repel the mess, drive somewhere for the activity, and gear up with all the equipment. When I used to read slush, I'd do it for a few hours at a time. Full focus, no breaks. I'd get in clear-eyed and get out when I started to feel Slush Psychosis creeping in.[4] And it's during one of these marathon sessions that you will have your opportunity to catch a gatekeeper's eye.

Now that you know how they read, you must also realize that agents have previously evaluated tens of thousands—if not hundreds of thousands or even millions, depending on the length of their careers—of queries and story openings. I'm not joking, and I'm not trying to freak you out, but many gatekeepers report receiving upwards of 50,000 to 60,000 submissions per year.

About half of those will be an easy rejection for a number of reasons. The queries aren't in a genre or for a target audience the agent actively represents; the submissions aren't personalized;[5] the work doesn't seem literate at all (writing is an odd choice of hobby in those cases, but the heart wants what it wants); the query or manuscript are just batshit insane;[6] the writing itself is suffering from various common issues (see the Common Opening Clichés and Recurring Notes chapters); or the writer is known to the agent

---

3. I have no idea what possessed me to think of this analogy as I haven't played paintball a day in my life. But stick with me for a second.
4. **Slush Psychosis**: A psychological affliction that sets in once you've read so much slush in one session that you lose all sense of your own taste. Beer goggles, but for queries. Weird things start seeming oddly attractive. You can't tell if promising things are actually good. It's disorienting, like spending time in a sensory deprivation tank. Which way is up? Do words even have meaning? This is why many agents keep a "maybe" pile that they'll come back to with a clear head.
5. Lack of personalization isn't the biggest deal in the world, but many agents explicitly ignore submissions which misspell their names. When I worked at the Andrea Brown Literary Agency, which is proudly and entirely female, I'd regularly get queries addressed to "Mr. Brown." This told me the writer somehow managed to do less than zero research, which is an accomplishment in and of itself with the many resources available (see Appendix A).
6. I am bursting with stories but don't want to specifically identify any writer or creative work, even fifteen years later.

—and not in a good way.[7] Once the agent applies this kind of filter —which also takes time and energy—they're still left with tens of thousands of submissions to read.

Sometimes an agent evaluates their own slush. Often, they'll have a reader or intern do the first screening process. (Working as a reader or unpaid intern for a literary agency or publisher and going through submissions is a time-honored rite of passage for anyone looking to work in the industry.) Over time, agents start to recognize patterns, types of writers (and writing styles), and common story opening clichés and errors. They start to build their tastes. They learn to very quickly judge whether a writer or submission is at that certain level of readiness for potential submission to publishers.[8]

I've often heard writers express downright *shock* that agents only spend between 30 seconds and two minutes per inquiry.[9] This is enough time to read the query and scan the first few paragraphs of the writing sample. (Even if there's something in the query that immediately turns them off, most agents will still at least *look* at the writing.) I currently run webinars and critique the first two double-spaced pages,[10] and I've had people complain: *How can you tell anything from the first two double-spaced pages???? Why not fifteen pages???? What if my story gets really good thirty pages in?????????????!!?*

Tough luck. No agent is going to hang on for thirty pages because you've inexplicably decided to hoard the engaging stuff for later. I'm sorry. If an agent likes your premise (see the Theme, Premise, and Promise chapter), they might skim the first ten pages and

---

7. They might be: a former client; resending a previously rejected submission; known to act rude or toxic on social media; creepily misusing an agent's personal information that they've found online; or a frequent flyer who regularly turns up with a seemingly endless portfolio of projects.
8. Nobody likes to hear this, but even agents get rejected. They're not a silver bullet.
9. These numbers are anecdotal, of course, but reflect my own experience and what I've heard from former colleagues.
10. This is the same sample length you will see critiqued in the Workshop section of this guide.

decide to ask for a partial or full manuscript. But nobody is hanging on your every word in the slush pile. Nobody.

Remember, they've already honed their internal rubric and are coming to your project having seen untold numbers of other aspiring query and manuscript submission examples. They know what they like and have a sense of what the market is seeking (which is another part of their job—to constantly be networking with acquisitions editors and learning *their* tastes). They can tell a ton from two pages. Heck, they've likely pegged you after a few paragraphs.

Again, I'm not saying this to discourage you. Yes, the game of trying to get a book deal is incredibly competitive. But if you know this and persist anyway, you're one step closer to potentially realizing your goal. Very few people who "have a book in them" ever complete a project. Even fewer gear up to take their hobby seriously, learn the industry, and prepare to submit or self-publish. Of those, only a small percentage are ready for serious consideration. And an even smaller cohort will get agent representation. (Unfortunately, not all of those authors will get a book deal, as agents can still get it wrong, despite their best intentions.)

It's a game of attrition. Of numbers.

And you are making yourself all the more competitive by devoting special focus to the crucial topic of story openings. By reading, challenging yourself, and growing, you're getting an edge, and I'm proud to show you the ropes in this guide.

One final thought on the topic of beginnings, which I hope might put your mind at ease: They're revisable. You should do your very best to intentionally include the craft concepts you'll learn here, but you can also put your first chapter away and focus on the rest of the narrative. Openings are the single most frequently revised portion of any manuscript. You don't even know the entire story yet— especially if you haven't finished your first draft. You'll figure out many of your theme, character, plot, and style elements as you write.

Once you have the whole scope of your story in mind, go back to your opening. It might change entirely—in fact, don't be afraid to do a blank-page rewrite. This takes some of the pressure off of "nailing it" on the first try. Do your best, then use the principles in this guide and insights gleaned from the provided examples to re-conceptualize and polish your beginning. It might never be entirely perfect, but that's not what we're after in the art and craft of narrative openings. Now get out there, and here's to the beginning of a good story!

Bonus Tip: You'll see articles and other resources cited in this guide. In ebook editions, all the links are clickable and will take you directly to the relevant articles, other chapters in this guide, and specific book titles I'm referencing. For print editions, all of the articles and additional resources discussed herein are also collected in the Recurring Notes chapter and Appendix A.

THEORY

WHY STORY OPENINGS MATTER

My longstanding mandate to writers everywhere is to make readers care. This is your only job when you're crafting or pitching a story opening. (Memoir and nonfiction writers are on the hook for this, too, as authors like Malcolm Gladwell have popularized the art of teaching and discussing concepts by couching them within narrative techniques.) If a reader cares, they will follow you—and your character or topic—on a journey, and that's what you want.

Of course, this is easier said than done. You're also competing for audience attention, not just against other books—and millions of those are traditionally and independently published each year. Your readers have a seemingly ever-decreasing amount of leisure time, and they must choose whether they want to spend it reading, doom-scrolling, gaming, bingeing TV or other media, or, you know, socializing with friends and family IRL. There are more distractions —digital and analog—available to us than ever before, and books occupy a small but mighty section of that footprint.

If you aspire to traditional publication, you must first impress a series of gatekeepers before you get access to that reader's time, emotional investment, and, of course, media dollar. These include literary agents—the middlemen who are able to pitch your project to acquisitions editors, including those at the Big Five publishing houses[1]—and eventually those editors, their pub boards, and in-house sales and marketing teams.

Your pitch, which we'll talk about in the Theme, Premise, and Promise chapter of this guide, can then carry you into the publisher's trade catalogue, to sales conventions, and into conversations with booksellers and buyers who will bring your project to *their* customers, the readers. There's a long distribution chain of excitement that must click into place before you reach your target market.

Human emotion and engagement are the energy that powers each link of this chain. Emotional connection is, of course, desirable because if a reader (or agent, acquisitions editor, salesperson, and bookseller) doesn't care, they're not going to be able to make anyone else care.

The opening of your story creates a gatekeeper and reader's first impression of your work. It also lays the emotional and stylistic foundation for the rest of the book. Expectations are powerful, as we'll also see in the Theme, Premise, and Promise chapter. Whether you know it or not (and it's better if you know this and intentionally use it to your advantage), you are manipulating your reader's experience from the opening line onward.

I'm often telling writers that "a book teaches us how to read it." This is especially true in picture books which may have, for example, a rhyme scheme.[2] Any pattern established early on in a story is going to reinforce what readers know about your project. If you break that pattern—or shatter, reverse, or upend a genre convention—readers

---

1. As the market currently stands, that's HarperCollins, Penguin Random House, Macmillan, Hachette, and Simon & Schuster.

2. This guide does not directly address picture book openings. For that, please check out my book, *Writing Irresistible Picture Books: Insider Insights Into Crafting Compelling Modern Stories for Young Readers*, as books for young readers have their own very specific conventions, expectations, and structures. There's an entire section on openings, as well as a breakdown of 154 published titles and subject matter analysis of 1,000 picture book deal announcements for forthcoming projects.

will notice. You not only want to hook a reader, you want to hook the *type of reader* who likes *your particular type of book.*

This should be done on purpose. If you wield the power of pattern and change with full knowledge of what you're doing, your readers will feel they're in the good hands of an expert storyteller.

Below, you'll find the essential ingredients of any story opening. These will form the framework of the later chapters in this guide:

- **Premise and Theme**: what your story is about in the most basic literal and figurative sense, respectively;
- **Curiosity Hooks**: any immediate intrigue, mystery, or conflict that catches reader attention;
- **Character**: which POV[3] you're using, who the protagonist is, how they might be relatable, and what they want or struggle with at the very beginning of the story, with room for an interesting growth or development trajectory;
- **Action and Conflict**: an opening in scene and action which serves as an introduction to a plot that seems like it will matter to the character (and therefore to readers), whether the initial action is quickly resolved or kicks off the story-wide arc of obstacles, antagonism, and tension;
- **Setting and World-building**: the temporal and physical location of the story, as well as the atmosphere implied by the environment; and
- **Tone and Style**: the use of language, mood, voice, syntax, imagery, and word choice, which creates an impression about the overall genre-appropriate vibes.

In addition to these elements, you'll also want to keep your eye on the balance of action and information, how and where you deploy important details, your pacing (the perceived speed at which your

---

3. This stands for "point of view" and is one of the most foundational narrative choices you can make. A much deeper dive into this topic appears in my book, *Writing Interiority: Crafting Irresistible Characters.*

action moves), and how you'll make and keep (or subvert) promises in the larger narrative itself.

Another thing to remember is that the promises you make (more about those in the Theme, Premise, and Promise chapter) help readers know what they're in for (even in a twisty thriller, where misdirects and surprises are part of the genre). When we treat every element of our story beginning with intention and care, we create a sense of consistency. Readers understand the point of view, tense, time period, flow of various threads (if you're using multiple narrators or timelines), language, voice, and other benchmark craft elements. There are no odd inconsistencies, pattern interrupts, or jarring trips and falls—except for ones you place into your story on purpose.

One small clarification I want to make. Throughout this guide, you'll see me refer to "category and genre." These are two distinct publishing industry terms and are not to be used interchangeably. "Category" refers to the target audience for your work, so "middle grade" would be a category, not a genre. "Genre" refers to the broad stylistic conventions applied to a project. "Romantic comedy" is a genre, not a category. It's possible to have a "middle grade romantic comedy," in fact, though the crush at the heart of it would have to be clean and light-hearted. I'll discuss categories and genres in more detail throughout this guide.

When we approach our stories, and especially our story beginnings, we must remember that readers are our partners in literary crime. They deserve respect and engagement, and they deserve to play a very important role in interpreting a creation. That's right—readers aren't just passively sitting there, turning pages. They're actually detectives.

Readers As Detectives

You might recognize this point from *Writing Interiority: Crafting Irresistible Characters*, but I maintain very strongly that readers actively engage in stories. They want to uncover your narrative without getting it explained outright, or, worse, feeling condescended to. This is the wisdom behind "show, don't tell," especially when it comes to character, but if you've read *Writing Interiority,* you know I devote an entire chapter to debunking that stale piece of advice and offering a better alternative. (More on this in the Recurring Notes chapter.)

The reason "show, don't tell" still has merit in the eyes of the writing and publishing establishment is that it reminds you to give readers something to do. In fact, as you'll see throughout this guide, a story beginning is a dish best served with action, showing, and scene. There are some elements you're "allowed" to tell about, including key story opening data points like:

- The character's objective and motivation (see the Characters chapter);
- The character's inner tension or deep longing, which might be hinted at in the first chapter (the Characters chapter again);
- Any immediate backstory which contextualizes the present scene, conflict, or tension (another topic in the Characters chapter);
- A more distant sense of the wound or backstory, *but only* if it adds resonance to a present situation, relationship, inner struggle, or emotional response (see our The First Chapter and Beyond chapter);
- What the character is presently doing and why (the Action and Conflict chapter); and
- Why any of this matters to the character and, therefore, the reader, otherwise known as the stakes (described in the Action and Conflict chapter as well).

Feel free to do *some* telling about the above. No, your high school English teacher will not burst through your wall like the Kool-Aid pitcher and bust you. You might contend with some longstanding guilt about breaking a Writing 101 rule, but that's between you and your muse.

By telling very selectively and putting the rest of your story ingredients into scene from the beginning, you'll allow readers to indulge in their favorite activity—digging around inside your narrative, spying in the character's head, and otherwise becoming emotionally engaged (more on this in the Theme, Premise, and Promise chapter). They're probably good at their detective work and enjoy it, too. That's why they've shown up to the printed or digital page instead of indulging in the infinite scroll on social media or watching a movie (or, if you're me, both at the same time).

By telling and explaining, you rob them of the joy of discovering your story for themselves. You take away the desire, curiosity, spark, and satisfaction of guessing, interpreting, and reacting. Don't do this. Writers who tend to get and keep ever-expanding readerships over the course of their careers know to treat their audiences well. In fact, in my work as an IP developer and book packager with Bittersweet Books, our unofficial motto is: *The only thing we take seriously is the reader's experience.*

Your opening goal should involve giving readers something to do. Start with intrigue, a secret, a relatable character, someone with juicy inner tension, a conflict, a universal theme, clear voice … then put these elements into motion. We'll learn how to do all of this and more in the following pages, and we'll see aspiring writers like you attempt the same in our workshop samples.

Don't be afraid to pick up twenty books in your genre and see how their authors start them. Monitor yourself as you read—are you responding as the author might've intended, or are you thrown from the action by inconsistent details, lack of information and context, or a subjective element (like voice) that you simply don't like? If the character is tricky or maybe even a full-blown antihero, is the writer doing anything to try and get you to relate, perhaps even despite yourself? Analyze the craft on the page, but watch yourself, too. Are you being manipulated? Are you actively participating? Stop after a paragraph. Do you honestly want to read more? If so, how has the author created that yearning?

Before we get into the craft theory, let's take a look at published story opening and see the wide variety of available approaches. This will act as a lovely little introduction to your available options.

PUBLISHED FIRST LINES

Though the topic of this guide is first pages, I wanted to sample some compelling opening *lines* from current and popular published works. Why? To see how the craft concepts you're about to learn are used by writers at the top of their game. To demonstrate that you can tell a lot from a line or two. I'll add commentary as we go, and I hope you get some ideas as you read.[1]

In the below examples, I've retained any identifying headings. You can see which books start with the first chapter versus a prologue, for example, and note any location/time/character name markers. These are all elements you can leverage in your own work.

I've divided the published examples by genre. Sometimes there are multiple applicable genres—historical fantasy, for example—but I didn't get that granular in identifying each book. I've also noted which books are debuts, and which are part of an established series.

Literary First Lines

There's controversy about what, exactly, "literary" means, as all

---

1. You'll be treated to longer writing excerpts in the Workshop section.

books could be labeled literature. Readers, publishers, and gatekeepers generally use this term to indicate works that prioritize language and style while potentially focusing less on plot, thrills, tension, and other markers of genres like mystery/thriller/suspense. These stories are generally told through the lens of character experience first and foremost, but this is a broad generalization.

Louise / August 1975: The bed is empty.

Louise, the counselor—twenty-three, short-limbed, rasp-voiced, jolly—stands barefoot on the warm rough planks of the cabin called Balsam and processes the absence of a body in the lower bunk by the door.

The God of the Woods by Liz Moore (2024)

This novel was a breakout hit. The heading defines both time and character perspective. Immediately, we have intrigue and danger—a counselor has just discovered a camper missing. High stakes from the start!

Didn't seem fair on the young lad. That suit at the funeral. With the braces on his teeth, the supreme discomfort of the adolescent. On such occasions, one could almost come to regret one's own social brilliance.

Intermezzo: A Novel by Sally Rooney (2024)

A rather sad young lad is described here, but the POV narrator immediately raises some curiosity. Who's the kind of person who implies they have "social brilliance," and at a funeral, no less? Whose funeral is it? How are the lad and the narrator related, if they are?

Prologue: Here are the ways I could start this story:

Olivia was breathtaking.

For a long time, I was convinced that she was responsible for everything that went wrong.

No one will love you more or hurt you more than a sister.

Chapter 1: I was afraid to wake up my dad. He was stretched out on the couch in his den, late afternoon, his brown loafers kicked off on the shag carpet, resting on each other like rabbits.

Shred Sisters by Betsy Lerner (Debut, 2024)

I've provided both the prologue and the first chapter opening for this debut. The prologue sets a very clear tone and character worldview. But as you'll see in the Common Opening Clichés chapter, I'll call this "throat-clearing." The actual first chapter introduces tension ("afraid to wake up my dad"), a sense of place, and some interesting imagery.

Before Mazer invented himself as Mazer, he was Samson Mazer, and before he was Samson Mazer, he was Samson Masur—a change of two letters that transformed him from a nice, ostensibly Jewish boy to a Professional Builder of Worlds—and for most of his youth, he was Sam, S.A.M. on the hall of fame of his grandfather's *Donkey Kong* machine, but mainly Sam.

Tomorrow, and Tomorrow, and Tomorrow by Gabrielle Zevin (2022)

Gaming features heavily in this novel, and that world-building is clear immediately. We also get a curious introduction to Mazer, one of the main characters, through an omniscient lens. Readers may be intrigued to see the ramifications of this backstory and his various transformations on the present narrative.

Cyrus Shams / Keady University, 2015: Maybe it was that Cyrus had done the wrong drugs in the right order, or the right drugs in the wrong order, but when God finally spoke back to him after twenty-seven years of silence, what Cyrus wanted more than anything else was a do-over.

Martyr! by Kaveh Akbar (Debut, 2024)

An attention-getting opening if I've ever seen one. We're positioned in time (college) and immediately introduced to humor and a rather controversial connection between drugs and seeing God. Whether you're on board or scandalized, I doubt you'll stop reading. You might also wonder why Cyrus wants a do-over, and why God has broken his silence now (if he, indeed, did, and it's not just the drugs).

Bad Mommy: The young mothers were telling each other how tired they were. This was one of their favorite topics, along with the eating, sleeping, and defecating habits of their offspring, the merits of certain nursery schools, and the difficulty of sticking to an exercise routine.

Little Children by Tom Perrotta (2003)

A two-sentence plunge right into the world and value system of suburban motherhood. There might be some sardonic judgment from the omniscient narrator, but we'll have to keep reading to find out what *about* these "young mothers" is story-worthy.

Sender: I come back to the apartment and find the worst thing in the world. A yellow postcard has been shoved between the door and its frame.

Greta & Valdin by Rebecca K. Reilly (Debut, 2021)

You'll notice several opening examples which begin with a mysterious phone call, letter, or visitor. This is a tried-and-true way of creating curiosity, but you'll want to bear it out with a truly consequential reveal if you go this route.

I was half asleep when Mamá dressed my brother, Pablo, and me, hurried the two of us into the car, and cranked the starter.

The Things We Didn't Know by Elba Iris Pérez (Debut, 2024)

Lots of action right away. Why is Mamá collecting the kids seemingly in the middle of the night? The verbs ("hurried," "cranked") suggest this happens in a rush, which conveys immediate danger.

I wanted the girl to know the truth. I wanted her to know who I was—who I really was—instead of a white man who had lived across from her all her life and watched her grow up from this side of the river.

Fire Exit by Morgan Talty (Debut, 2024)

We introduce the theme of racial dynamics right away, as well as a parasocial relationship between neighbors. That the narrator has been watching "the girl" invites some curiosity, but the main hook is the implied question: Well, who *is* the protagonist then? What's "the truth"? The intimate first-person POV offers close psychic distance.

Upmarket First Lines

"Upmarket" is a term used to describe a certain subset of the literary marketplace which can also be called "women's fiction" or "book club fiction." The focus is still very much on character, but these books often have a clear premise that's larger than life in some way.

> The hotel looks exactly as Phoebe had hoped. It sits on the edge of the cliff like an old and stately dog, patiently waiting for her arrival.
>
> *The Wedding People* by Alison Espach (2024)

This character has many complicated reasons for coming to this hotel at this point in her life. Immediately, we get the sense of how important it is to her, which makes readers wonder why.

> The first time we have sex, we are both fully clothed, at our desks during working hours, bathed in blue computer light. He is uptown processing a new bundle of microfiche and I am downtown handling corrections for a new Labrador detective manuscript.
>
> *Luster* by Raven Leilani (Debut, 2020)

Does she mean literal or figurative "sex" here? A quickie, or electrifying emails sent between a literal uptown and downtown? The naughty idea of mixing arousal and microfiche is enough to pique curiosity.

> Some things I need to tell you here at the beginning. To get them out of the way.

The Labors of Hercules Beal by Gary D. Schmidt (2023)

This is a middle grade coming-of-age novel. Here, the second-person direct address ("you") grabs reader attention by virtue of the protagonist immediately breaking the fourth wall to talk to the audience.

Prologue: A sister is not a friend. Who can explain the urge to take a relationship as primal and complex as a sibling and reduce it to something as replaceable, as banal as a friend?

Chapter One / Lucky: Lucky was late. Irresponsibly, irreversibly, in-danger-of-losing-this-job late.

Blue Sisters by Coco Mellors (2024)

Some more throat-clearing and philosophizing about the nature of sisterhood, which is understandable, given the title. But before this gets too ponderous, we're plunged into a specific POV and some immediate action and conflict: Lucky is very late, the stakes are high, and there's also the dramatic irony of someone with her name caught in a decidedly unlucky situation.

Part 1 / The Snakes / Charlotte / Tennessee / 1974-1977: Charlotte repositioned herself in her hospital bed to get a better look at the crying baby. Though she could sympathize with the feeling of outrage that came from being torn violently from a position of warmth and comfort, she did nothing to comfort the child. Instead, she watched it wail desperately until a nurse forced the warm lump of wiggling flesh into Charlotte's arms.

Grown Women by Sarai Johnson (2024)

This is an intergenerational saga about four women, so it's fitting that we meet Charlotte at the moment she becomes a mother. However, her emotional detachment upon seeing her baby is palpable, and this engenders immediate reader empathy for her and, of course, that baby, who's alone and "wail[ing] desperately."

The man is tall and has dark tousled hair, and when she gets back quite late from Elena's hen do, she finds him waiting on the landing at the top of the stairs.

The Husbands by Holly Gramazio (Debut, 2024)

Elena encounters a surprise handsome man on her doorstep after a night of partying. She might be drunk or in a reckless mood. What might happen next? Is this a man she knows, one she met earlier in the evening, or a total stranger?

Sorry to trouble you was how the note began, which is such a great opener. Please, trouble me! Trouble me! I've been waiting my whole life to be troubled by a note like this.

All Fours by Miranda July (2024)

Voice welcomes the reader in this excerpt. We have a mysterious note, then commentary about it. Not only will readers want to know what's in "a note like this," but also why this particular character is so eager to be troubled.

This Could've Been an Email: There will be questions. Ones I don't have socially acceptable answers for. I know because today is my birthday, and a last-minute meeting has appeared on my calendar.

I Hope This Finds You Well by Natalie Sue (2024)

An immediate plunge into some meme-worthy office culture with the chapter heading. Instead of a curious note, we get a curious weapon-of-the-modern-middle-manager: the calendar ambush. Corporate workers know that surprise meetings tend to happen with high-stakes events like layoffs. But it's her birthday! And what are the socially unacceptable answers she's hiding? For that matter, what are the questions?

> You are about to begin reading a new book, and to be honest, you are a little tense. The beginning of a novel is like a first date. You hope that from the first lines an urgent magic will take hold, and you will sink into the story like a hot bath, giving yourself over entirely.
>
> *Margo's Got Money Troubles* by Rufi Thorpe (Debut, 2024)

Another instance of second-person direct address, with the character guessing what the reader might be experiencing. This can be polarizing. Is she right about what you're feeling? If so, you might be intrigued. If not, you might bounce because it's not an instant connection.

Historical First Lines

Historical fiction takes place in a different time (or sometimes an alternate re-imagining of history). Certain projects also layer on another genre, like fantasy, as we'll see below. Tone and style can go from serious to comedic.

Coronado Island, California, May 1966: The walled and gated
McGrath estate was a world unto itself, protected and private.
On this twilit evening, the Tudor-style home's mullioned
windows glowed jewel-like amid the lush, landscaped grounds.

The Women by Kristin Hannah (2024)

We're oriented in time right away with this opening. Then there's
some intrigue with an estate that's "a world until itself, protected
and private." The sense of place is obvious, and readers are invited
to learn what makes this locale so special.

Chapter 1: Those little bastards were hiding out there in the tall
grass. The moon was not quite full, but bright, and it was
behind them, so I could see them as plain as day, though it was
deep night.

James by Percival Everett (2024)

We get a narrator seeing "those little bastards" attempting to hide in
the "deep night." There's instant action, scene-setting, and danger
here, but readers will soon realize that the character, Jim, is
watching Tom Sawyer and Huck Finn makes fools of themselves, so
the audience's initial expectation is reversed.

December 1942 / I Hear a Rhapsody: It is early evening in the
lobby of an elegant Manhattan hotel. Crystal prisms dangling
from the chandeliers glow with soft electric light. On velvet
couches near the fire, couples sit close, the men in officers'
uniforms, the women in evening war, resting their heads on
their gentlemen's shoulders.

Lovely War by Julie Berry (2019)

This YA novel instantly plunges us into the world with lush description. It's also a bit aspirational. Who wouldn't want to enter this kind of "elegant" space? Historical novels have to work harder to establish their specific setting and historical context ("the men in officers' uniforms" ground us in the World War era, as does the year in the heading. (Though most of this action takes place during WWI, there are some chapters from WWII.)

Prologue: There were children, and then there were the children of Indians, because the merciless savage inhabitants of these American lands did not make children but nits, and nits make lice, or so it was said by the man who meant to make a massacre feel like killing bugs at Sand Creek, when seven hundred drunken men came at dawn with cannons, and then again four years later almost to the day the same way at the Washita River, where afterward, seven hundred Indian horses were rounded up and shot in the head.

Wandering Stars by Tommy Orange (2024)

Immediate unflinching human cruelty is introduced in this prologue, as is racial division. The thematic idea of "the children of Indians" being reduced to "nits" to make killing them feel justified is heartrending. Readers might be wondering which POV they'll inhabit—the indigenous peoples' or the drunken men's. The initial description suggests the colonizer's view of the scene, but the "so it was said" shifts the perspective.

Charlotte / Philadelphia, 1873: The city of Philadelphia wasn't what it claimed to be. But after four years of living here with her father, Charlotte knew there was a lot of that going around.

All We Were Promised by Ashton Lattimore (Debut, 2024)

Right away, we get a subverted expectation. Charlotte has moved to Philadelphia and is disillusioned—not only by the city, but by her father. She suggests there's "a lot of [deception] going around," which offers some sharp commentary and suggests readers will want to know this plucky, virtuous character.

Syracuse / 412 BC: So Gelon says to me, "Let's go down and feed the Athenians. The weather's perfect for feeding Athenians."

Glorious Exploits by Ferdia Lennon (Debut, 2024)

This is obviously an *alternate* historical story, given the voice. Right away, there's a sharp disconnect between the colloquial, modern dialogue style and the year in the heading. This is an important signal to send. Readers looking for a strait-laced historical account of the Peloponnesian War will put the book down, which is probably for the best, as this novel is targeting audiences more interested in humor or satire. (The cover features a classical bust with googly eyes on it, so I'm not sure a serious historical reader would've picked it up in the first place.) This opening is a perfect example of demonstrating tone and signaling the vibe.

Chapter 1 / Cecily / Bintang, Kuala Lumpur / February 1945 / Japanese-occupied Malaya: Teenage boys had begun to disappear. The first boy Cecily heard of was one of the Chin brothers, the middle of five hulking boys with narrow foreheads and broad shoulders—they were Boon Hock, Boon Lam, Boon Khong, Boon Hee, and Boon Wai, but their mother called them all Ah Boon, and it was up to the boys to know which one she was calling for.

The Storm We Made by Vanessa Chan (Debut, 2024)

A very interesting cultural tidbit about names in Malaysian culture, which also seems to have a matriarchal bent (the boys have to be so attuned to their mother that the right brother must answer her call). We also learn there's a Japanese occupation happening and that boys are disappearing. We get danger, mystery, and some world-building into two sentences.

Fantasy, Science Fiction, and Speculative First Lines

A "speculative" story has a magic, fantasy, technology, magical realism, or other element that takes place outside of our reality. Fantasy generally deals more with magic, creatures, or other worlds entirely, while science fiction focuses on how humans interface with advanced or ancient technology in building their societies. The elements involved can be as varied as an author's imagination.

At the end of Oak Leaf Lane, dawn arrived fifteen minutes early. Most folks didn't notice, as they rarely did about such things, but eagerness circled the air like a hungry buzzard, watching and waiting.

The Courting of Bristol Keats by Mary E. Pearson (2024)

This is a romantasy (a portmanteau of "romance" and "fantasy") for young adult audiences. Though we don't get any concrete magic right away, it's interesting to think of "dawn arriv[ing] fifteen minutes early." Literally or in terms of perception? Are the people anxious for something? Though we're told "most folks didn't notice," should they have? The buzzard and "watching and waiting" images introduce an ominous tone.

I don't want to be here.

Rain slashes my face, the wind turning my long hair into whips.

Court of the Vampire Queen by Katee Robert (2022)

Another YA romantasy. We get a statement full of tension, then some imagery which underscores it (rain that "slashes" and the whip-like hair). This kind of dramatic voice signals a high-stakes and emotional read.

Home: Isla Crown watched the man she loved disappear as the world fell away.

The other man she loved gripped her arm with the desperate hope of holding onto a dream before waking.

Skyshade: A Lightlark Saga Book by Alex Aster (Series Installment, 2024)

And yet another YA romantasy (this trend might be leveling out now, but there was an explosion of them published in 2024). This opening isn't shy about its tropes—we get an immediate love triangle and desperate emotions. This is a series installment, so while some readers know these characters already, others might not. It's a unique challenge to continue a series without a giant info-dump to kick off sequels.

When I was a kid, my mom constantly invented games. The Quiet Game. The Who Can Make Their Cookie Last Longer? Game. A perennial favorite, The Marshmallow Game involved eating marshmallows while wearing puffy Goodwill jackets indoors, to avoid turning on the heat.

The Inheritance Games by Jennifer Lynn Barnes (Series Debut, 2020)

Though this is a YA fantasy, we're not immediately plunged into a speculative world. Instead, we get the family culture—how Mom turned these obvious cost-cutting measures into "games." This engenders empathy from readers and makes them curious about the title, which also references a game (but a different kind).

If the bread hadn't burned, this would be a very different story. If the cook's son hadn't come home late the night before, if the cook hadn't known he was hanging around that lady playwright, if she hadn't lain awake fretting for his immortal soul and weeping over the future fates of possible grandchildren, if she hadn't been so tired and distracted, then the bread would not have burned and the calamities that followed might have belong to some other house than Casa Ordoño, on some other street than Calle de Dos Santos.

The Familiar by Leigh Bardugo (2024)

The approach taken in this historical fantasy introduction is rather convoluted (which is a risk). We hear about what *might not* have happened, as the author obviously lays out what *did*. Along the way, we're treated to some fun and dramatic characters, and the promise of "the calamities that followed." Normally, I suggest that debut writers show the current tension instead of hinting at future conflict, especially in the beginning, but this is a beloved author with a fanbase that'll stick along for the ride.

Out of the corner of Jemma Barker's eye, the woman flickered, a shadow of light shimmering at the edges of her vision.

Don't look at 'em, Jemma. That was Mama's voice.

This Cursed House by Del Sandeen (Debut, 2024)

A Southern Gothic novel with a ghostly twist. We see the specters immediately, and they're made mysterious by "flicker[ing]" at the "edges of [the character's] vision. That Jemma hears Mama's voice in her head is also a shot of intrigue: Is Mama gone? And then: Is this ghost dangerous?

The Madness Years / China, 1967: The Red Union had been attacking the headquarters of the April Twenty-eighth Brigade for two days. Their red flags fluttered restlessly around the brigade building like flames yearning for firewood.

The Three-Body Problem by Cixin Liu, translated by Ken Liu (2006)

Some dangerous imagery and historical grounding kick off this sci-fi novel. The omniscient narrator overlooks the action, so readers might wonder if they'll soon inhabit the POV of someone from the April Twenty-eight Brigade. Notice how first-person POV can suck readers in, but omniscient POV and a more prominent narrative distance can make audiences yearn to be included, too. How interesting that opposite storytelling choices can have similar effects. The image of "flames yearning for firewood" promises immediate danger.

Prologue: On the second Sabbat of Twelfthmoon, in the city of Weep, a girl fell from the sky.

Her skin was blue, her blood was red.

Strange the Dreamer by Laini Taylor (Series Debut, 2017)

A YA series opener here, with some world-building about the calendar (and potentially religious culture) in this world, as well as a jarring event. The intrigue comes from the girl's blue skin, and the danger comes from her red blood.

Prologue: You may think you know the story. It goes like this: once upon a time, there was a sixteen-year-old girl named Jane Grey, who was forced to marry a complete stranger (Lord Guildford or Gilford or Gifford-something-or-other), and shortly thereafter found herself ruler of a country. She was queen for nine days. Then she quite literally lost her head.

My Lady Jane by Cynthia Hand, Brodi Ashton, Jodi Meadows (2016)

Another alternative historical fantasy, though for the YA audience this time. From the chatty second-person direct address introduction and flippant voice ("then she quite literally lost her head"), readers know they're not getting the usual snapshot of English history. This version has magic, too!

Prologue: Greetings, Mother—I do not have much time. This change (this wondrous, wondrous change) is at this very moment upon me. I could not stop it if I tried. And I have no interest in trying.

Chapter 1: I was four years old when I first met a dragon. I never told my mother. I didn't think she'd understand.

When Women Were Dragons by Kelly Barnhill (2022)

This speculative fiction novel features women turning into dragons during the McCarthy era. In the prologue, we see the protagonist transforming and loving it. Then we go back in time to the character's childhood, when it seems she was very shy about bringing up the topic of dragons with Mother. This invites the obvious question: How did we get from the past version of the protagonist to the current one?

On winter nights, they burned heavy bundles of dried peat in the hearth and inhaled the scent of sacred ground burning while their father paced the length of the room, reciting the history of the Haddesley compact.

The Bog Wife by Kay Chronister (2024)

An atmospheric Appalachian gothic novel with a unique family culture. Right away, readers are pulled in with sensory details. The idea of burning "sacred ground" invites some questions and suggests danger. Readers might immediately want to know what the "Haddesley compact" involves, and the answer to this question drives much of the story.

The sky was strewn with pepper-pot stars, reflected in the pond below. On the water's surface, the mirror image of Ying Yue's face floated, pale and moonlike, distorted by ripples.

The Girl with No Reflection by Keshe Chow (Debut, 2024)

We'll discuss how to introduce a character's physical appearance a bit later. Here, we have some lovely writing and a "distorted" vision of the protagonist, which suggests tension (external, but maybe internal, too).

Liv: This had better be worth it.

With a grunt, I help Celeste push a piece of warped sheet metal aside to reveal a rusted drone.

The Dividing Sky by Jill Tew (Debut, 2024)

This YA sci-fi dystopian gives us strong character emotion right away, and the suggestion of high stakes ("This had better be worth it"). Liv is obviously in the middle of doing something dangerous, and the drone points to the kind of technology readers will see in this world.

Chapter 1 / Faron: Faron Vincent had been a liar for longer than she'd been a saint.

So Let Them Burn by Kamilah Cole (Debut, 2024)

There's an obvious question in this YA novel opening: How the heck did Faron Vincent go from liar to saint? And is she still a liar, despite the suggested virtue of her new identity?

Chapter 1 / Day One—Feast of the Dragon / Early Evening: My father always says: 'You can't run from your responsibilities,' but he lacks imagination. Besides, I'm not *running*. I'm sidestepping.

Voyage of the Damned by Frances White (Debut, 2024)

An immediately engaging voice in this YA romantasy. There's ideological tension between the character and father, and then a weaseling around the suggestion that she's running away from her responsibilities. Immediately, this suggests an unreliable narrator, which is another signal to readers.

The Quiet Death of Mr. Webber: In Kellner Books on the Upper East Side of New York City, a few minutes before his death, John Webber was reading *The Count of Monte Cristo*.

The Book of Doors by Gareth Brown (Debut, 2024)

This is a time traveler fantasy, and right away, we get the suggestion of future calamity, just as we did in *The Familiar*, above. There's an ongoing trend in publishing to feature cozy book- and library-related places, so readers who gravitate to that world will feel at home right away.

They killed themselves. All of them. All at once.

Sky Full of Elephants by Cebo Campbell (Debut, 2024)

Jarring, just like the girl falling from the sky in *Strange the Dreamer*, quoted above. The questions are immediate: Who are "they"? Why did they do this? Why "all at once"? Is this a cult or religious event? Is there a fantasy element? A curiosity hook at its finest.

Keila never thought the flames would reach the library. She was dimly aware that most of the other librarians had fled weeks ago, when the revolutionaries took the palace and defenestrated the emperor in a rather dramatic display.

The Spellshop by Sarah Beth Durst (2024)

This romantasy has a sardonic voice as well—"a rather dramatic display" is used to describe the emperor being thrown out a window. ("Defenestrated" is a great verb.) The second sentence gives great context for the current revolution, and we also get a library on fire, which introduces high stakes. It also begs the question: Why did Keila stay if everyone else "fled weeks ago"? And what now?

Romance and Romantic Comedy First Lines

Romantic relationships are at the plot and character-development heart of these stories. These books also tend to be trope-heavy and aimed at experienced readers who love the genre. Romantic comedy relies more on ridiculous, over-the-top, or contrived situations, such as a "fake dating" scheme, while romance can be more earnest (but isn't always).

March 2023: Tanner Hughes stepped onto the porch of the cottage that had once belonged to his grandparents and locked the door behind him. In one hand, he held a duffel bag, in the other a garment bag protecting the suit he'd worn to his grandmother's funeral five weeks earlier.

Counting Miracles by Nicholas Sparks (2024)

This wistful opening comes from romance juggernaut Nicholas Sparks and is designed to tug at reader heartstrings. There's some elegantly inserted backstory, as well as a sense of departure—the cottage "once belonged" in the family, and Tanner is holding a bag. Where will he go now?

In an ideal world, Marc Compton would be acting like a total dick.

I'm not asking for much. Some gloating, maybe. Obnoxiously raised eyebrows. A sneered, "Well, well, well. Look who showed up unannounced on Christmas Eve."

Cruel Winter with You by Ali Hazelwood (2024)

Some classic snappy romcom voice from one of the bestsellers in the genre. But we're also thrust into an unfolding situation. The character has "show[n] up unannounced on Christmas Eve," which can be a risky or unexpected move, depending on the family dynamics involved. Also, who wants someone to "be acting like a total dick" to them? The enemies-to-lovers potential flies off the page.

Chapter One / Ford: "Dude. *Forbes* named you the World's Hottest Billionaire." My best friend, Weston Belmont, announces the title with extra flair to mock me. He makes it sound like I'm a stripper about to take the stage.

Wild Love by Elsie Silver (Series Debut, 2024)

Some fun, sassy humor here. Romance and romantic comedy readers tend to gravitate toward specific tropes, and this opening screams "billionaire romance" right away, but with some teasing, suggesting these good-looking rich bros aren't total assholes. (The character from *Cruel Winter with You*, above, might not like them, then!)

Mystery, Thriller, and Suspense First Lines

These stories are often plot-driven and focus on the mechanic of figuring out what happened in the past (mystery) or preventing something high-stakes from happening in the future (thriller). Horror broadly falls under this label as well, though it's a distinct genre. These novels can use a global scale or, in the case of domestic suspense, be centered in a home or marriage. Sometimes we get a cozy variation, where the gore happens off-page, or a graphic, high-stakes story full of death and destruction.

The pain hit first, then the sound followed, the way lightning beats thunder in a storm.

The pain was in Jack Reacher's right wrist.

In Too Deep: A Reacher Novel by Lee Child and Andrew Child (Series Installment, 2024)

Fans of the Jack Reacher series will immediately worry about their favorite protagonist. This opening not only begins in action, but plays to the audience by threatening the main character.

The phone rang. Again.

It was the fourth time in eight minutes.

The Grey Wolf: A Chief Inspector Gamache Novel by Louise Penny (Series Installment, 2024)

Another long-running series installment from a fan favorite author. There's an insistent phone call, but we also learn a detail about the narrator, who seems fastidious enough to count and time the calls. This personality type might intrigue readers.

Travis Devine sat in the cab staring at the note he'd just found in his coat pocket, and wondered how many more minutes he might have to live.

To Die For: A 6:20 Man Novel by David Baldacci (Series Installment, 2024)

We're introduced to present action, a mysterious note, and some rather alarming concern for Travis's life. Where is he going in the cab? Is he fleeing someone or something? What's in the note that makes him feel like death is imminent?

Later, not a single person will recall seeing the lady board the flight at Hobart Airport.

Nothing about her appearance or demeanor raises a red flag or even an eyebrow.

Here One Moment by Liane Moriarty (2024)

This opening takes us into the future, like *The Familiar* does, above. It's notable that nobody will "recall seeing the lady" later. Are they lying? Or is she really that unremarkable? The suggestion here is that something bad has happened and the omniscient POV makes readers feel helpless as they watch it unfold.

Chapter 1 / Lucy: A podcaster has decided to ruin my life, so I'm buying a chicken.

I make plans for this chicken as I sit in my cubicle at Walter J. Brown Investment Services, waiting to be fired.

Listen for the Lie by Amy Tintera (2024)

Lots of tantalizing questions and some engaging humor here. What does the chicken have to do with anything? How can a podcaster ruin someone's life and why have they chosen Lucy's? Why is she getting fired? One might say there's a lot going on, but we can't deny the hooks!

Prologue: Never open a book with the weather.

Who was it who said that? I can't remember—some famous writer, I expect.

The Fury by Alex Michaelides (2024)

A self-conscious and self-referential opening. However, I use these terms to mean "self-aware" rather than "embarrassed." In self-conscious storytelling, we are intentional about what we're doing and let readers into the process. This helps them feel like insiders—a great engagement strategy, especially since starting with the weather is one of the most boring story beginnings, as you'll see in the Common Opening Clichés chapter. This prologue also lets us into the narrator's jaded first-person POV, suggesting a storyteller inviting us along for the ride.

---

7 December 2022, 7:30 p.m.: I am a ghost in the room tonight. A shadow no one will notice, exactly as it should be.

You Can't Hurt Me by Emma Cook (2024)

An intriguing tone to set at the beginning of a story: Is this a literal ghost, or a figurative one? Why does the character want to go unnoticed? (Spoiler alert: She's a ghost*writer* at her client's book event, but the fake-out is dramatic enough to pique curiosity.)

Outsiders: They'd rung the doorbell unannounced on a chilly Friday night.

The strangers on Eve Palmer's doorstep seemed harmless enough.

We Used to Live Here by Marcus Kliewer (Debut, 2024)

We've had mystery notes and phone calls, but a mystery stranger on the doorstep is the most immediate and potentially dangerous. Here, the heading "Outsiders" sets an ominous tone, as does the "unannounced" visit. Though the "strangers" (more danger suggested) look "harmless enough," many thriller readers know that any character who lets their guard down is likely to get it. Now audiences might be curious what "it" will be.

Perhaps he'll die this time.

He finds this doesn't worry him.

The Ministry of Time by Kaliane Bradley (Debut, 2024)

A classic intrigue play. Why is this person so cavalier about death? How have they come to the precipice of it before?

Saturday, July 16, 1994 6:37 a.m.: Morning sunlight seeps into the tent like a water leak, dripping onto the boy in a muted glow.

Middle of the Night by Riley Sager (2024)

The header notes the date and time right down to the minute and suggests something noteworthy is about to happen. The peaceful imagery also creates some subtle intrigue and danger. Thriller readers might immediately worry for "the boy," as innocents tend to fare poorly in these types of stories.

Prologue: He knew any biographer would decide that the story of his life could be summarized by this: When Liam Samuel Noone began accruing his fortune, the first thing he did was buy a piece of land as far away from his hometown as he could possibly get.

The Night We Lost Him by Laura Dave (2024)

The character sees himself through a potential future biographer's lens, which is unusual. He seems to take for granted that his life will be written about. We also get a bit of background, and readers might wonder if the surface narrative is, indeed, true. Did he really run as far away from home "as he could possibly get"? He suggests this isn't the case, which might make audiences curious to learn the truth. It could also signal another unreliable narrator, bent on shaping the story to his satisfaction.

Memoir First Lines

Contemporary memoir, or narrative nonfiction, uses a lot of the same hooks and opening gambits as fiction does. Except the subject matter is the author's life (often organized around a specific theme), and the protagonist is a version of the creator. These stories tend to draw in readers with a number of variables—shock value, an incredible lived experience, or relatable realizations and transformations which can inspire audiences, no matter what they're going through in their own lives.

All Persians are liars and lying is a sin.

That's what the kids in Mrs. Miller's class think, but I'm the only Persian they've ever met, so I don't know where they got that idea.

Everything Sad Is Untrue by Daniel Nayeri (2020)

This memoir is for young adult and adult readers and tackles the author's coming of age (more on the target category for such a work in the introduction to the First Pages for Adult Readers chapter in the Workshop section at the end of this guide). Note how the author plays with expectations. We get two declarative sentences which suggest Persians are liars and sinners. Then we hear that others think these things about the author, too. Has he created these narratives in his own life? A memoir with a potential unreliable narrator, or at least an obvious raconteur, is immediately intriguing. The title suggests we will be confronting what's true and "untrue," also, so a theme is set into motion right away.

Chapter 1 / Honest Girl: Whenever I ask my mother if she remembers the time in second grade when I stabbed a kid in the head with a pencil, her answer is always the same:

"Vaguely."

Sociopath: A Memoir by Patric Gagne, Ph.D (2024)

This beginning is jarring, especially since the voice is clinical, delivering the facts without emotion. Of course, the title suggests the author is a sociopath. Many readers will likely show up to the page already curious to get into the head of someone with this taboo diagnosis. This beginning delivers immediately.

> *Prologue:* This was my fault. I chase him up the stairs.
>
> At the top of the landing, I caught his right sleeve. When he spun around, his forearm cuffed my cheek. The force knocked me to the wood floor, shocked and dizzy. The bedroom door slammed behind him.
>
> *A Well-Trained Wife: My Escape from Christian Patriarchy* by Tia Levings (2024)

Instant danger and empathy for the character. Readers who gravitate to stories of religious fundamentalism and women escaping the patriarchy are already primed to feel for the author, who seems to believe the dangerous situation unfolding is "[her] fault." This sets up a rock bottom from which she will grow and suggests potential future triumph, which is a common strategy to kick off memoirs with a survival or redemption theme.

> *Prologue: 5:00:* You will surely forgive me if I begin this brief time we have together by talking about our enemies. I say *our* enemies and know that in the many worlds beyond these pages, we are not beholden to each other in whatever rage we do or do not share, but if you will, please, imagine with me.
>
> *There's Always This Year: On Basketball and Ascension* by Hanif Abdurraqib (2024)

Memoirs tend to be more expository in nature—the author is speaking about themselves and is obviously and self-consciously spinning a narrative. Here, the idea that we're bonding over common enemies is intriguing, and the author quite literally invites readers to "please, imagine with [him]." This is similar to the *Everything Sad Is Untrue* opening, above, as audiences get the feeling that they're in the hands of a storyteller. It's a masterful approach because I'm pulled in by this entreaty, whether or not I feel I can relate. Readers might become more willing to go along for the ride either way.

> All burglaries are alike, but every burglary is uninsured in its own way. On June 27, 2019, at 5:15 p.m., I leave my apartment for one hour and come home to find all my jewelry missing. This is the front entrance of the story, the facts of the case.

Grief is for People by Sloane Crosley (2024)

This opening riffs on the famous introduction from Leo Tolstoy's *Anna Karenina*.[2] The author, who is a novelist and essayist, adds a dash of humor right off the bat and invites readers to come through "the front entrance of the story." The cut-and-dried facts of the case are necessary, but without the voice accompanying them, audiences might not be as compelled.

———

WHEW! IF YOU MADE IT ALL THE WAY THROUGH THIS CHAPTER, YOU GET a gold star. This was a lot of material and analysis. You might also have gotten some inspiration for your own story opening, which is great. But before I turn you loose to write your beginning, let's spend a bit more time learning about the ingredients you just saw in action. First, we'll dive into the foundational elements of your story

---

2. "All happy families are alike; each unhappy family is unhappy in its own way."

—the theme and premise—before we drill into individual craft topics. If you're already on the submission trail, you might know—and dread—industry-leaning terms like "premise." But I promise I'll unpack these concepts in a way that demystifies them and brings them back down to earth.

THEME, PREMISE, AND PROMISE

Theme and premise, together, encompass your main idea. The difference between these two terms, to me, comes down to how they're used. Theme is the implicit, deeply human answer to the question: What's this story about? Premise is the explicit, audience-facing response to the same.

Themes are generally universal and simple, as you can see in the following examples. You might not write a project with a theme in mind, but you'd do well to figure yours out before too long. (Sometimes the essence of our creative work isn't clear to us until we're able to take a step back, say, during revision, or as you prepare to submit.)

I strongly suggest hammering out your theme before you pitch your project, though, so you can revise at least one more time with your guiding North Star idea in mind. Theme can be expressed using characters, relationships, imagery, setting, world-building, and the events of your plot themselves. However, theme shouldn't be stated aloud or explained in the text—this is something for the reader to figure out. Remember our detective readers, from the Why Story Openings Matter chapter? They especially like to discern theme for themselves.

Examples of themes are:

- Love
- Human resilience
- Finding one's voice

Premise is closely related to theme, but it's also more outward-facing. When we start to talk about the premise, we think about translating our work for an external audience of gatekeepers, readers, or even curious family and friends, possibly for the first time. Premises tend to be specific and multi-faceted, and their goal is to convey the essence of the story in terms that someone else can easily grasp.

Examples of premise statements are:

- A mysterious millionaire becomes entangled in the lavish and destructive world of the past while attempting to rekindle a love affair. (*The Great Gatsby* by F. Scott Fitzgerald)
- An alienated teenage boy grapples with coming of age and authenticity as he navigates disillusionment in New York City. (*The Catcher in the Rye* by J.D. Salinger)
- In a dystopian future controlled by a totalitarian government, one man stands up to the regime with independent thought and love. (*1984* by George Orwell)
- *The Terminator* meets *Cinderella*. (*Cinder* by Marissa Meyer)[1]

Note that the example premise statements offer specific data points about character *and* plot. Often, theme and premise work together to shape a big-picture impression of your project. If you were to boil down your book idea into a premise statement, what might you say? A lot of writers include a premise statement, logline, elevator pitch (industry terms which refer to a short expression of a book's

---

1. I was one of the many agents who offered representation when this manuscript came in. It hooked so many people right away!

concept) in their query letters. It is the currency of the publishing and marketing world.

If you don't know your premise, why not? Push beyond the simple details of your category and audience. For example, "A coming-of-age story about one magical summer" is an okay start. You offer the broad category and hint at theme with "coming-of-age," which suggests a character growing into their own sense of self and identity. We also get a sense of potential world-building and tone with the commonly used nostalgic summertime setting.

That said, I can't tell you anything else about this story. Who is the character? A young man grieving a dead parent can have a "coming-of-age" summer. So can a girl going to horse camp for the first time. But the tones of these projects will be different. "Magical" is vague and sits at the border between the figurative and literal. Is the summer tonally "magical" because our protagonist falls in love for the first time, or is it literally "magical" because the story takes place at a retreat for young witches?

When you prepare to pitch your book idea, there's a serious information imbalance. You have all the data—you know your project best of all—and the gatekeeper or reader has none. We'll talk a lot more about the balance of action and information in the Action and Conflict chapter, but your job is to convey a strong and clear sense of your story as vividly and succinctly as possible. This is why there's so much emphasis put on the query letter and first pages. They have to accomplish a lot in very few words.

Many writers struggle with boiling down the essence of the book of their hearts, which they've been working on for years, to one page, one sentence, or a single "meets" comparison. Yes, this is hard to do. It can absolutely feel like a punishing exercise or, worse, a silly contrivance that you resent participating in. However, this is all part of the process of presenting your creative output for evaluation and purchase by either readers or literary agents and publishers.

Let's face it, nobody has the time to sit and listen to you explain the intricacy of your world-building, the nuance of your intergenerational character relationships, or the ins and outs of your twisty thriller plot, point by point. This is why you have to zoom out and offer the broad strokes. Your job is to make sure you convey the most appealing impression of the work, in the shortest amount of time. You also need to remember that, with everything you say, you're making promises.

Storytelling Promises

Telling a story to an audience is, as it turns out, a serious responsibility. You're expressing to the reader (or literary agent or acquisitions editor) that you intend to take them on a specific journey. Now, let's first do away with our pearl-clutching at the notion that there are certain *types* of books, writers, or readers. Yes, art is art, and each creation is absolutely a beautiful and unique snowflake, but unless you're swinging for the fences with a genre-busting, postmodern, uncategorizable, never-before-seen idea, your project is likely to fall into at least a broad target audience label. It might also have a genre. Beyond that, your writing probably has something in common with one set of stylistic conventions or another. Your theme and protagonist arc are likely appealing to a certain type of reader. The events of your plot might scratch the itch of, say, heist fans, or police procedural buffs.

Of course, when your book is published, this categorization process is largely out of your hands. The product itself will be shelved in a specific area of the bookstore, or in a certain category online. Projects will be broadly divided into target audiences, from one of the six children's book categories, to fiction for adult readers, to nonfiction. As I mentioned in the Introduction, your story will have a cover and marketing copy, which will generally further reflect its topic and vibe. Are there flowers on the cover (women's fiction, memoir, romance, cozy)? A snake threading through a skull's empty eye socket (fantasy)? An archival photo of a military officer (military, historical fiction, nonfiction)? An illustration of two lovers in a clinch (romance, romantic comedy)? Blood or an ominous-looking house (thriller, suspense)? I could go on and on. Even merchandizing—where it is displayed, how close to the door, facing out on the shelf, on an end cap, grouped with other BookTok favorites on a table—sends signals.

Sure, readers aren't a monolith, only purchasing one type of story. Writers and audiences and books contain multitudes. But it's downright silly to pretend these generalizations, categories, and styles don't matter in today's market, especially given how many other ways audiences can get their pop culture yayas. The idea of a book's promise stems directly from this understanding.

Each of the details described above—cover, marketing copy, target audience, genre, how prominently the book is displayed—starts setting audience expectations, like:

- This will probably be funny;
- If you like dragons, you'll like this;
- This is by your favorite author, and they have a few signature styles and tropes you tend to enjoy;
- The pacing on this one will be fast, and you'll feel suspense as you read; and
- Beautiful writing ahead!

Audiences have different moods and needs, too. Sometimes they're shopping for themselves, their children/grandchildren, or for their mother-in-law's holiday gift, etc. They're going on vacation and want a trashy beach read, or they just listened to a podcast and want to do a rigorous deep nonfiction dive on a topic. All of the external promises detailed above help them try and zero in on their next purchase or library borrow.

But we don't have any of these markers yet when we're talking about a manuscript. Instead, we have the query letter, premise statement, or in-person or virtual pitch at a conference (if applicable). And, of course, the opening pages. With each of those submission package ingredients, we're making implicit and explicit promises about our work. Most writers don't approach their projects this way, and they are often less prepared to pitch competitively. But if you're aware of the promises you're making, you stand to fulfill them and get the attention of gatekeepers and readers alike.

The most important notion to take away from this chapter is that promises are in the eye of the beholder. They are completely out of your control. This can feel like a jarring wake-up call. You've been tinkering with your project and driving the bus for the entire process of its creation—at least until you start to get some third-party critique, which we'll talk about in the Revising Your Opening chapter. Now, you're throwing open your doors and showing your wares, and this is a big proof-of-concept moment.

Is your story coming across as you intended? Is it being received at least somewhat as you'd hoped? If so, you're on the right track. If not, consider the promises you're making, because the people receiving your pitch and pages aren't picking up what you're putting down—and that's important feedback.

Of course, personal taste comes into play here as well. It's not just a form-letter brush-off: Publishing *is* extremely subjective. If your pitch is *"The Notebook* meets *Wednesday,"* which I'd interpret as a weepy, epic love story with a goth twist, and that perfectly encapsulates the essence of your work, it's up to the gatekeeper or reader to decide if they're compelled. And guess what? They're either going to respond favorably to the top-level pitch or they're not—*and they're not wrong.* Their taste is their taste, and your taste is your taste, and if the two overlap … great! But if not? That's okay. They're allowed to like what they like, and your work ain't it.

You'll either find someone else who's into your project, or you won't, and the world will keep spinning. Some writers mistakenly believe they have to be everything to everybody. When I had a slush pile, I'd consistently see statements along the lines of: *This book will be a hit with everyone from zero to one hundred!*

No, it won't. Even a Marketing 101 student will tell you that you can't capture such a broad audience—all 7.5 billion people alive, with the exception of a few centenarians, apparently. Nor would you want to. Not even oxygen, which you might agree has a crack

PR team, is poisonous to anaerobic bacteria.[2] There's nothing that appeals to absolutely everyone, and that's okay.

But you can powerfully connect with audiences by correctly identifying the type of book you're writing, then pitching it as such. And then, in the substance of the book itself, you'll want to leave little breadcrumbs that fulfill your promises.

The Promise of the Premise

The promise of the premise is a craft idea that's relevant to entire projects, not just openings. That said, story openings are a very powerful place to address some of your promises. For example, when you start to really communicate the essence of your work in your beginning, you will be pre-empting gatekeeper and reader questions such as:

- **Character**: Who is the story about? What kind of person are they? What are they struggling with and what might their growth (or, less commonly, devolution) arc be? Do they have a lot of admirable qualities, or are they an antihero? What's the theme of the story, and how might it play out in the protagonist's attitudes, worldviews, choices, and relationships?
- **Plot**: What's the kind of story I can expect? What are its tropes or common genre features? For example, in a heist story, I might get the research/preparation sequence, vetting the team (and attendant interpersonal conflicts), training montage, heist itself, high stakes and danger, aftermath, showcase of the spoils, and maybe a twist ending. You might not have all of these ingredients, in this order, but readers will start formulating expectations once they know the broad strokes of your plot. Chekhov's gun is an important idea to keep in mind—this is the storytelling

---

2. I made this joke in *Writing Interiority: Crafting Irresistible Characters*, and I'm not sorry to repeat it.

maxim that if a gun appears in the first act of the story, it should go off by the end. What other kinds of plot beats are you implying with your beginning?

- **Genre**: Most genres have tropes and common elements baked in. A sci-fi story will be heavy on tech and world-building and might include themes of humans pushing to the outer reaches of their known worlds or battling dystopian regimes on moral grounds. A romance or romantic comedy better have an HEA ("happily ever after," or at least a "happy for now" ending). Horror will include violence or suspense at the very least, and offer a snapshot of the darkness and monstrousness inherent in human nature. (For a great breakdown of genre basics and themes, check out *The Anatomy of Genres* by John Truby.) How are you fulfilling or playing with these expectations?
- **World**: Even contemporary realistic stories have a sense of world-building. Part of sinking into a story is getting to know its world, culture, society, conventions, and whether the main character fits in or feels excluded. In speculative worlds, there are also other considerations. For example, if we're in a fantasy and a character is awakening to a set of powers, readers will want to learn the rules, boundaries, and origins of the magic, the attitude about magic in the larger story world, and how magic enhances or challenges some part of the protagonist's sense of self.
- **Theme**: Which ideas might this story leave me with when I close the back cover? How might it be relevant to my life, or even change the direction of my future evolution? (Might it offer some hope? Lift me up? Be a slap in the face?)
- **Style**: Language, imagery, and overall vibe can tell us a lot about the kind of book we'll be enjoying. Is the dialogue comprised of fast, witty banter in a romantic comedy? Or is that expectation subverted with a dose of dark humor? Is your intergenerational saga told with an eye toward beautiful language and imagery, or is your postmodern antihero narrative rendered in terse sentence fragments and across bleak landscapes? Tone and voice can be confusing

topics for writers, but these should eventually click into
place with enough reading and writing practice. For the
time being, pay attention to your word choice, pacing,
sentence lengths, syntax, and the connotations of your
choices (the implied meanings, rather than the literal ones).
All of these are sending a message to your detective readers
about the vibe, energy, and mood of your work.

You might notice this list has a lot in common with the list of broad
strokes beginning ingredients from the Why Story Openings Matter
chapter. Every element you choose to include in your beginning is
planting seeds and making promises, whether it's a curiosity hook
(see the following chapter) about the character's backstory which
won't be revealed until the stunning climax (see the The First
Chapter and Beyond chapter), or an introduction to a secondary
comedic relief character who you bring on for a chuckle every few
scenes.

Every time a reader learns a new piece of information, meets a
character, takes note of a detail, or sees your protagonist make a
choice, they're likely to ask themselves: Does this matter? Will I see
this element again? Why is this included *here*?

This line of inquiry tends to be heightened at the beginning of a
story, where *everything* is new and readers don't yet have a sense of
what'll end up playing a big role in the long run. This is why you
must direct their attention intentionally, with full command of what
you're doing. You must be aware of the promises you're making—
or, at the very least, aware *that* you're making promises in the first
place.

I love to use the image of the writer as a spotlight operator.
Audiences, and readers, tend to look where the spotlight is shining
brightest. If we are meant to pay attention, we appreciate the heads-
up. The more description, prose, dialogue, or action you lavish on a
specific storytelling element—be it a setting, plot point, secondary
character, or protagonist inner struggle—the more readers will
perceive that puzzle piece as important. At the beginning of a story,

all elements have the potential to be signals. Make sure you're sending the right ones.

Once you've relaxed into the plot and character development a bit in the opening chapters, and then into the first act and beyond, the promises you're making take on a different role. Readers are no longer wondering what kind of story this will be—at least I should hope not! They've settled in and are picking up what you're putting down. You have a larger time horizon to play with. Now, whenever your protagonist and antagonist get together, you're planting seeds about what their ultimate climactic scene might be (or "the obligatory scene," as Robert McKee calls it in *Story*). Whenever the protagonist sees his crush, we're tracking what happened between them last time, his expectations for their next encounter, and her shifting reactions and what they might suggest about her level of interest. Will he finally confess his feelings in this chapter? Is he likely to be rebuffed or successful?

You'll also want to consider how the promise of the premise plays out on a story-wide stage. If you think about *Save the Cat Writes a Novel* by Jessica Brody and the "fun and games" beat, this is the essence of your story dramatized on the page. What can *only* happen in *your* plot? With *your* specific protagonist? If it's a heist, let's meet the rough-and-tumble group of unlikely allies. Let's see them clash against one another but pull together at the last moment. Maybe you'll even have some unexpected sparks fly or throw a twist into the works courtesy of a secret connection in two characters' backstories.

What's catnip for fans of Southern Gothic and how can you highlight your particular unique spin on this element? What's only available in your specific setting? Don't forget that writing a book is supposed to be fun. You've gravitated to your genre and category for a reason—don't hesitate to show your choices off and make them aspirational, larger-than-life, and deeply gratifying for the readers who have, likewise, gravitated to your specific premise.

To reward them for showing up to the page, you'll want to consider placing some curiosity hooks, and that's what we'll talk about next.

CURIOSITY HOOKS

Remember our goal as writers: to make gatekeepers and, eventually, readers care. To this end, curiosity is a powerful key to emotional investment. It's also a fairly easy feeling to arouse because most people are naturally draw to even a small, insignificant mystery. We just can't help ourselves.

The night before I wrote this chapter, I was reading a book called *The Quarry Girls* by Jess Lourey, a thriller based on a true crime story. One of the POV protagonists seemed to have low self-esteem, even for a teenage girl, and hid while her more glamorous and, ahem, developed friends got male attention. Then she mentioned "I tugged my hair to hide my deformity."[1] Now, this story is set in the '70s, so the term wasn't necessarily polite, but I couldn't help wanting to know what'd happened to her. Not so I could *gawk*, but because this detail hinted at an interesting piece of her backstory and was connected to her inner struggle and self-consciousness in the present moment.

A visual difference doesn't automatically make a character more interesting (or somehow less-than, obviously). But the way this part

---

1. Jess Lourey, *The Quarry Girls: A Thriller* (New York: Thomas & Mercer, 2022), 13.

of her appearance was introduced, I got the feeling there was more to it, and I was curious. (As it turns out, her mother set her ear on fire during a mental health episode. Their relationship continues to be a present-moment conflict for this character, so this mystery ends up being quite relevant.)

This author knows it, too, because they drop a breadcrumb about the physical element in question every couple of chapters but save the full reveal for later. Details small and large can create a sense of mystery or intrigue. I tend to call them "curiosity hooks" or "open loops." They operate with the same logic as the promises we read about in the previous chapter. The promise, in this case, is, "This is important, and you'll find out why." The spotlight shone on that detail, and I was hooked.

That tantalizing "later" is irresistible for most readers, especially if we have a reason to care about the character (they're relatable, in active pursuit of a want or goal, struggling internally, and maybe just a bit flawed or incomplete). In fact, a protagonist who presents as having room for growth and development constitutes an open loop in and of itself—only this time, the loop is as wide as an entire character arc. (We'll talk more about introducing an engaging protagonist in the Characters chapter.)

For now, think about any small or medium mystery that you can build into your opening. An envelope that arrives with no postmark, delivered by hand. A conflict with a romantic partner the previous night that's alluded to and putting the protagonist in a bad mood the morning the story starts, but the crux of which we won't know until later. Distant backstory. Recent backstory. Anything that creates a sense of tension, like a perceived slight or a very real trauma. Go back to the Published First Lines chapter and reread the numerous first lines which kicked off with intrigue.

Defining a Hook

A hook is a compelling opening sentence or paragraph that grabs the reader's attention and entices them to continue. The hook creates immediate interest and introduces the story's tone and style. More importantly, it provides a reason for the reader to care about the narrative. It can also raise questions about the characters, setting, or situation, and hint at the central conflict or a situation that promises further tension. A novel hook is a compelling, intriguing, or captivating opening designed to grab the reader's attention right away. It can be an unusual scenario, a thought-provoking question, an evocative description, or a dramatic event.

The right balance of information and mystery in your story's opening can captivate readers, providing enough context to ground them while inviting them to keep reading.

When we meet your character, we only know who they are on the page and in the current moment. But there are all kinds of experiences and events hiding in their past—you can tease readers with these, but only if the payoff reveal affects the present. That they won state in figure skating when they were six doesn't matter at all if nothing in the story bears any relevance to sports or ice or childhood. But if the character is now twenty-one and has just lost her figure skating scholarship because she's ranked dead last at her university? Then this backstory matters.

You can also tease using the future, as we saw in several examples in the Published First Lines chapter. When a character can't wait to see if they've been chosen to participate in a dating show because they gave up on finding a spouse any other way after a break-up, readers will be eager for a text message, call, or email that could come at any time.

Or maybe you'll set a ticking clock on it: If she's picked, she will hear by Friday afternoon. The hours drag by, each one more unbearable than the last. Readers start getting antsy. The suspense thickens if we know what a character wants, why they want it, and why it matters. Maybe this character's siblings are already married, and her parents are starting to loudly worry, so a successful love match might feel like the most important thing in the world. Once readers know this context, they will become invested in what happens.

Yes, this guide is primarily concerned with story beginnings, but I'll play this example out for a few more beats to make a point. Let's say she gets the call—she made the show!—and that particular loop closes. Well, we still know what's important to the character, why she wants her goal, and why it matters. Now, we begin to envision the upcoming plot mechanic of a dating contest.

But then she gets an email from her one true love—the college boyfriend who got away. It's an attachment but it's encrypted. Is this a scam? Spam? Or might he be thinking about her all these years later? Another loop opens. Masterful authors are constantly opening and closing loops and planting curiosity hooks throughout a narrative so readers are always left wondering about something. As long as the answer is relevant to both story and character, it almost doesn't matter what the question is.

So what mysteries or basic curiosities are you stirring up in your story opening? Is the character waiting for something or someone? Fresh off an upsetting or jubilant experience? Still dealing with the ramifications of a traumatic past event? Driving hard toward a goal?

All of these are extremely viable options for putting your character into action, giving them inner struggle, or both. What questions will a reader have once they read your opening? If you're unsure, try this: Give your opening page or two to a trusted reader or critique partner. They shouldn't know too much about your story ahead of time, as you want them to come to the scene with fresh eyes. Then ask them: What were you curious about? What seemed like a mystery?

If they don't identify anything, you know you need to add some intrigue to your opening scene. This is such a powerful reader engagement strategy that I wanted to mention it first and foremost.

A Word of Warning

See what I did there with the above section heading? I bet you want to know what the warning is. You might not want to know *that much*, but I bet you care just a tiny bit.

You see how I'm drawing out some suspense before revealing the answer?

Are you getting sick of me yet?[2]

I'm lightly torturing you to demonstrate a strategy and, as a matter of fact, deliver the warning. When I said that you want to "tease" your reader in the previous section, I didn't mean jerk them around or abuse their natural inclination to be curious. Reader manipulation is a fine art, especially in the beginning of a story. They are putting their trust (and time, emotion, and money) in your hands with the implicit understanding that you'll entertain them and make the experience worthwhile.

But because you have all of the story information and they have none, it's easy to get this symbiotic relationship—of entertainer and audience, artist and appreciator—off on the wrong foot. Incidentally, this warning is why most prologues don't work, which we'll talk about in the Common Opening Clichés chapter.

It's very easy to starve a story of information in an effort to pull off intrigue. But confusion is not the same as mystery. Far from it. If you read crime, thriller, mystery, or suspense stories, you know that most of the information is available. I'd say the ratio of the known to the unknown is 80% or 90% to 20% or 10%, respectively.

The trick isn't to withhold *everything,* it's to shape a reader's reaction to information by using the available point-of-view character(s) as a proxy. (I say "character(s)" here because these stories tend to feature multiple point-of-view protagonists.) How the character(s) interpret the information, their reactions, and their potentially contradictory takeaways all come together into a delicate balance of truth and misdirection. It's not until later in the story that the other 10% or 20% of your information—which changes everything—comes to light. Suddenly the truth snaps together.

The point isn't to withhold as much data as you can, it's to provide

---

2. If so, you're in good company with my husband and children!

context for why the missing detail matters, then intentionally omit the answer.

We can't, after all, solve an equation if we don't have a number of known variables at our disposal. Your call to action at the beginning of a story is to be generous with information, which seems to go against storytelling common sense. But keep something back or make the available data wrong or incomplete. Something about their existing knowledge won't sit right with your character, and they'll want to know more or to bring any dissonance into consonance. By extension, readers will become more invested. (If you want a deeper dive, I did an entire chapter on information reveals in *Writing Interiority: Crafting Irresistible Characters*.)

The toughest beginnings to pull off are those where the writer offers absolutely zero useful data for readers. A character is running for his life from unseen assailants. We don't know why he's running, where he's running to, or what/who/where he's running from. I'm assuming his goal is to save his life, but he could very well be a bad guy running from a superhero or secret agent. Same thing for the dream sequence opening (more on that in the Common Opening Clichés chapter as well) or a character surfacing from being drugged and feeling completely disoriented—no idea where she is, who she's with, how much time has passed since she was last conscious, etc.

If the character doesn't know the very basics of their own story—or is choosing not to reveal anything in a misguided attempt to seem more mysterious—readers have very little reason to care. Openings like this are too slippery, with no concrete foothold to help the audience into the story. (Static beginnings full of information are another issue, but we'll deal with those in the Action and Conflict chapter.)

So offer plenty of information, but keep a few details back. Wrap it all up in action. Use curiosity hooks and open loops. It's completely possible to do this in the first paragraph or on the first page of your story. In fact, I strongly encourage you to find something serious and something light-hearted that you can withhold. What it is will depend on the overall characterization of your protagonist, what matters to them, any genre or category expectations readers might have, and where your plot ends up going (with its relevant sources of tension and conflict).

If the very first curiosity hook you plant is easily and quickly resolved, make sure it's at least tangentially connected to something with higher stakes for the character. After all, if you arouse a reader's curiosity, you want to reward them for becoming engaged. If the envelope with the postcard is a personal-looking sales pitch for new windows or the encrypted attachment from the one true love is just a random computer virus, readers might think—and rightfully so—that you're abusing their willingness to go on a storytelling journey with you.

Don't take their trust for granted, and once you have them on the hook, it's time to work your magic. You can do that with the most potent writing craft element in any arsenal: your character. This is the topic that kicks off our Craft Concepts section.

CRAFT CONCEPTS

CHARACTERS

It's almost impossible to offer general guidance for the creation of an engaging protagonist (or set of protagonists), but I won't stop trying. It actually doesn't really matter who your main character[1] is, as long as they have several things going for them. Those are:

1. **Relatability**: Human qualities that attract readers, whether a universal experience, a desire, inner struggle, self-consciousness, bald-faced optimism, or another attribute that readers might recognize from their own lives;
2. **Passion/spark**: Now this is a controversial point, but I firmly believe that readers want to inhabit someone who's a bit larger than life, embroiled in something interesting, and harnessing passion or energy, even if it's underdeveloped, misguided, or chaotic;
3. **Striving**: We all know what it feels like to care for and/or about something, so it's only natural for us to relate to characters who are in pursuit of an external goal, an internal

---

1. From now on, I will refer to your primary POV protagonist in the singular, as a "character." If you have multiple protagonists in your story, feel free to substitute the plural "characters."

goal, an internal need, or all of the above. (More on these characterizing elements in a moment.) Plus, if readers know what your character wants or needs, you have endless opportunities to throw obstacles and conflict at the situation. As long as your character keeps going and doesn't allow themselves to be deterred (they're allowed the occasional wallow, though), their stock will rise in a reader's eyes;

4. **Proactivity**: The ability to drive the action forward and make choices rather than being dragged around by the plot or simply reacting;

5. **Foibles/flaws**: Whether generated by the character's backstory and wound or not, these are negative or self-limiting elements of their personality. We all make bad choices and even act against our own best interests, and seeing a character with weaknesses, misbeliefs, needs, and other perceived negatives may help readers empathize and relate. Overall, though, the character's good and moral traits should outweigh their maladaptive and negative ones, unless you're offering an antagonist or antihero POV;

6. **Room for Growth**: Characters who are too self-aware and perfect aren't fun to read. If readers compare themselves to a perfect protagonist, they might invariably feel bad and judge that character instead of aligning with them. ("What's wrong with her? She's so fussy!") If you offer a protagonist who's clearly still working on themselves and has the room to do so, readers will become naturally more engaged in their potential growth arc and seeing where they end up;

7. **Inner Struggle**: We all have issues and experiences which stir up self-doubt, denial, cognitive bias, and—especially—vulnerability. In fact, most humans have a tough time being totally open, honest, and authentic. If your character has an inner self they're guarding—as long as this self is accessible to the reader, even if nobody else in the story sees it—this is the kind of "secret" that can bond protagonist and audience and make the reader feel like an insider. Both of these are potent engagement strategies;

8. **Rationale and Logic**: Even if your character isn't always rational, they should have a *rationale*[2] for their choices and actions which readers are privy to. If audiences understand your protagonist's emotional or mental logic and their actions flow more or less in a cause-and-effect sequence, readers are much more likely to attune with them; and

9. **Moral Code/Value System**: No matter what, the character should have a belief system which drives them, and it should be more or less good on a fundamental level (unless, again, you're introducing an antagonist or antihero). If readers get the sense they're a "character worthy of the journey," even if they have shortcomings, you will engender relatability.

Basically, you'll want to focus on introducing a compelling, relatable, or interesting character with a unique voice, worldview, and/or situation. This engages the reader by presenting someone whose story they might want to follow right away. Instead of telling audiences about your character, you must use action, interiority, and dialogue to reveal key characterizing traits and fold in necessary (but sparse, especially at first) backstory details.

It's a tall order to develop all of these storytelling elements for your protagonist. It's an even taller order to communicate them in the opening line, paragraph, or page of a story. Don't worry, you don't have to go down the entire punch list and tick all of these boxes immediately. The above are just qualities which are easy to care about. But what if you're not writing women's fiction or young adult? What if your character is hard-boiled and doesn't care about saving any cats?[3]

Then lean on the protagonist's moral code and appeal to your audience's sense of humanity or theme. If your character firmly

---

2. Thanks again to Scott Marasigan for this turn of phrase. You always know the right thing to say!
3. The entire opening premise of *Save the Cat* by Blake Snyder, which spawned *Save the Cat Writes a Novel* by Jessica Brody, is that even prickly characters need to demonstrate some inherent goodness in action, or readers won't root for them.

believes that "no good deed goes unpunished" and goes through the world with a chip on her shoulder, your challenge is to give her an understandable stance and value system which your readers can understand. Maybe she's a special prosecutor who's an expert at going after shady NGOs and others who take advantage of people's best intentions. She sees the worst and slimiest and is frequently disillusioned. But this is also what keeps her showing up to a demanding job day after day, and readers like seeing a mission-driven character in action.

Audiences might not like or share her specific attitude, but if they understand it and, more importantly, respect it, they'll potentially go along for the ride. Especially if they anticipate that the character will let her walls down, exhibit some vulnerability, or otherwise become less rigid as the story goes on. Maybe her beliefs will be confirmed, or maybe she'll be pleasantly surprised by the end. (But this isn't a guide about endings! You'll have to wait for my plot framework project which—*deep sigh*—I'm sure will be forthcoming shortly after I swear off ever writing another nonfiction book.)

The point here is that any kind of character can be made compelling, even an antagonist or antihero. All you need to do is give your character a sense of purpose, show them in proactive action, and offer both intellectual and emotional logic for the way they are. The following craft topic can help you do this.

Objective and Motivation

The objective is what your character wants, and the motivation is why they want it. Easy-peasy, lemon-squeezy. Now, if you've done any major character work, you know your protagonist will likely have an initial objective and motivation, scene-level objectives, and also a wound and need (discussed a bit later in this chapter) powering them throughout. While we're not overly concerned with how their objective and motivation develop over time—this is a guide to story openings, after all—we will want to be aware of how these forces were forged in order to contextualize an initial objective and motivation.

A character's first goal/want (and sometimes the reason for it) is likely superficial, especially if your protagonist will go on a growth journey and pivot from chasing their objective to their need (usually around the midpoint). This is totally fine. Your call to action is to give them *something* or *someone* to want, even if these first, external, and extrinsic desires transform after some introspection and development.

Putting your character in pursuit of a goal—even if it's a silly one, like catching the mysterious office prankster and unmasking them, which also leverages a curiosity hook—is key. This gives them something to do in the present moment and introduces what matters to them. What they care about, after all, hints at who they are, at least in that moment. They want to be a hero to their peers, in a small way, and that's endearing.

While your story opening should happen in action (a lot more on this in the following chapter) and be focused on the present or the future, you'll also want to introduce a dash of the past when readers meet your protagonist.

Backstory

I'm absolutely not telling you to offer deep and comprehensive backstory for your character in your opening pages, or even the first few chapters (more on this in the Action and Conflict and the The First Chapter and Beyond chapters). That said, you should know a few crucial elements of your protagonist's backstory for yourself. (One thing you absolutely don't want to do is enter a flashback or leave the present moment in the opening pages, as you'll see in a bit.)

Where the protagonist came from, after all, influences where they're going and what they're pursuing, just as it influences their wound and need (discussed below). If readers know a little bit about their recent or distant past—even if it's just one sentence of context—they might feel like your character is three-dimensional and dynamic, with a history and foundation. A small detail or two—as long as they're characterizing and offer some insight into your protagonist's deeper sense of self—in a story opening goes a long way. This is especially true if you also plan on hinting at your protagonist's wound and need early on.

Wound and Need

Some characters have led relatively peaceful lives and don't have overwhelmingly traumatic backstory in their rearview mirrors. (Must be nice!) Some are troubled and still working to heal and reconcile their formative years, while others find their negative experiences galvanizing. No matter your character's relationship to their particular wound (if applicable), you might want to think about introducing important or impactful backstory as the genesis of your protagonist's need.

For example, the protagonist might say they want control over their lives because they grew up as a latchkey kid with no reliable adults to depend on. But, paradoxically, what they *need* is to learn how to cede control and let others in. Not everyone is a disappointment, and the character might learn this by the end of the story and enjoy their first fulfilling relationship. In this case, their want and need are diametrically opposed, which introduces an interesting dynamic.

You won't generally explore the wound and need in the opening pages because these character-building elements don't often emerge until later. Readers might become aware of them before the character does, though, especially if the wound involves a lot of present-day inner struggle. For this reason, you might want to hint at the protagonist's arc, either by addressing your theme in an abstract way in the first few chapters, or planting another character in the story who demonstrates the need in action.

That's right—secondary characters and the protagonist's relationships throughout the story can (and should) offer insight into your primary POV.

Secondary Characters and Relationships

In your effort to make the protagonist dynamic, consider putting them into scene as soon as possible. (More on this approach in the following chapter.) One way to do this is to add another character (or group of characters) to the page and have them interact with your lead.

Why is this important and dynamic? Whenever we have multiple people in a room together (or on the flight deck of spaceship, or wherever your opening scene is set!), you potentially introduce conflict, tension, and stakes. It's very unusual for an entire group of people to want the same thing without any disagreement or power imbalance. Even if they have the same objective—to rescue the ship from an alien takeover—and motivation—to save themselves and their loved ones—they might approach the action differently. Character A is sure his strategy is the best and doesn't want to hear anyone else's input; Character B wants to prove himself as a competent captain but is currently the ship's waste management engineer; Character C is sick of her domineering shipmates and actually wouldn't mind a thinning of the herd; and on and on.

As you'll see in the following chapter, characters are always angling for their own objectives and needs in scene, even if they're allies and friends. For the purposes of your story beginning, throw a character who has some conflict with your protagonist into the mix. Maybe it's the antagonist (if you have one), but the protagonist/antagonist relationship often involves a lot of backstory, especially if they're longstanding enemies. Same for family members—a lot of positive and potentially negative baggage goes into defining these bonds. What if—instead of doing such a big lift in your opening sequence —you introduce readers to the protagonist and an ally during a rocky moment?

The best friend has "forgotten" to invite your main character to a more popular girl's party. The co-founder has been taking secret meetings about the business with a powerful investor. The wife is counting on this anniversary dinner to either rekindle the marriage or confirm her suspicion that the magic is gone. One character has one desire or need and another character has thrown an obstacle or betrayal wrench into the works.

Starting with an ally, friend, or lover character adds instant emotional engagement to the proceedings. Sure, your protagonist cares about their nemesis (if applicable), but they care about their loved one *more*. And if they're invested in the relationship, readers get a shortcut to becoming emotionally involved, too. There's power in showing a protagonist's relationship conflict with secondary characters, especially in the first few pages.

Spark

Speaking of characters who care about something, think about my advice to give your protagonist some spark in the Why Story Openings Matter chapter. A protagonist with a passion not only suggests a built-in objective, motivation, backstory, need, and set of relationships, they also become more relatable, human, quirky, or aspirational. Remember, your readers want to walk in the shoes of someone who's engaging, cool, or weird (in a good way).

Your protagonist doesn't have to be perfect. They don't even have to be good at their secret hobby (let's say it's roller derby). In fact, they can downright suck at it, but as long as they're driven to do it—and get back up when they're knocked down, at least most of the time—their reader appeal will skyrocket.

The bummer character who sits in his room and ruminates about everything going wrong in his life is certainly relatable. We've all sulked, and if you're writing middle grade or young adult,[4] you might think your job is to capture realistic teenage doldrums and snark.

I'd strongly advise against making your protagonist too negative or

---

4. The Workshop section of this book features writing samples from several middle grade (MG) and young adult (YA) novels, as well as discussion of those markets. For a deeper dive, you can pick up my guide, *Writing Irresistible Kidlit: The Ultimate Guide to Crafting Fiction for Young Adult and Middle Grade Readers.*

overly obsessed with what's going wrong. This doesn't actually create conflict or tension—in fact, it flattens it. A protagonist who's passionate about something, who pursues a goal, and who's invested in their close relationships has so much more potential for triumph and strife *because* they care. If they don't care or don't become caught up in hope and excitement, you lose the ability to create stakes, which we'll read about in the following chapter.

Decide what makes your protagonist unique. Give them something they love to do—and love about themselves, too. Especially in the children's book market. I'm seeing more and more stories with coming-of-age themes in everything from picture books to teen novels that feature a character who already knows what they love about themselves. We're not learning that "the magic was inside them all along" at the very end. We start with the magic, the passion, the spark, and watch how it grows or shrinks throughout the plot, and how this self-love (or at least self-knowledge) might spread to others and change the course of a character, relationship, or community in surprising ways.

Of course, crafting a character who loves themselves takes a writer who can practice self-love (easier said than done!). If this is the result of your writing endeavors, even if you don't score a book deal right away, I'd say it's a huge win.

Proactivity

Finally, the most powerful way to create an engaging character is to make them proactive. This underscores all of the other character qualities and strategies we've discussed in this chapter. If the lead is sitting there and hoping something exciting will happen, they're passive. Ruminating about the past? Passive. Putting their desires aside? Passive.

When we first meet Grace, from *Amazing Grace Adams* by Fran Littlewood, an upmarket women's fiction novel, we see her sign up for a linguistics championship. This might seem like small potatoes, but we learn she's denied herself this chance three years running. She has low self-esteem and doubts herself, but when we meet her, she decides to take a risk. She hasn't always been this brave, but now she is *proactive*. This courageous action puts her other self-defeating tendencies into a new context and allows readers to bond with this brave new version of Grace right away.

The opening action doesn't have to hook into the larger thrust of the plot just yet, as we'll see in the following chapter. But there should be opportunity for conflict, action, and consequential choice for your protagonist immediately. Otherwise, they risk coming across as passive in your story's opening, and this is perhaps the cardinal sin of any aspiring beginning.

Identifying these protagonist elements is fine and good, and you might understand—in vague terms—how to include them in your opening, but you still need scene, context, action and setting to make your characterizations sing. Let's take these concepts from the abstract to the tangible and talk about action and conflict next.

ACTION AND CONFLICT

Once you have an idea of who your character is, you want to give them something to do. Ideally, this something will matter to them and will put them in pursuit of an objective. As a result, they'll seem proactive and driven. You'll want to potentially introduce another character who can throw an obstacle—physical or emotional—in their path. And all of this should happen in the present moment and in scene.

The Greek term *"in medias res"* means "in the middle of things," and this is how you'll ideally want to catch your protagonist. Then the trick becomes *sustaining* the present action, rather than scurrying away.

One of the most stubborn and preventable errors I see in many story beginnings is the writer's tendency to leave the moment. This can be subtle, and you might not even know you're doing it. For example, we meet the character in action as he's fighting with his best friend. So far, so good. This is a dynamic relationship, and we have conflict on the page. Then there's an offhanded comment like:

Jack and I met when his family moved next door to ours in kindergarten. I could always count on him. Always.

This might not seem egregious to you. Sure, there's some backstory dropped in here (we can learn about the circumstances of the family's arrival later, if it's really important to the current plot) and it's telling, but readers get a sense of the friendship's length, which serves to make it matter more to the protagonist, right? However what *also* happens in this snippet?

We leave the present moment. Not literally, of course, unless this turns out to be a time travel story. But figuratively. The first-person narrator, our protagonist, has abandoned the current timeline and started digging around in the limbo of memory. It only happened for a moment, but the narrative flow *was* interrupted to shovel in some context. (We'll see some examples of subtle present moment departures from real-life writing samples in the Workshop portion of this guide.)

Until you get more confident in writing story openings, I'd strongly discourage you from doing this. Why? Because I want you to be comfortable choosing a present moment you can sustain for several uninterrupted pages. Most writers can't do this without immediately adding backstory, outright flashback, philosophizing, or thematic explanation (see the Common Opening Clichés and the The First Chapter and Beyond chapters).

But when you begin a story, your goal should be to move it forward. If the story's past is more immediately interesting to you than the present and you really want to showcase what you've developed for the character's backstory, start the narrative earlier. Conversely, if the character is simply sitting there and fretting about a potentially high-stakes future event, start later. They must have enough going on in the present moment that you are able to devote several uninterrupted pages to it, or you're not opening in the right place.

This reminds you to stay in scene. It also reminds you to use all of the trappings of scene, which we'll discuss in a moment. Finally, it keeps you focused on action, without getting distracted by the backstory and characterizing information you've developed—possibly entire notebooks filled with details, many of which will and should ultimately remain off the page.

Choose a moment. Stick inside of it. Sustain it. This is how you lay the first brick of your plot. Sound simple enough? Well, when all you have are choices—because you're making the whole story up out of whole cloth[1]—it's easy to go astray. That's why I offer the below suggestion for selecting a dynamic first scene.

When Do I Start?

Believe it or not, choosing *when* to start is an art form in and of itself. I'll give you a few considerations as you dream up the perfect opening event. In no particular order, you should come up with a scene that:

- Has its own introductory action and conflict, or hooks into the larger plot tension you'll be developing throughout;
- Contains potential for conflict and tension (see below);
- Can showcase at least one other character;
- Involves something that matters to the protagonist—they're either striving to achieve it or losing an important opportunity, chance, or (less commonly) object;
- Showcases the character's unique attributes and allows them to be themselves while they're in action;
- Lends itself well to a difficult choice—the character is at a

---

1. Unless you're writing a memoir, of course, but even then, you have to be selective about where you start. After all, you have millions of lived experiences to choose from, and their sequencing and intended effect on readers are up to you. The work of memoir is shaping these events into a cohesive and theme-focused narrative. How much manipulation you'll do to finagle a narrative from your life story depends on your comfort level with changing the letter—not the spirit—of the raw material. Check out the excellent guide, *The Art of Memoir* by Mary Karr, for more on this juicy topic.

crossroads, must make the next move, or can otherwise display what matters to them in the moment; and

- Introduces an important story location or uses a setting which suggests the premise, theme, and protagonist's growth arc.

First and foremost, though, your opening scene should answer a major question: Why today? As in: Why does this story start *today*? (We'll see this question become relevant in several of our Workshop pieces as well.) The first few chapters should show a character in their relatively normal state, then tilt them toward a new abnormal, which they'll generally only realize the full ramifications of after the inciting incident.

This is why it's always a good idea to show off a familiar setting, longstanding relationship, or protagonist objective in the beginning. These can help to justify starting in a specific moment. The protagonist doesn't know it yet, but their life is about to change. The inciting incident—the first major plot tentpole in traditional story structure—is often thought of as a "one-way door." Once a character crosses the threshold into the rest of the story, there's no going back, either physically, emotionally, intellectually, or all of the above. They can no longer be who they were because they've realized something about themselves or life, or they've been called to challenge themselves in new ways.

Your opening scene, therefore, is one of the last times we'll see your protagonist living their status quo. So give us the old with a hint of the new in the present moment. What are they satisfied with on the surface? Deep down? What are they dissatisfied with or wish they could change? Do they show this side of themselves to anyone or keep it hidden? If the former, maybe put that scene partner on the page. What else about the ordinary baseline (including their world, society, or culture, more on this in the following chapter) might they struggle with?

Once you've seeded some of these elements, unleash a conflict or challenge. If it's a normal day at the office, pipe the rumor of layoffs into the whisper network, have a meeting with the boss pop up last minute on the protagonist's calendar (as we saw in the *I Hope This Finds You Well* published example!), or dangle a juicy, high-stakes client lead in front of them. You can get tension out of desired wins and threatened consequences, though showing your protagonist pursuing the former makes them naturally more dynamic.

Ask yourself why your story starts on the day it does, rather than two months before or six months after. If you don't have a good answer to this question, put everything else on hold and add some strong logic for beginning the way you do. Nothing else is going to happen with your character, writing, setting, or imagery until you crack a compelling *raison d'être* or "reason for being" for the first scene.

Scenework Makes the Dream Work

When you're writing a scene, remember to use some of the following dynamic elements in your writing:

- **Setting**: The location of the present-moment action, as well as any emotional relationship your protagonist has to this place. As readers get to know your world, I'd avoid offering too many locations which are new or neutral. You should showcase symbolic places with an emotional charge;
- **Sensory Details and Physicality**: This is a reminder to put your character into scene and setting by using all of the senses at your disposal and getting into their body, not just their mind (the latter is the essence of this interiority stuff I keep talking about). I'll offer a few caveats about telling with the body in the Recurring Notes chapter, so this suggestion takes some nuance. By remembering that your character has a physical presence, you can engage readers and remind yourself to stay in the present moment, too;
- **Tension and Conflict**: Tension is what we feel whenever there's conflict, especially if we're emotionally invested in the proceedings or outcome. A character can—and definitely should—feel tension in any given scene, whether there's overt external conflict or covert inner struggle. As the

character's proxy, the reader should also have reason to become invested. Remember curiosity hooks and the emotion of intrigue, discussed in the Theme, Premise, and Promise chapter? Leverage audience interest and empathy; and

- **Dialogue**: The spoken exchange of beats, ideas, gambits, efforts, and strategies exchanged between characters as they pursue objectives.

Dialogue is, in fact, so essential to contemporary writing of all kinds —even nonfiction—that I have a cautionary tale to share. Many agents I've spoken to in my career report scrolling through the opening of a manuscript to see where the first instance of dialogue lands. If you've formatted your project correctly, with industry-standard .5" indents for every new line,[2] you'll make it easy for a gatekeeper to tell.

If the opening contains page after page of beautiful prose, lush scene-setting, voice showcasing, and philosophizing, odds are you're not putting any action on the page. We might not even be in the present moment. The story is in limbo while you do housekeeping, explanation, showboating, and throat-clearing. (You'll read more about these issues in the Common Opening Clichés chapter.)

But most contemporary novel and creative nonfiction openings should explode on the page with present-moment action. Your odds of attracting a gatekeeper go down the longer you keep your story in suspended animation. Writers often ask about exceptions at this point. "What about literary fiction?" they wonder in my webinars. The implication seems to be that the rules don't apply in the literary arena. Writers feel exempt from the restrictions of more "lowbrow"

---

2. For a free downloadable manuscript formatting cheat sheet I created, head on over to this URL: https://bit.ly/novel-outline

commercial fiction or think pulling a James Joyce and starting with a sentence that goes on for 4,500 words makes them unique.[3]

Well, take this anecdotal advice as you will, but I'd argue that even books considered literary—and it's important to note that this designation has no formal definition and is extremely subjective— should plunge readers into present-moment action, even if the writer's focus is on descriptive language. Is your intention to entertain and glorify yourself as a wordsmith or to engage your audience? It's possible to do both, but it's very obvious when writers pursue the former. I'd strongly suggest learning the rules and guidelines, then playing around with them intentionally. You have nothing to lose if you start with action and dialogue, regardless of category and genre. But you might lose the all-important attention of your gatekeepers and readers if you don't.

When you're constructing a scene, consider pitting your protagonist against another character. If a protagonist has a strong objective, they can then play actions—or individual "beats"—to try and obtain it. It'd be helpful for story purposes if the other character blocked them or surprised them in some way, which would make them reset their expectations or adjust their strategy or desire. (Though you want a scene partner to make things tough for your protagonist, the objective should theoretically be achievable—if it's downright impossible, readers might disengage.)

When it comes to dialogue, remember that speech is limited by the mechanics of breath, so spoken sentences tend to be shorter than narrative descriptions. It's considered contrived to have characters explain themselves or their goals too obviously to others—people simply don't talk like this. There's also a lot of room for subtext and subterfuge in every character exchange.

If your protagonist doesn't come right out and demand their objective, how might they try to get it? Flatter their scene partner? Disarm the other character partner by reminding them of a recent

---

3. None of Joyce's novels *start* with a 4,500-word sentence but *Ulysses* does *contain* one.

failure? (And how might this gambit reflect on the protagonist's moral framework?) Offer a favor without being asked, in the hopes the scene partner will feel generous or indebted in the future? It's not enough to simply have words between quotation marks on the page. Dialogue, in and of itself, must be finely crafted and active.

Though I strongly encourage you to choose a first scene the protagonist can participate in, I understand that's not always possible. They might need to eavesdrop on some high-stakes action or to observe while other characters are talking (we'll see this dynamic in one of our Workshop examples). In this case, make sure to give them active material in interiority—their thoughts, feelings, expectations, reactions, and inner struggle—or they'll seem passive by just listening and recording.

Above all else, though, make sure your opening scene—and every other scene you include in your story—generates tension and conflict.

Tension and Conflict

As we saw in the previous bulleted list, conflict is what happens in the plot to create trouble for your main character. Tension is the internal discomfort they feel when things don't go their way. Paradoxically, it can also arise when things seem great. (Some characters and humans can't relax and enjoy their good fortune for fear that the "other shoe" will drop. This is called "foreboding joy.")

What's creating conflict in your opening scene? If you've put two characters on the page in opposing positions over a common objective, you have a great start. If there isn't an overt fight or power imbalance, though, how else might you introduce the key scene ingredient of tension? What might the character be thinking about as they go through their day? What are they dissatisfied by? You don't want to have them simply whining, per the previous chapter, but you can always give them a sense of frustrated or unmet expectations, no matter what else is going on. Remember, your opening scene will often feature a glimpse at your protagonist's status quo—something about it will be *itchy*.

Otherwise, there's no reason to change anything or embark on an internal and external character and plot arc.

Your extra credit assignment, once you start thinking about the tension in your first scene, is to then introduce conflict in *every* scene of your story, whether with imagery and voice, interiority, or outright plot. All of these elements add conflict to your protagonist's experience. Speaking of the plot arc, I'll briefly discuss how your opening scene might relate to the bigger storyline you've planned.[4]

Plot

If you've read *Writing the Breakout Novel* by Donald Maass or were paying attention to the plot portion of my book, *Writing Interiority: Crafting Irresistible Characters,* you'll remember the concept of the "bridging conflict." This refers to lower-level action which might not yet connect to the main plot. The point here is you want to offer readers enough tension that the opening still seems to matter. In fact, starting with a medium-level conflict is a relatable strategy.

If you go too small—with no tension or action—readers might not engage for all of the reasons we've previously discussed. But if you go too big—similar to the disorienting "too slippery" opening described in the Curiosity Hooks chapter—you could also lose your audience. First, they might not know enough about the characters or story to care yet. Second, if you start with 11/10 tension, you'll have trouble topping it.

Most plots tend to begin at a relatively settled point and get much worse for their characters (physically, emotionally, or, often, both). If you blow the opening scene out of the water in terms of conflict, you'll have to keep pulling out the stops and raising tension and stakes. Can your chosen plot sustain this escalation, or will your story become melodramatic and cartoony after a while?

---

4. Or, if you haven't sketched anything out in advance and are going to pants it, you'll likely still have a climax you're writing toward. Otherwise, how do you know where to point your first scene and then each sequence of scenes after?

(Paradoxically, too many high-stakes events in a row can have a numbing effect, invoking the Law of Diminishing Returns.)[5]

First, you must decide whether to lead primarily with internal conflict or external struggle. Ideally, your idea will be able to support both, but it's also true that some categories and genres—women's fiction, coming-of-age middle grade and young adult, literary fiction—tend to have less overt plot action and adventure. Others—thriller, fantasy, sci-fi, crime—tend to have more, with perhaps less focus on their character's internal arc.

Once you have a sense of where your larger story might go—and whether character or plot development will lead the way—you can reverse engineer a compelling opening scene. If you're more interested in exploring the growth journey of a wallflower character and the theme of finding one's voice, you might start with a lower-stakes work meeting where the protagonist desperately wants to speak up—but doesn't. This will send readers a message about the kind of growth arc they can expect from your set-up.

On the other hand, if your thriller character doesn't really change over the course of the story but does bring down an extremely powerful entity from the inside by using their wiles and training, perhaps the first scene can involve a higher-stakes scenario where the protagonist successfully tricks an enemy (as long as it's done with virtuous intentions) or showcases their personal strengths and talents. When you think about the set-up of your opening scene, start the way you mean to continue, and make sure the events of the first few pages matter to both your character and to readers. That's where stakes come in.

Stakes

If you've ever wondered, "What's the worst that could happen?" or even "What's the best that could happen?" in a book or movie, that's stakes in action. A story's stakes define why a specific

---

5. Consider this: https://kidlit.com/the-law-of-diminishing-returns/

moment, action, or development matters to the character—and, by proxy, the reader. In the above section, I discussed options for lower-stakes and higher-stakes opening scenes because stakes exist on a spectrum. A low-stakes event might wound a character's sense of self, negatively impact a relationship, or bruise a protagonist's feelings. Perhaps a misunderstanding sends them away from their best friend's house wondering if the two are drifting apart, only to set up a reconciliation later.

High stakes, on the other hand, can and should be emotional (the loss of a love partner, alienation from a parent) but can also negatively affect a protagonist physically and mentally. A character is thrown into a basement, blindfolded, and either starves or loses their grip on reality. Remember, you don't necessarily want to start with the highest possible stakes, unless, of course, you're offering readers a prologue. *The Quarry Girls* by Jess Lourey flashes forward to show a character getting abducted. But if your story has very little to do with danger and mayhem, this kind of opening would ring false and feel like an unfair tease to readers.

You can build a sense of stakes into your opening by having your character think about what they stand to gain or lose if an event does or doesn't happen. You get bonus points if we already know what's important to the protagonist. The first thing we learn about Grace Adams in *Amazing Grace Adams* by Fran Littlewood is her knack for linguistics. When we see her vacillate about entering a contest, her decision gains perceived importance. If she was reading an algebra book and thinking about how much she wanted to win the linguistics contest, there would be a disconnect. What signals are you sending about your protagonist's priorities? How might you come up with an opening scene that puts these very elements on the line, or at least throws them into question?

Anything that impacts a character's sense of identity has the power to generate the most significant stakes. You can threaten my hobby, sure, but if you come after what I consider to be my essence as a human being? I will do anything in my power to hold on to this piece of myself. Using stakes is easy: establish what your character cares about, challenge their ability to do or be it, and/or have someone else come after it. Key characterizing elements of your protagonist's personality are especially vulnerable to attack, and even if you don't threaten their deep self in your opening, you should be hinting at their essence by establishing their nearest and dearest passion. (Sound diabolical? Well, yeah! You don't craft a compelling plot by taking it easy on your characters.)

Once you've created a strong protagonist, fleshed out some secondary characters, and put them all into action which outlines and then challenges the POV's sense of self, priorities, and desires, you should be off to a good start with a dynamic beginning. But readers coming to your page for the first time have more questions than "Who is the main character?" and "What will the story be about (in terms of theme, premise, and plot)?"

They also want to discover the kind of world they'll be plunged into, and that's what we'll talk about next.

SETTING AND WORLD

This chapter isn't intended to be a comprehensive guide to scene-setting and world-building, especially for those of you who are writing in historical, fantasy, and sci-fi genres (which naturally tend to involve more robust story worlds). For speculative writers, I'd strongly suggest *Wonderbook* by Jeff VanderMeer. That said, each story has a specific world, and each environment should be designed to both challenge and illuminate your protagonist and plot. For example, a story about a rebellious teenage might fall flat until we set it in a dystopian, authoritarian society. Then you'll be adding tons of stakes and potential conflicts for your character to explore as they test their value system and boundaries.

Even our real world has setting considerations. No matter the location—domestic or international, rural or urban—the story will also have official and unofficial, spoken and unspoken cultural dynamics, power hierarchies, domestic environments, and social mores. As a result, your characters will have certain worldviews, beliefs, blind spots, prejudices, assumptions, and goals which may have their genesis in the outside world. Did that rebellious teenager want to excel as a leader on her own steam and for her own reasons? Or is she doing so in part because she perceives her mother's generation as weak and powerless? Is her inner self constantly whispering, *You can't end up like her*? Your protagonist will always be a combination of nature and nurture, and the story world should play a role in the latter.

Setting can also be extremely powerful in, well, *setting* up your story. Here are some elements to consider as you design the actual location component of your story beginning:

- Where are we? Is this place new, or does it have significance for the protagonist? As you know from the previous chapter, I prefer a known and resonant location, but a strong argument could also be made for a new and startling environment—as both options present opportunities for conflict.
- What's the vibe or tone of the setting? You might want to go beyond "It was a dark and stormy night"[1] as your objective correlative to portend trouble ahead, as this is a big story opening cliché, as we already saw in the Published First Lines chapter.
- What kind of emotional resonance does your protagonist have with the place? Do they feel comfortable there, or are they out of their element?
- What kind of images, sensory details, and descriptions might you use to underscore the tone of the location?
- When are we in the day? What's the season? A scene set in an abandoned church on a winter night conveys a very different mood than one which takes place during a springtime Sunday morning Easter egg hunt on the same building's front lawn.
- Are there any circumstances that make the setting different the first time we see it? Is Mother's bedroom usually a comforting place, but does it seem eerie now that she's gone missing? How might you sow confusion or tension by using a character's existing relationship to a place?

---

1. And the author of this famous phrase is the namesake of the Bulwer-Lytton Fiction Contest "worst first lines" contest.

- Does the setting reappear in a similar or starkly different context later in the story? One of my favorite tricks is tying character arc to place. Who your protagonist is in this setting offers an example of where they are in their development. The next time we visit a location, they might act, react, feel, or think very differently. (You can also set your final scene in the same spot as your opening to really bring your story and character arc full circle.)

Moving beyond setting, you might want to answer the following world-building questions about the larger universe of your story:

- What's the political landscape of this society?
- What is the social structure here? Is the character on the inside or outside of prevailing power dynamics?
- If there are magical powers, what are their rules and boundaries? If you're writing a speculative story, how does the addition of magic, legendary creatures, paranormal elements, etc., alter the protagonist's situation and the larger plot?
- If there's technology, what are its rules and boundaries? If you're writing sci-fi, how does the specific type of technology and its abilities and limitations alter the protagonist's trajectory?
- If yours is a historical world, how do the rules and restrictions of the time period affect your protagonist and plot?
- What is the history of this world? Does everyone agree or is the prevailing narrative controversial? How does the character relate to the world's culture and background?
- What are the myths and fables of this world? What kinds of stories do the inhabitants tell themselves about their people and society?
- Are there any faith traditions? How pervasive is organized religion (if applicable)? What does this world think about a higher power, and how does the society enforce moral value systems? How do people self-actualize?

If you're able to introduce some noteworthy details which touch upon these questions and issues right away, you can spark curiosity about your world, time period, setting, culture, etc., and its rules, which only encourages readers to learn more. The ideal approach is to have your character interact with the world in the opening scene, which will lend some momentum to the world-building context. (Avoid simply explaining the above elements at all costs.) In general, you should be intentional with how you present this data, when, and, especially, how much of it you offer. This is where the balance of action and information comes in.

Balance of Action and Information

A lot of writers get into trouble trying to balance action and information, especially those who develop their worlds first and foremost (speculative and sci-fi writers, as well as those who've done a lot of historical research, tend to be guiltiest here). They get so into their worlds and settings that character and story become afterthoughts. If you have nothing *but* world-building to present to the reader, you'll have to be especially careful to avoid info-dumping—especially in your story opening. The goal is to reveal information gradually, allowing readers to piece together the context as they go. The more they connect the dots and start building a sense of your world in their heads, the more engaged they'll feel.

For your opening, I strongly encourage you to give readers only what they absolutely need to know to understand your character and the conflict of the first scene. This information should also be presented in context.

For example, the middle grade novel *The Spirit Glass* by Roshani Chokshi is set in a Filipino-mythology-inspired fantasy world. Our protagonist is on the verge of a significant birthday and fully expects to receive the magical power to commune with spirits. There's a lot of potential for lush world-building, but readers don't meet the various creatures and fantasy elements right away. We also don't immediately look beyond the veil which separates the dead from the living, even though we will journey there over the course of the story.

Instead, audiences start with simple context: Corazon expects to get her powers any second now, but they don't arrive. These are the first lines:

Corazon Lopez possessed a rare and secret power.... The only problem was that this secret power was apparently just *so* humongous and *so* hard to handle that it remained a secret ... even from Corazon.

But not for much longer.

Hopefully.

The Spirit Glass by Roshani Chokshi

Immediately following this opening are three sentences of detail about what *babaylan* powers generally do, then we go into the present moment and see Corazon standing in her kitchen, convinced she's about to be thunderstruck by magic. Her unmet desire pulls readers in.

This is a relatively light approach to the fantasy world-building, as we only get information which is immediately relevant to the character and her predicament. We see her yearning and interpret with her inward struggle with impatience and doubt, and we understand the conflict—a lack of expected powers.

Filipino mythology is quite intricate, and, as mentioned, we learn a lot more about it. But this always happens through the lens of character and action. At no point does this author go off on a lecture, putting dense information on the page for its own sake. This is also a middle grade fantasy, and that category and genre expect a lot of action and adventure, leaving little room for ponderousness.

We meet the character first, get a headline about the world (there are spirit realm-related magic powers here), and see the strange or upsetting thing that's happening. This opening demonstrates careful restraint.

Just as David and Moira must "fold in the cheese" into their heirloom enchilada recipe,[2] you can always layer in information as you go. If you have a world-building-heavy story to tell, you'll have to do a lot of folding and layering. But you don't have to do it all immediately. (It's also entirely possible that you don't actually need all of the information you've invented. Some of it can and should be left on the cutting room floor, as it was more useful in your own creative process. It doesn't impact the story nearly enough to merit its inclusion.) Offer the most relevant and impactful data up front, then save the rest for later.

From then on, it's up to you to make changes or tweak character (and reader) understanding of the world when you establish new story developments, twists, reveals, and surprises. It's a tricky balancing act, and I'll talk more about how you can relax and spend more time on establishing information after the first few pages in our The First Chapter and Beyond chapter.

If you notice that your world-building comes across as dense right away, try to identify between one and three tidbits readers absolutely need to know for the opening scene to make sense. (This is also my advice for world-building information overload in query letters. Include what's absolutely essential for a gatekeeper to understand your premise, then leave the rest for the synopsis and manuscript sample itself.)

Now that we've covered character, plot, and story world, you might think we're done with our exploration of the core story opening ingredients. And you'd be partially right. These are the quantifiable elements most manuscripts start with. But two more craft topics have the potential to wrap everything together into a cohesive whole. I'm talking about tone and style, and we'll cover them in our next chapter.

---

2. If you don't get this *Schitt's Creek* reference, do yourself a favor and check out this beloved comedy series.

TONE AND STYLE

A story's beginning sets the tone for the entire narrative, and we saw some notable examples of this in the Published First Lines chapter. POV is one of the first signals you can send to readers, from the immersive invitation of first person, to outright second-person direct address, or the more versatile third person, which can vary widely, from detached and objective to deeply subjective and intimate. In the case of *The Three-Body Problem* by Cixin Liu, translated by Ken Liu, the omniscient narration creates a paradoxical desire to close the narrative distance gap.

Moving on from perspective, tone and style can be difficult for writers to grasp because they are, by their very nature, ephemeral. Sort of like the topic of writing voice. Many agents and acquisitions editors say things like, "I know it when I see it." And they're right. Tone, style, voice, vibe, etc., are very much in the eye of the beholder, as are some of the elements discussed in the Theme, Premise, and Promise chapter.

But watch out: You shouldn't leave them completely up to the reader to determine. My challenge to you throughout this guide has been to make more intentional choices. And thousands of small yet precise decisions come together to influence an audience's sense of tone and style.

Tone can be described as the mood of the writing or scene. Style is the set of artistic conventions with which the tone and narrative are rendered. Your choice of words with specific denotations and connotations can evoke distinct emotions. For instance, using dark, heavy words can create a somber tone, while light, whimsical language can come across as playful. Short, choppy sentences can convey tension and urgency, while long, flowing ones can evoke a sense of calm or even awe. The imagery and motifs you choose in an opening can hint at the thematic elements of the story to come. Recurring scenes set in a crumbling building, for instance, might set a tone of decay and decline.

It's also possible to create combinations. You can, for example, have a mysterious tone with a literary style. Or a high-fantasy tone done in a witty, banter-driven style. There's obviously some overlap between these concepts. By working on one, you'll also be developing the other.

Remember our discussion of categories and genres in the Why Story Openings Matter chapter? I talked about each type of book having broad conventions which tend to attract certain audiences, like the classic HEA expectation in a romance or romantic comedy. A book teaches us how to read it, and a book with a specific tone or style promises related emotions and experiences. If I'm lounging on a chaise by the pool with what I believe is a breezy beach read, I'm going to be jarred out of a lighthearted experience if the story begins with an earnest, weepy funeral. (There are also funny funerals, as we saw in the Published First Lines chapter, or at least funny characters behaving inappropriately at earnest funerals, but here, I mean a gut-wrenching, tragic funeral.) If the beach read starts with the right tone and style but then veers into thriller pacing or an irredeemable antihero protagonist, that might also sour my experience.

That's not to say books can't shift tones or trajectories, either subtly or abruptly. But I'd say that change should be foreshadowed early, maybe with a peek at a POV section in a different voice or with scenes and character interactions which suggest the theme of duplicity. If that breezy beach reach becomes a morally gray postmodern slog, you might lose me as a reader, as I wasn't in the mood for such a book poolside. (Readers, like characters and writers, have moods and appetites. They contain multitudes, which is also why it's important to clearly broadcast your book's category, genre, tone, and style, so you can guide the *right reader* to the *right project, right when they want it.* Win-win-win!)

Unpacking Tone and Style

Let's make these concepts concrete. To look at tone, let's see the same scenario done four different ways. First, here's the "naked" description that I wrote, without any tone conventions applied:

She looked at the vista.

Now let's see it as a romance or romantic comedy:

As she peered over the sun-dappled vineyard from the balcony, a pair of strong hands covered her eyes, the smell of cedar and musk suddenly overwhelming her.

"What took you so long?" she asked, and her date chuckled, a deep rumble against her back.

Next, let's try a high-octane thriller:

As she peered over the sun-dappled vineyard from the balcony, a pair of strong hands covered her eyes, the smell of something chemical singeing her nose.

"Wait, who are—"

But she couldn't finish the sentence as darkness claimed her.

Finally, here's horror:

She crouched low, satisfied that there was no one beyond the balcony. The surrounding vineyards stretched into the night. Only a few hours ago, they'd felt peaceful. Now she was acutely conscious of how far she was from the next house.

Snap. Something moved outside the wall.

Too close.

She couldn't bring herself to look again.

Is this idea starting to make more sense? The tone is the underlying emotional current of a piece. Your protagonist can contribute to the emotion of a scene or passage, especially if you're in their close-third-person or first-person POV. An intrusive narrator can also tell the story in such a way that their interpretation of events establishes the tone. Your imagery and setting can offer a moody wash over everything and evoke specific reactions from the reader. These will ideally be in line with your audience's category and genre expectations, as well as the existing conventions for your specific type of project.

If we then go to the sentence level of the writing itself, we'll find style, which aligns itself most closely with voice. Style can move quickly or slowly (also known as the story's pacing). It can be silly or serious. There can be evocative language to savor, or choppy sentence fragments to trip over. Style also encompasses sentence length, word choice, imagery, and syntax.

A manuscript's tone and style might remain consistent throughout, or they can shift. For example, the style of the writing could transition to better reflect what a character is going through over the course of the story. The prose might be relaxed as the protagonist experiences an upswing but could grow terse during the climactic sequence.

Let's do the above exercise for style. Here's a basic text again, without any stylistic leanings:

> He walked into the restaurant. His date was already sitting at the bar.

Now let's make this warm and energetic:

> He strode into the restaurant, leaving the January flurries behind. There she sat, laughing with the woman next to her at the bar, her hair tumbling in soft waves down her shoulders. That was Catherine—she could make fast friends with anyone.

Here it is again, filtered through a cold voice:

> He swept past, noting a B grade from the health department hidden in the corner of the window. His date had suggested this place, but he didn't know her taste. And there she was … at the bar and at least one espresso martini deep, from the looks of it. He steeled himself. Was this about to be a problem?

Shifting it over to claustrophobia might look like:

> The restaurant din rang in his ears, too loud, the tables too close. He wanted to leave immediately, but it was too late— she'd spotted him.

And, now, breathless passion:

> The client meeting falling apart at work didn't matter. Nothing
> did. He had to see her. The restaurant was packed, but as soon
> as he locked eyes with Catherine, everything faded into the
> background. "Hello," he breathed and closed the distance
> between them.

When combined with your character choices, plot, world, and
action, tone and style can create a kind of alchemy that pulls
everything together. All you have to do is be aware of what your
sentence-level writing is doing, what your audience might expect,
and how all of these elements filter through your narrative choices.
Notice the in-your-face immediacy of first-person POV and present
tense. It can feel quite relentless to experience an entire story written
using this combination. There's more psychic distance and remove
in omniscient POV and past tense, on the other hand. What kind of
novel or memoir might benefit from the former? What about the
latter?

Learn to love exploring the rhythm of your writing and being more
selective with imagery, word choice, sentence length, and syntax.
Consider matching a different style to each of your POV characters,
if you're working with multiple narrators. How does your
protagonist's mood and position in the story affect how they think
about and describe the world around them? All of these
considerations are part of tone—the overall expectations of your
particular category and genre—and style—how you express your
specific story in your unique voice.

What's the vibe you want a new reader to interpret from your
opening pages? If you're still stuck on these concepts, try applying
several tones to your writing until you find a combination that
works for the story you want to tell, character, events of the plot,
world, and, of course, impression you want to make. Who are you

as a creator? What's your personal signature? How might you add this layer to whatever you write?

This is definitely a skill you'll develop over time—even across multiple books—so don't feel you have to nail down a permanent answer now. But know it's never too early to start thinking about your authorial signature, as this is something else that, with any luck, your audience will eventually know and expect from you.

Now let's talk about what happens beyond the all-important real estate of the first page. Each of these concepts applies not only to your opening lines, but to the scenes and chapters which follow.

MOVING FORWARD

THE FIRST CHAPTER AND BEYOND

Given what you've read so far, you might be wondering how anyone gets published. (Or, rather, how you might pull off a story opening that's compelling enough to get *you* published.) The bar for creating captivating first pages might seem too high. The to-do list comes off as too rigorous. Well, don't despair.[1] As I also said in the introduction, you have time to write, rewrite, and even throw the whole opening out and start over. This is totally okay. (We'll talk about this in the Revising Your Opening chapter.)

For your opening line, aim for something short, punchy, and character-led which captures your curiosity hook, if possible. Don't start with unattributed dialogue (if we don't know who's speaking, to whom, or what else is going on, we don't care). Try to avoid ponderous scene-setting and imagery. Fight the urge to start explaining your theme or world. A good first sentence can be funny (depending on your tone and style) or unexpected. At the very least, it should seed some intrigue or raise an eyebrow.

Go back and reread the Published First Lines chapter. Notice how each example has some kind of hook (also discussed in the

---

1. Easier said than done, I know!

Curiosity Hooks chapter). It could be a relatable character observation, action, or reaction. We might be thrust into the middle of an engaging or tense situation. Or you could blow readers away with your voice and writing chops (while also embedding them into a present-moment scene, of course).

The length and style of the first line also sets the tone and leads by example. What do you focus on, and how do you express yourself? This helps show readers what's important not only in the story but to the POV narrator and author. What does the story value? How do you convey that? Which promises are inherent in your opening, and how will you deliver on those—or subvert expectations—as the story moves forward?

Now it's time for your opening paragraphs. How do you build on the energy and curiosity you generated in the opening line? Read on.

The First Paragraphs

Once you've gotten over the hurdle of that first-line impression, you might think you're safe from a gatekeeper losing focus on your submission or a reader putting your book back on the shelf or clicking out of the ebook sample. Wrong. You now have to capitalize on the momentum of your opening.

But your options for doing so become quite diverse. You must, at the very least, establish your character, what they're doing in the present moment, where they are in space, and what's motivating them to act. This will also be buttressed by tone and style, but you can always fine-tune those as you become more and more familiar with the story you're telling.

Every choice you make in the first few paragraphs steers reader expectations. As you start layering sentence after sentence onto your story opening, you will want to be extra conscious of any promises you might be making. For example, if we meet a secondary character in scene and learn a few things about them, readers will wonder if they're going to be important to the larger narrative. This is why I recommend starting in action with a character who has a long-standing or nuanced relationship with the protagonist. They'll be more likely to stick around and matter in the long run.

One of the first manuscripts I worked on when I opened my freelance editing business in 2013 was primarily about a pilot—let's call him Jake. He would make dozens of flights over the course of the story. In the opening chapter, however, we met his co-pilot—let's call him Chad. In fact, the first scene was in Chad's POV. In the second chapter, we went into Jake's perspective … and stayed there for the rest of the story. And guess what? Not only did we never experience Chad's POV again, we never saw *Chad* again. It was as if he never existed in the first place.

This example has stuck with me because it was such a misuse of the beginning. To offer a character who doesn't reappear and to assign them a point of view—a powerful position usually reserved for the protagonist—you have wasted your most valuable real estate. Everything I learned or engaged with as a reader went out the window.

Not only did this writer squander the opportunity to foster audience connection to Jake, the actual protagonist, but I, as a reader, felt a bit misled and disrespected. I had my detective hat on and was starting to pick up on the promises and signals of the chapter, only to go back to square one when the real main character showed up. (My *feelings* aren't *hurt* or anything. In my work, I tend to keep projects at an emotional distance so I can react as objectively as possible. But I say this to demonstrate a point. A reader might resent a manuscript or book that doesn't seem to respect their time and energy, or they might even lose trust in the writer's skill.)

The above is an extreme example, but an important one. What you include in the first few paragraphs—then the first few pages, then the opening chapters—must earn its keep. It should either move the reader's understanding of the protagonist forward, advance the plot, introduce mystery or intrigue, suggest theme, offer world-building or character development context (such as defining why the objective matters to them), or add a little stylistic or tonal frisson

—though the creative writing bells and whistles should be your last priority in the opening, unless you're specifically working in a literary genre or the execution of your premise depends on a specific voice.

Notice where you're establishing theme, character, plot and conflict, setting and story world. Track any hooks and loops. In fact, I'll ask you to do this in a more intentional way in the Revising Your Opening chapter. The first page's level of information density will dissipate as you hit your stride, include more dialogue, and push ahead on your action. Not every line of your manuscript needs to be laden with multiple levels of meaning once you've reached your cruising altitude.[2]

The order in which you introduce your storytelling elements might also send meta-signals to your audience. If you're writing a coming-of-age young adult contemporary and we spend the first paragraph or two in the character's interiority, that tracks. This combination of genre and category is often concerned with the protagonist, their thought processes, and inner struggles.

A hard sci-fi story might introduce a character interfacing with their technology or engaging in some significant action (though, remember, you don't want to start off with level-ten stakes right away unless you're writing a prologue). This reassures your sci-fi reader that you've got plenty of world-building in store. A detective in a police procedural might be running a crucial piece of evidence to the lab—which offers a sneak peek of the conflict and action to come. The intergenerational literary saga could open with the heavy subtext of a conversation between spouses—except the dialogue "about" what to eat for dinner that night manages to imply some of their fears, hopes, dreams, and disappointments.

When you're revising your entire manuscript, I suggest you ask these questions of each *chapter*: Does it add to a reader's understanding of the character, any secondary characters, and the relationships involved? Does it move the plot forward in a

---

2. Maybe you'll find Chad *there*?

discernible way? Does it develop a reader's curiosity about and relationship to the story? Does the protagonist have the opportunity to be proactive? In other words: Does it earn its keep? In your first chapter, though, you should be asking these same questions about each *paragraph*.

The First Chapter

You'd obviously keep reading your own story past the opening paragraphs—you wrote it, so I'm assuming you think it's worthwhile. That said, you're going to have maximum emotional investment in the project, for obvious reasons. Nobody is going to care about it as much as you do, not even its eventual literary agent and acquisitions editor, who are going to be the book's professional champions. And that's okay. (A creator is always the most invested party, and that's the natural order of things.)

Of course, you'll want readers to emotionally invest as much as possible alongside you. To accomplish this goal, you'll need to give them reasons to keep going, stay up all night and be grumpy at work or school the next day, and recommend the story to all of their friends.

Once you read your first line, then your first paragraphs, and into your first chapter, can you honestly say whether you're compelled enough to continue? If you give the same section to a critique partner or freelance editor, will they simply force a smile, or will they ask for more?

We can create an irresistible sense of curiosity by stoking the fires of mystery and bringing a character to life on the page who's in hot pursuit of something (or someone) that matters to them. Maybe we've just seen them triumph and want to see whether that success carries. (Success can also be a double-edged sword because it raises expectations and pressure.) Or, more likely, we've witnessed them being knocked down a peg or two, and our empathy engines are revving up.

You must now make several creative decisions about the substance of your first chapter. How long will you make your scenes? Sometimes a chapter contains many smaller moments strung together. Other times, it's just one scene, which can be long or short. As we'll see in the Workshop section, you might want to err on the side of making your opening chapter compact, especially if you're working with multiple narrators or in more than one timeline. This way, gatekeepers can evaluate each of your voices from the writing sample. Consider also turning the screw and embedding another curiosity hook or source of intrigue at the end of each scene. You'll want to start hinting at or overtly plugging into the bigger story conflict that'll end up driving the rest of the plot, too. What are you waiting for?

Every time a reader encounters the white space at the end of a section or chapter, you should be fighting to keep them. It's quite easy to slide in a bookmark and go to bed at a natural break in the story. That's why you want to end your first chapter on a question, hook, surprise, reveal, or cliffhanger that changes something for the character. How do we know the event we just witnessed is a big deal? Ideally you've done your work to establish what's important to your protagonist and why. Using many of the strategies in this guide, you can threaten what's nearest and dearest to your main character or seed a sense of vulnerability and self-doubt. Yes, even in the opening, where we're just getting to know your protagonist.

This is especially important to do at the end of the first chapter, so readers might feel they *have to* keep reading. The same goes for gatekeepers. If you've managed to keep their interest from the first line all the way to the end of the first chapter (if it's included in the ten double-spaced pages you'll send as part of your submission, and, as I said above, I strongly recommend you make your first chapter short enough to fit in its entirety), you'll want to pull the fishing rod and hook them in a very visceral way. The end of the first chapter is a real make-or-break moment.

While you don't want to abuse the cliffhanger, I strongly suggest using one in this instance. Keep the action in the present moment. Raise the stakes for your character. Avoid the whole, "If I only knew then what I know now, I never would've followed Kevin to his parents' cabin that Saturday night." Don't zoom off to some hazy future POV and see the scene through the eyes of experience. Focus on the character's nerves as she makes the decision to go. Give us a sense of the risk involved through her interiority. Has she never done anything like this before? Will her parents kill her? Does she believe hooking up with Kevin is going to give her status? Paradoxically, might it tank her reputation? Or is she in love with him? Do we know why sneaking off to meet him is so important to her? Why is it worth forsaking her values or getting in trouble?

What's her inner struggle? Maybe she doesn't really like him, but her best friend just lost her virginity, and she feels left out in the whole "maturity" game. Maybe Kevin used to bully her, and this is all a ploy to humiliate him in retaliation. This might seem like the most obvious statement I've made in this guide, but when readers genuinely don't know what's going to happen, you have their attention. Create mystery and uncertainty when you end your first chapter, or introduce a complication that'll hook into your main plot.

The Following Chapters

If your first few sentences and paragraphs are a microcosm of your story, the first chapters build on that foundation and expand the universe you're presenting to your reader. All of the ingredients will be the same, including insights into the protagonist via their actions, dialogue, and interiority; introductions to important secondary characters and relationships; initial conflicts transitioning into the larger plot tension as you approach the inciting incident; consistent tone and style which reinforce the genre and set expectations; and even more world-building data once readers are warmed up. If you're still cloudy on any of these opening building blocks, feel free to reread the relevant craft chapters for ideas.

Now there's good news: Once you've launched the story and readers or gatekeepers are still with you beyond the first chapter, you have a little bit more time and room to play around. You should never allow the pressure of pacing your story and moving it forward to droop—as some writers do when they struggle with their muddy middles, for example—but you *can* relax a little. Unless you're writing action adventure or thriller, you won't be able to sustain breakneck pacing on every page, nor should you want to.

In Chapter 2 of your story and beyond, you can add more dimension to the ideas you've already established, introduce more characters, and add layers to your protagonist. Readers might have a strong sense of who your characters are—or pretend to be—from the first chapter. Now you can reinforce or even subvert these notions. Does the protagonist act immorally or outside of their best interest? Do they go back on a promise or betray a friend? Are readers becoming more aware of a wound, piece of backstory, or underlying need which might be driving their behavior?

The above suggestions point to change and growth, which will start to kick in beyond the opening chapter. Unfortunately, what you've established about your character in the beginning is not enough to flesh out a compelling narrative, in and of itself. Stories, protagonists, and plots are dynamic. In fact, if you go on too long without adding layers of nuance to any element of your project, readers might get bored, and you'll risk losing them again.

This is especially true of your main character, who should start to show multiple sides of themselves as the pages roll on. A one-dimensional protagonist or secondary character, after all, is a caricature or stereotype. (While it's true that some characters need more development, like your protagonist, and some need less, like the dance instructor we meet for two scenes total, you still want to identify potential layers for most of your *dramatis personae* to make them surprising, intriguing, and engaging, even if you're building them from recognizable archetypes.)[3]

You'll also want to continue intentionally revealing and establishing

---

3. For a deep dive into character roles, I highly recommend *The Writer's Journey* by Christopher Vogler.

two elements you weren't able to fully develop in the first chapter: backstory and flashback.

Backstory and Flashback

Once you're able to move beyond your beginning, you can present more information about your character and world's backstories. To be clear, you should absolutely not do a giant info-dump, even in the second or third chapter. All information is dense and impedes action and should therefore be parceled out gradually, whether you're writing Chapter 2 or 20.

Some stories don't rely on backstory to get started and are based mostly in the present. Instead of requiring past context, they're rather forward-facing. If this is you, great. You might still want to deploy relevant backstory at some point, especially if your character ever pivots from chasing their objective to pursuing their need (which might be rooted in a past wound). Other stories rely on a crucial reveal from the character's past during the climax. In these cases, important information is intentionally withheld for later. (But remember, readers and characters need *some* data to work with in the current timeline, as originally discussed in the Curiosity Hooks chapter.)

Protagonists don't often self-actualize in the present or future without a sense of what came before and what's buried beneath their foundations. Once the first chapter is over, you have more breathing room to potentially even indulge in some flashback. To clarify the terms: **Backstory** is the sum total of a character's past experiences which have come together to define who they are in the present and to suggest their future. A **flashback** is a specific type of scene with setting, dialogue, sensory details, interiority, and action. It just so happens to be taking place in the past.

Essentially, backstory is the information, and flashback is the delivery method. Flashback often gets a bad reputation in creative writing, and that's because aspiring authors often indulge in it right away, before audiences have a reason to care about the character *or* their history. Gatekeepers and readers tend to hate it for the same reason they hate info-dumps. It's too much, too soon, before anyone has formed a meaningful connection with the story.

But flashbacks can indeed be helpful. For example, if we can't meet an important secondary character in the present because they're dead or otherwise unavailable, you can showcase their personality and the particulars of their relationship with the protagonist in flashback. This is especially desirable if a protagonist's deceased parent or other mentor was instrumental in shaping their identity. Without flashback, we can only be told about this important character. With flashback, however, we can see them in action, watch how they treated the protagonist, see their worldview in dialogue, and otherwise interpret them with our reader detective hats on.

I'd do everything in my power to avoid leaving the present moment for the first few pages, bare minimum, or even the first chapter, if you want a challenge. This means no lengthy presentation of backstory and definitely no flashbacks. (You can *allude* to backstory, but only offer those details which immediately contextualize the protagonist's actions or reactions in the present scene.)

In the example of the best friends on the rocks in the Action and Conflict chapter, I demonstrated a small instance of the character leaving the present moment to time travel and establish details about the friendship. If the origins of the relationship are important to the present and future story, we should probably see a flashback to their first meeting (or another significant past moment) at some point. However, labeling them "lifelong friends" or "best friends" and showing their interactions could also be enough to cement the idea of an ongoing, long-standing, nuanced, and important relationship.

Some writers fall into a toxic pattern of introducing an element of the protagonist's life or identity, then immediately zooming off to fill in its origin story. If the protagonist is into tennis, we then get a memory of her first time on the court. When we talk about the friend's mother, we flash back to Mom helping the neighborhood kids run a lemonade stand. A similar mistake is pausing the action to insert a character's physical appearance the second we meet someone (which I'll talk about in the following chapter). This pattern will grow stale after a while.

As with all kinds of other information, you have to be selective with backstory, and especially with backstory that's important enough to merit the flashback treatment. The more something matters, the more attention you should pay to it on the page—its past, present, *and* future. However, the bulk of your story should be forward-looking rather than obsessed with what already happened. The past cannot be changed. It can only be used to explain the present or combed over for missed clues. Of course, many stories, especially mysteries, rely heavily on current interpretations of the past, and rightfully so. The detective or amateur sleuth is trying to solve a case and needs to be somewhat backward-facing in their focus.

Some stories, like *Eleanor Oliphant Is Completely Fine* by Gail Honeyman, hinge on the climactic revelation of an incendiary past event. This is a very specific structure, and the withheld detail should snap many things about the character or plot (or both) into focus. This only works if the information will pay off emotionally and be worth the wait. That said, even those protagonists who are missing an essential piece of their history should also have consequential relationships and conflicts in the present. They can't get far if they're waiting for backstory to give them momentum or an identity. In most cases, focus forward on what characters can do and change about their circumstances, as the past is fixed and static, which translates to low stakes. Yes, backstory and flashback have a place in many kinds of stories, but it shouldn't come at the expense of the current plot or a protagonist's nuanced sense of self.

Growing the World

Once readers learn the bare minimum about your story world in the first chapter, you can start to fill in the blanks as the narrative gets underway. Remember, specific segments of our contemporary realistic universe deserve world-building, too. For example, a college campus bursting with secret societies in a dark academia novel, or a quaint hometown ripe for a Christmas romance can become characters in and of themselves. Here, you can play with setting, tone, and style to deliver on your genre expectations, as well as focusing on the cultural and social rules (spoken and unspoken). A lot of dramatic tension can be created if your protagonist falls outside the "ruling class" of their family, school, or workplace. Readers are naturally primed to root for the underdog, so this can also be a nice audience engagement strategy.

When we pivot to historical, fantasy, and science fiction world-building, your to-do list is likely longer. In those genres, we're dealing with the history of the world, magical or technology rules and limitations, and how these elements directly impact the protagonist and plot. Don't worry if you want to lay the facts on slightly thicker once you clear the first chapter. For readers in these genres, the world-building detail is part of the promise of the premise, and they'll expect you to elaborate on what you've already established.

What I'd avoid, however, are big info-dump sections of dry explanation. Whenever possible, bring up world-building details in the context of character and action. Your protagonist has to do the spell *this* way because they've been banned from using magic for thirty days. Readers might already know what the character did because you've shown them getting in trouble in present action or flashback. Or you might be building mystery and intrigue about what happened by showing only their punishment.

Either way, the protagonist is now hampered and will stumble over obstacles in doing what they have to do to achieve their objective, or they might be sidelined altogether and unable to participate. This, I'd imagine, will increase tension and maybe even conflict with other characters. If your protagonist was the top magic user in their guild, for example, their enemies might now come crawling out of the woodwork to fill a power vacuum—literally and figuratively. If, on the other hand, your protagonist is barely clinging to their mage status, you have an opportunity to raise stakes—this could be the last straw for their education, career, or sense of self (if they define their identity largely by their powers).

Once you've set the character and plot ramifications of your world-building detail into motion, you can weave in additional information. Magic used to be much more powerful, but rules, boundaries, and prohibitions were put in place a century ago. For the most part, this has worked well to curb dangerous overuse, but a rebellious faction is seeding discontent and wants the rules relaxed or reversed. They believe society has gone soft and lost its former focus on progress and power. This, in turn, could set up a plot conflict with big ramifications, an antagonist, and a belief system challenge for the protagonist. What does the main character think? Where do they stand? How might they react to clashing worldviews in their own guild?

If you were to visualize this distribution of story information, it'd go something like this:

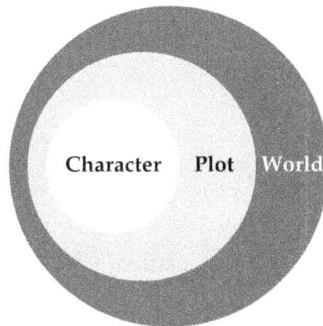

Notice how character is the basis of everything, then is fully enclosed by plot, while world-building surrounds and affects the story but is also peripheral.

You should aim to have all of your world-building more or less complete by the end of the first act so readers get their footing and understand the confines and possibilities of your story world once the plot really kicks into gear. If you're still tweaking the basics of the world right before the climax, you need to streamline your process and thin out the sheer volume of information you're presenting. Readers need to understand the world in order to understand why certain events, dynamics, and stakes matter. If we get a download of the antagonist's family history right before they swoop in for their big attack, you're not pacing the data correctly. Most of the villain's context should already be known. Unknown elements are only withheld toward the end to hamstring the protagonist.

Once the world's rules and foundations are laid, readers will focus on changes, shifts, surprises, twists, and reveals—all the ways in which your setting transforms throughout the story (if it does) and how these revelations affect your character, their objective/need, and their action throughout the plot. If readers know the normal, they can sense when it becomes abnormal, then extrapolate and appreciate the consequences and ramifications. When audiences are confident in their understanding of your world and how it operates, they can do much more informed guesswork as you deploy obstacles and reversals.

World-building Rules

On this note, let me add something here about putting boundaries on your magic and technology, for those of you writing in speculative genres. Open-ended abilities or talismans with near-unlimited capacity are actually a liability. Sure, it's fun to wield such powers. But if your speculative element has no rules, boundaries, or restrictions, you will never be able to create stakes in your plot and stir up true conflict for your character.

If your protagonist can, for example, call on the powers of all four elements to get out of a jam, no threat will ever seem to matter. Why? There are just too many tools in the arsenal and readers will be trained to believe that, more often than not, your protagonist will rescue themselves, evade capture, or dodge consequences. There's simply no reason to worry, especially if audiences have already seen several instances of dangerous situations dissipating with a spell or technological assist. When you get to your climax and want readers to care, they won't. There's no doubt in the audience's collective mind that this will be another triumph for the protagonist.

This is exactly why you want to bind up the magic or tech and introduce limitations. The protagonist is useless at wielding flame magic in the presence of iron, for example. Obviously, their nemesis will trap them in iron handcuffs at the first opportunity. Now the protagonist must rely on their wiles, passion, knowledge, ingenuity, and spark to get out of a bad situation, rather than simply muttering an incantation. Your stakes become more robust as a result. Readers will be anticipating seeing the magical rule in action and will worry when it comes into play. This is only possible if they know what iron means in the world of your story and why it's such a powerful weapon against the protagonist in particular.

Teach readers your world-building rules early and amend or add to them as the world develops, if need be. Don't establish a rule seconds before it becomes relevant. The boundaries and laws of your magic or tech should be clarified in your early world-building efforts so they become part of the tapestry of your unique fantasy or science fiction realm. Once readers have their feet wet and develop an understanding of how things work in your world, bring that logic to bear on the plot.

As a gatekeeper or reader chooses between near-endless options for their next client or book, respectively, they'll want to know what makes your speculative world compelling and marketable. What's the fresh premise, unique combination of world-building details, type of magic or technology, or other feature that's going to set *this* fantasy or *this* science fiction project apart? Simply making yours an orc or unicorn story isn't enough. There are plenty of those on shelves and in slush piles. You should aim to innovate even further and make your world-building more specific.

The same is true of historical projects. That's right, books set in another era of our reality aren't off this hook, either. Another World War II book? Various periods of the twentieth century, especially, have already been explored to death. What's the unique slant, undiscovered event or setting, or forgotten historical character you'll be adding to our collective knowledge of a specific period? If you don't have a good answer for this question, or you're setting your thriller in the 1980s just to get away from the plot convenience of cell phones, you need a stronger reason for showcasing the timeframe you've chosen.

Now that we're talking about standing out in a crowded market, you should be aware of (and stay away from) some well-known opening clichés, if at all possible. That's what we'll cover in the next chapter, before we dig into our real-world writing sample Workshop.

COMMON OPENING CLICHÉS

If you go back to the Why Story Openings Matter chapter and put yourself in the shoes of a gatekeeper reading slush, you might start to understand that in those 300 or so queries and story openings an agent or acquisitions editor might read in their two-hour submission binge, there will be commonalities. Of course there are. In fact, they appear much more frequently than you might imagine.

Does this mean the onus is on you to come up with a story beginning *that has never been done before*? No. Not at all. In fact, trying to do something completely "innovative" could be risky, because you could send the wrong message, set incorrect expectations, and limit your story's commercial potential. Of course, not every writer wants to write a mainstream novel or memoir with best-seller potential for a Big Five publishing house. And that's okay. But a lot of my readers do, if you check the "If you let yourself dream, what does success look like for this project?" question on my potential client intake form.[1]

---

1. Sure, I do ask for pie-in-the-sky hopes and dreams, so the question invites these big goals, but it's telling that most aspiring writers will admit to wanting *New York Times*-best-seller-dom, a multi-book series, or to make a living with their craft.

If you want to let your freak flag fly and you don't care if another soul on the planet ever validates your efforts, that's fine. Pure self-expression is as worthy a goal as any other. Try to do the thing that's never been done. Have fun. Send me a postcard. If, on the other hand, you want to impress and compel gatekeepers and readers, you'll want to try and thread that elusive needle of a story opening that feels fresh but isn't too familiar *or* strange.

The techniques detailed in this guide will definitely help you narrow down your story opening options. Avoiding the clichés listed below will, too. You can, of course, decide you're the exception to the rule and you should be able to start your story with one of these well-known set-ups. Some writers suffer from some exceptionalism bias and delusions of grandeur, especially when they're new to the craft.

I'm here to tell you, as someone who has evaluated literally millions of submissions and story openings: You're probably not a unique snowflake. And you don't have to be! Gatekeepers and readers want to be entertained and intrigued, as simple and as complex as that. They also don't want to see the story beginning they've already seen three dozen times in the same slush session. Once you know what to avoid, you can fine-tune your creativity and find a different approach. But before we list the clichés, let's talk about the elephant in the story opening room: the prologue.

Prologues

It wouldn't be a guide to opening pages if I didn't tackle the hot-button issue of prologues. Why are they controversial? You might hear agents and acquisitions editors talking or posting about hating prologues. Yet they're quite common in the wild. A lot of books have them, especially in genres like fantasy, science-fiction, and mystery/thriller/suspense, where we hear from either the antagonist or an unnamed victim in an early bid to create intrigue.

In my book, *Writing Irresistible Picture Books: Insider Insights Into Crafting Compelling Modern Stories for Young Readers,* I discuss a common writing and publishing catch-22. Most agents flat-out say they're not looking for rhyming picture books. But when I analyzed

154 recent picture books as part of my research, 35 of them featured rhyming texts. This isn't an overwhelming number but, at 22.7% of the sample, it's not insignificant, either. I cite this example to say there can sometimes be a big disconnect between what gatekeepers say they want, and what they sign. When I was agenting at the height of *Twilight* mania, I sat in a meeting across from a HarperCollins editorial director and listened while she categorically denied wanting any vampire paranormal stories. The following week in Publishers Marketplace, which is the industry's deal announcement database, the news broke that she'd just bought a YA vampire trilogy.

Sometimes agents will say something just to say it. Sometimes they'll find a really great example of something they didn't think they desired. In fact, an agent once got in hot water for posting to their Manuscript Wish List that they wanted something *exactly* like a pitch they'd just received. So they liked the premise, but not *that specific execution of the premise* that'd come into the slush. Of course, the writer who submitted that project was horrified to see the agent broadcasting their idea to the world—and doubly insulted that this gatekeeper seemed to think their own premise wasn't done well enough to represent. This kind of stuff, regrettably, happens.

The business is subjective. Agents and editors are merely human and can be subject to whims or find themselves swayed. Their true impression completely depends on the project, the timing, their mood, whether they're reading slush after a glass or two of wine, or any number of other factors. So yes, sometimes an agent will express disdain for prologues but pick up a project with a prologue. Sometimes an editor will speak at a conference and tell writers not to use prologues in theory, but if we look at her list, prologues abound.

It's a yes/and situation. Yes, plenty of agents and acquisitions editors say they hate prologues. *And* plenty of books on shelves have prologues. What can you take from this data? Whether you use a prologue depends on whether your story needs one. How do you know? First let's talk about the advantages prologues can offer:

- A peek into backstory (flashback rendered in full scene);
- A flash-forward (usually to an exciting scene from the run-up to the climax); and
- A visit to another time entirely (ancient history, the far future, or anything else relevant to the world or character).

You already know to start your story with present-moment action. But what if you need to establish action from outside the now? What if readers really need to know that an old crone spoke a prophecy over an oracle five-hundred years ago, and now the fated destroyer of the world has been activated, unbeknownst to everyone? We'll probably follow their story for the duration of the plot—where they're either the protagonist or antagonist—and see how the prophecy plays out. But if the circumstances of the original casting are important, a prologue can take readers there.

You can always introduce this kind of information after the narrative gets started. The origin story doesn't *have* to be the first thing readers learn. You can weave the particulars in later via a flashback or another data source. You can also have characters discussing it, which is more passive but also keeps you from interrupting the present-moment narrative flow. There are many ways to deploy information, and that's basically what the prologue is: just another way to insert data. For every useful prologue, know there are several other ways to accomplish the same task … they just might not establish the relevant information *first*.

Now let's talk about why most people hate—or claim to hate—prologues. They can be a cheap thrill, just like a chase sequence or dream in a story opening (more on those in a moment). The tension is high—especially if you're sampling from an action-packed past event or flashing forward to your story's climax. And then? All that tension drops as you move into your "real" beginning. We were just swinging a battle axe, now we're in homeroom. Or, worse, waking up to another boring day.

This kind of energetic comedown won't be well received. If this is your current opening strategy, do something about it. Try to equalize the energy between your prologue and opening by adding present conflict and tension for your protagonist in the first chapter that follows. Or take the risk of cutting the prologue and rewriting the first chapter to hook readers instead. What's currently so wrong with it that you felt the need to insert a high-octane, high-stakes, big-swagger prologue? Take a big step back and try to evaluate your work with clear eyes.

This advice goes double if you're using a cliché story opening, and I'll unpack some from publishing's Least Wanted list next.

Cliché Story Openings

For every familiar beginning I present here, I'm also going to offer the rationale for avoiding it:

- **Waking Up/Going to Sleep**: This is perhaps the most insidious and cliché opening, and many writers don't like to be called out for it. However, if you have your character waking up on the first page of your story rather than starting *in medias res*, which we talked about in the Action and Conflict chapter, you are sending an unintended message, which is: *I have no idea how to plot.* Why? Because we all start our days with waking up and end them with going to sleep (though the latter is more of an issue at the end of a chapter). However, a plot is a carefully selected and intentional sequence of events—a highlights reel of your character's life. If you're going through their days step by step, you're not cherry picking what's happening. Gatekeepers and readers want to make sure they're in good hands, and this common opening cliché doesn't instill that confidence.
- **Dream Sequence**: This is hated for the same reason prologues are. Dreams are exciting and high stakes, which is why writers are tempted to use them. That said, dreams often have their own nonsensical logic, setting, tone, etc., which won't necessarily carry over to the character's real world. So we've just spent time learning one set of rules and details, only to have this understanding ripped away. We're also likely thrust into a much more boring beginning once

the dream ends, which feels like a cheap bait and switch. Finally, dreams aren't real—unless you're in a very specific speculative world where harm visited on a character in their dreams carries over into real life. Otherwise, the danger and conflict vanish when the protagonist wakes up and stakes immediately drop.

- **Mirror, Mirror, on the Wall**: Some writers feel passionate about establishing their character's physical appearance in vivid detail, right away, while others don't. If you find yourself wanting to convey a very clear picture, avoid the stereotypical mirror scene to start. Find another way to establish what your character looks like. Believe it or not, not every reader cares to have this level of detail about a protagonist's looks. Many are happy to mentally fill in the blanks themselves. As with any other scene-setting and world-building detail, keep physical appearance description to a minimum and focus on putting the protagonist into action instead.

- **The Chase**: If a reader doesn't know what's going on, who's chasing the character, why, what the stakes are, etc., it's much harder to become engaged in the story. It's also entirely possible to start with stakes that are *too* high. Readers don't care yet, so they might empathize with life-or-death danger on the first page, or they might feel numb to it because there's no connection or reason to relate yet. With story openings, once you confuse 'em, you lose 'em. This is why I recommend starting with a character who knows what's going on in the scene, as well as opening on a small-to-medium conflict instead of ripping out all the stops right away, as initially discussed in the Curiosity Hooks chapter.

- **Weather Report**: Unless you're talking about the weather ironically, as one of our samples in the Published First Lines chapter did, we don't want to start with a dark and stormy night. This technique, known as the objective correlative, has become a giant cliché. Yes, weather can set the tone right away, but many other writers have abused this gambit to death. Start with character, put them into action, and add a dash of mystery. Use tone and style to give your pages a specific emotional wash. We don't need to see lightning cleaving the sky to get a sense of ominous things to come—you just need to work a bit harder on your initial plot conflict.

- **Info-dump**: As we saw in the Setting and World chapter, you might be tempted to put everything you've created on the page at once. This is akin to asking readers to leap over a raised drawbridge to reach your story. In school, most of us read our textbooks because we *had* to. But readers new to your story don't have any reason (positive or negative) to start learning fact after fact about your character or world just yet. They're not going to be motivated to metabolize all of the data you're throwing at them, not until they become engaged with your protagonist and plot. I strongly advise you to withhold as much world-building information as possible until you absolutely can't move forward without it. Besides, if your opening is too information-heavy, are you creating any intrigue amidst all that telling?

- **Setting Flyover**: Similar to the above, if you're in love with your story's setting and can't wait to show off your descriptive writing chops, you might be tempted to offer readers the lay of the land with paragraph after paragraph of specific visual detail. Certain genres and audiences—historical, literary, fantasy—might tolerate this more than others. That said, readers don't care about imagery showboating or gratuitous landscapes until you've given them a reason to hook into the story and character. You have a captive audience for only a few seconds—use this time wisely. If readers get the sense that you're only pleasing and glorifying yourself in your opening, they might not want to endure the whole showcase.

- **Philosophizing**: Here's an example:
    - *Love is a funny thing. The highest of highs, the lowest of lows. And you cannot truly know yourself in love unless you fall…*

- ○ Sounds deep, doesn't it? This is some philosophizing about the theme of love. But there's no story here, at least not yet. Character and action specifics are much more grounding, as is an opening scene. (With the above, we're just floating around in limbo, without a sense of the present moment.)
- **Throat-clearing**: This is similar to philosophizing, but is basically the writer explaining the type of story they're about to tell. Here's an example:
  - *Sometimes a story surprises you, takes you by the lapels and shakes you. A story like this doesn't come along every day...*
  - ○ This is all just telling *about* the story. Stop it and actually start the story in action, with character (not an intrusive narrator who's a thinly veiled version of the writer, unless your story has a very clear omniscient narrative voice which represents a character in its own right, like a memoir author or self-conscious POV engaging in direct address, as we saw several in the Published First Lines chapter).
- **"How did we get here?"**: This is a technique similar to a prologue. It goes something like:
  - *What's an HR director like me doing running for my life from a grizzly bear on the Pacific Crest Trail? Well, to answer that question, we have to rewind for a moment...*
  - ○ You start with high stakes, but those quickly dissipate as we take a step back into the "real" story. The tension created in this flashforward is unlikely to last.
- **Birthday Powers**: This is a holdover from the glory days of 2008 or so, when every manuscript featured a character waking up on a significant birthday to discover they're now some kind of paranormal creature and the brooding new hot guy in school will suddenly take notice of them. When I discussed *The Spirit Glass* by Roshani Chokshi in the Setting and World chapter, it was to call attention to this book's subversion of this common Chosen One trope. Corazon expects powers and doesn't get them. A

straightforward, earnest take on "I woke up and can now command elemental magic" may be a tough sell, especially in today's middle grade and young adult markets.

If your current story opening uses any of these gambits, don't panic. You can revise it, and I strongly recommend you do. For those of you who *simply must* use one of these openings, you can do whatever you want. I'm not here to stop you. However, know that gatekeeper eyes roll back in their heads when they hit one of these clichés. That's a big deficit to overcome. Do you want to start off your audition scrambling because you tripped and fell flat on your face? Submitting to gatekeepers or trying to impress readers is hard enough without prejudice working against you. Sure, you *can* use one of these clichés, but do you really want to? Even if you're intentionally playing with a familiar beginning, gatekeepers speeding through the slush might not pick you out as different and revolutionary—they might lump you in with one of the many cliché openings they've already read that day.

As I've already mentioned, you're making the whole thing up. If you think you *must* do something, realize you're the one calling the shots. There is no law that says you have to start a certain way or follow a familiar story structure. If you believe you're stuck in a corner, it's only because you've put yourself there. The mime is only trapped if they believe they're surrounded by glass. They can simply take a step forward. Nothing bad will happen. I promise. Just try another way before you hamstring yourself with a familiar story beginning.

Readers are not only detectives, they're savvy to the many available storytelling tricks. If you're using a prologue as a ploy, it will be obvious. Even if you're inadvertently using a prologue because you might feel self-conscious about a low-tension, low-stakes, or boring opening, readers will be able to tell.

If you're struggling to start your story, it should be abundantly clear by this point that you're not alone. That said, if I've caught you in time, you can take another pass at your beginning. If you've already contributed a cliché to someone's slush pile, that's okay, too. At least you're not alone there, either.

In the Workshop section which follows, we'll see some of these theoretical concepts applied to real writing samples from aspiring writers like you. This is your chance to see the creative writing and feedback process in action as we peel back the curtain on story beginnings in progress.

WORKSHOP

ABOUT THE WORKSHOP

In August, 2024, I solicited my mailing list of aspiring writers for submissions of their first two double-spaced pages (with industry-standard 1" margins and 12-point font, or approximately 500 words) from their works-in-progress in exchange for comprehensive notes. Many writers responded, and I ended up with 26 examples across three target audiences (middle grade, young adult, and adult).

I'm incredibly grateful to all of the writers who contributed their work, as it can be very enlightening to see what others are working on, as well as their strengths and opportunities for growth. Writing is a solitary endeavor, and that's exactly why I love to place you over a fellow aspiring writer's shoulder.

I've labeled the samples by genre, as I want you to be able to quickly and easily find example pages which relate to your own project. That said, I strongly believe that all kinds of writing and critique can offer an educational benefit. Consider reading all of these and seeing what you pick up from the workshop pieces, even if they seem to have little in common with your own work at face value.

Each submission will be marked up with in-line comments and some corrections. In an editorial setting, I would be using Word's

Track Changes function to modify the text and make margin notes. For this guide, I've tweaked the formatting to replicate this kind of editorial mark-up. Overview feedback follows each sample.

Here's a key for deciphering the editorial marks you'll find on the workshop submissions:

- **Footnotes**:
  - These contain comments. I will react to a single word or phrase, or a full sentence or passage, and my feedback appears directly below the referenced text, though sometimes the footnote's contents might carry over to the following page.
- **Underlines**:
  - <u>Underlines</u> point out "word echo," or word/phrase repetition in close proximity. These instances tend to unconsciously catch the reader. It's important to note that I'm not simply suggesting the writer go to the thesaurus and dig out a synonym. A lot of word echo comes from poor phrasing. The fix is to ask yourself: *Do I have to repeat these words and phrases here? Or is there a syntactical revision I could apply?*
- **Bolding**:
  - **Bolding** calls attention to repetition (also generally in close proximity). Trust your reader to retain what you're saying, and trust that you're saying it well enough without resorting to redundancy. (Easier said than done!) Instead of hitting readers over the head or invoking images which repeat the same idea, consider trimming, condensing, or choosing one strong image.
- **Brackets**:
  - My additions and changes are surrounded by [brackets]. Sometimes these contain insertions, other times, they indicate formatting changes.
- **Strikethrough**:
  - When I've deleted the writer's original text, I use ~~strikethrough~~ formatting. Sometimes this accompanies a revision, made in [brackets].

- **Italics**:
  - Some italics are original to the text. Other times, I've added them (in which case, I will also use brackets). In prose, italics are generally used to indicate verbatim thought, for emphasis, to offset written elements, and in other special cases, like for book/periodical/movie/show titles, and ship names. (Unpublished manuscript titles are generally formatted in caps or with quotation marks.)

In the following chapter, I will also outline a series of recurring notes that I found myself giving to several samples in this workshop. Read these over to bolster your own craft knowledge, and know that these frequently given notes will sometimes be referenced in sample comments.

RECURRING NOTES

Every writer and project is different, but over the years, I've found some common pieces of feedback that apply to manuscript after manuscript. To streamline the notes on the samples themselves and to give you easy reference going forward, I'll reproduce my most frequently offered notes below, organized by craft topic.

Telling

Many writers struggle with balancing showing and telling. (There's an in-depth discussion of this in *Writing Interiority: Crafting Irresistible Characters*.) Long story short, not all telling is bad, and you can, indeed, use it to introduce certain information—especially in a story opening.

However, there are a few common issues with what I call "bad telling" present in some of these samples. They are:

- **Naming Emotions:** You want to be wary of telling the emotions a character experiences directly. This is vague. Go into more specific interiority instead. For example, a character might be described as feeling "sad." Don't leave it at that. Why are they sad? About what, specifically? A million different people can be sad a million different ways about a million different things. So simply saying "sad" doesn't conjure sadness for the reader. You need to go a level deeper and give context for that particular bout of sadness. More thoughts on this here: https://kidlit.com/emotional-writing/

- **Physical Clichés:** Physical markers of emotion tend to be rife with clichés. Stomachs churning, chests tightening, eyes widening, cheeks flushing, hearts racing, etc. Avoid them if you can and go deeper into interiority. I don't care as much about the fact that a character is crying, for example, as I care about the specific thought that finally pushed them over the edge into an external display of their feelings. Sometimes it's fine to describe the chest tightening, sometimes it's richer and more complex to get the interiority instead. (Don't get me wrong, you can describe what the body is doing, but not if those physical details are our primary stand-ins for all emotion.) Consider this: https://kidlit.com/describing-emotions-in-writing/

- **Telling About Tone of Voice:** Avoid describing the tone of voice that a character uses to speak. This is the same as telling the reader what that character is feeling, it's just sneakier! How a character is feeling should be clear from what they say (dialogue) and what they do (action). Describing tone of voice is a crutch.

- **Telling with Body Language:** The problem with rendering body language on the page is that it's visual. The old maxim of "a picture is worth a thousand words" applies here. As humans, we can interpret mood from glances and subtle bodily cues. It takes a lot to translate this to the page, where our biggest ally (the visual) is missing. Avoid this type of telling and use dialogue and action to convey what a non-POV character might be experiencing instead.

- **Shown Versus Told:** Sometimes readers are *told* one thing but *shown* otherwise. Audiences will usually believe what they're shown and their own interpretation versus what they're told. And if their interpretation differs too much from what the writer tells them, the narrative, writer, or POV character will lose credibility.

- **Telling About Vibes:** Describing "vibes" or the atmosphere in a room/scene is yet another way of taking the joy of discovery away from readers. Saying that something is "ominous" isn't going to necessarily make readers feel tense. The real work is making this mood come to life by creating it with dialogue, action, voice, and imagery.
- **External Reaction:** Be wary of describing your POV character's reactions in a roundabout way, for example, by describing another character's reaction to them (e.g., "She rolled her eyes at my crossed arms."). You have access to the protagonist's interiority so you can draw a much more direct line.

Character

Here are some common character notes I find myself giving:

- **Head-hopping:** This is a POV note. Your opening should clearly express the point of view you plan on using, whether that's first person or close third or omniscient (these are your main options, but there are others). If you start off in one character's close-third perspective, you are locked in. They cannot know what another non-POV character is thinking, experiencing, or perceiving. The exception is if you're using true omniscient POV, but you still better have a good reason for going into another character's head. Otherwise, if you want to give POV access to a different character, use a section or chapter break. POV issues are rampant in aspiring manuscripts, and any instance of unintentional head-hopping conveys a lack of craftsmanship to gatekeepers.
- **Characters in Denial:** Sometimes a character must be in denial to make a plot mechanic work. But when readers know (or think they know) where a story is going, and the protagonist refuses to face reality, there's a disconnect.

Drag it out for too long, and audiences might lose patience. Consider this: https://kidlit.com/character-growth/

- **Caricature:** You want to create character, not caricature. Instead of hammering on the same few established attributes, try to find other characterizing details. Nobody is all good, and nobody is all villain. By portraying a character as one-note and one-note only, you reduce them to a stereotype, and those aren't interesting to read.

- **Thought Tags:** Italics indicate verbatim thought, so I'm of the mind that you don't technically need a "thought" tag after some direct interiority. However, if you'd like to use it the first few times, then drop it, that's fine, too. It's a stylistic choice.

- **Rhetorical Questions:** Characters who ask rhetorical questions—especially about what *they* might be thinking or experiencing—seem wishy-washy. When applicable, let them do critical thinking and take a position instead of simply wondering. Consider this: https://kidlit.com/using-the-rhetorical-question-in-fiction-writing/

- **Character Buy-in:** The story can't start until a character faces their reality, similar to my note about denial, above. If you're suggesting the plot is going in a certain direction, but the protagonist actively fights it, they might lose readers until they decide to engage with the facts. Consider this: https://kidlit.com/inciting-incident/

- **Third-person-style Self-description:** When you're in first-person POV, you have access to a character's interiority. Sometimes, though, writers are tempted to over-describe the character's physicality externally. This can sound like outside-in third-person narration, which clashes with the inside-out first-person lens. Consider this: https://kidlit.com/third-person-style-narration-in-first-person/

- **Acting Without Thinking:** Proactive characters are the gold standard in fiction and memoir. One thing that makes them heroic is their intentional ability to make choices. As such, characters who act without thinking or deciding can be less engaging. Consider this: https://kidlit.com/writing-dialogue-in-fiction/

Description

The following are some notes I commonly give about various descriptive issues:

- **Play-by-play Narration:** Play-by-play narration, or choreography, can clutter up your prose. Sometimes you need to render physical action or spatial orientation in step-by-step detail, but how much is too much? You could spend three pages on a girl making a sandwich because there are a lot of steps in the process (getting the bread out of the cupboard, slicing the tomatoes, etc.), or you could say, "She made a sandwich." The level of detail is up to you, but know that gratuitous action description can erode your pacing. The reader's imagination can also fill in a lot of suggested gestures, physical actions, arm movements, etc. Sometimes it's best to gloss over logistical description and focus on plot. Consider this: https://kidlit.com/descriptive-prose/
- **Filler:** It's assumed that if something is described, the character sees (hears, smells, etc.) it. They would have to in order to narrate it. So saying "He saw" or "I heard" or similar isn't necessary. Don't describe the character seeing/hearing/smelling/etc. the thing. Instead, cut right to the description of the thing itself. The rest is filler.
- **Turning Heads:** Describing people turning is largely unnecessary. If they're turning toward someone in conversation, that's expected. If they're turning in the direction of their movement, that's obvious because they're not going to walk backward or sideways. The only time you really need to describe someone turning is if they're pointedly turning away, which communicates emotion. Otherwise, turning in the direction of action is a no-brainer.

- **Mimetic Writing:** Practice mimetic writing, meaning matching the writing style to what you're saying. A long, somewhat congested sentence isn't good for conveying something that happens quickly. Short sentence bursts don't work for a languid, luxurious moment. The style and content are at odds, and the language should match what it's conveying.

Plot

Some frequent-flyer plot notes I find myself giving:

- **Why Today?:** Remember the Action and Conflict chapter? Every story should start at a certain moment in time (unless we're in limbo during a philosophizing or throat-clearing beginning, as discussed in the Common Opening Clichés chapter). The strongest beginnings consider why the story begins on that particular day, with your chosen action. If we meet the protagonist in their normal, and the story could kick off two weeks before or three months after, readers might wonder why you've chosen as you have. The first scene needs to matter, and there should be strong logic and intention behind the writer's selection.
- **Grounding the Reader:** Ground the reader when you begin a new chapter (or return after a section break, though that's less relevant in a guide to openings). I wouldn't suggest starting with dialogue, for example. It's great to jump into action, but you have to orient readers and answer some basic questions first. Audiences will naturally be curious about where and when we are, for example. Try to preemptively address those issues with some early scene-setting. More thoughts here: https://kidlit.com/how-to-start-a-chapter/

Dialogue

And now some dialogue notes:

- **Proper Dialogue Formatting:** Below is a list of correct dialogue formatting (note punctuation and capitalization patterns):
  - Speech tag: "Hello," she said.
  - Action tag: "Hello." She smiled.
  - Exclamation/question and speech: "Hello?" she asked.
  - Exclamation/question and action: "Hello!" She waved.
  - Continuation: "So," she said, "what's up?"
  - Lead-in with action: She smiled. "Hello."
  - Lead-in with speech (not commonly used): She said, "Hello."
  - Interruption with action: "Hello there"—she waved— "and nice to meet you!"
    - In standard U.S. English formatting, punctuation goes inside quotes (at least for dialogue), and single quotes go inside double quotes. British English formatting guidelines differ.
- **Expository Dialogue:** Avoid telling in dialogue, otherwise known as "As you know, Bob" exposition for the reader's benefit. When characters speak obvious facts to one another, it's not a "show, don't tell" workaround, it just sounds inorganic. Consider this: https://kidlit.com/obvious-telling-in-dialogue/
- **"Said" Synonyms in Dialogue Tags:** Fancy "said" synonyms get a very bad rap because they're distracting. "Said" and "asked" blend in without being too ostentatious. Synonyms are also a crutch. The point of dialogue is to convey emotion, not just information. If you give that job to the dialogue tag, you're not letting the dialogue speak for itself.
- **Adverbs in Dialogue Tags:** The same idea applies to adverbs in dialogue tags ("she chortled mockingly"). They're a shortcut for conveying emotion.

- **Trailing Off and Interruptions:** An ellipsis (…) means someone is trailing off in dialogue. An em-dash (—) means they've been interrupted. So if you use one of these, you don't also need to narrate that they've trailed off or been interrupted. Let the formatting work for you!

Voice and Style

These notes about voice and style tend to appear on a wide variety of projects:

- **Past Perfect Tense:** The "had verb" or past perfect tense is used to go even further into the past while already in past tense. While the past perfect is grammatically correct, all those instances of "had" do terrible things to voice. I recommend establishing the flashback, then reverting to plain past tense. As long as you make clear that we're doing some time traveling, you don't have to adhere to the past perfect for the duration of the flashback.
- **Contractions:** Use contractions whenever possible for more colloquial voice.
- **Expected Imagery:** If an image doesn't add much to a reader's understanding of what's being described, it's not effective (e.g., "flew like a bird," "glowed like a lightbulb," etc.). Aim for imagery that's unexpected or fresh and avoid the first comparison that comes to mind.
- **Dangling Modifier:** A subtle grammatical error called the dangling modifier can be tough to spot in one's own writing. Even I do it sometimes! Learn about it, master it, and avoid it. More about it here: https://bit.ly/dangling-modifier
- **Redundant Syntax:** Avoid constructing several sentences the same way in close proximity, with a specific focus on how you begin and end your phrases. The most common error is starting a whole paragraph full of sentences that begin with "Subject verb." Mix it up!

Without further ado, let's get into the opening page writing samples from the brave writers who volunteered their work for feedback so the entire community could learn.

MIDDLE GRADE FIRST PAGES

These writing samples have been categorized by target audience. It's important to note that the writers have identified their own categories. The following examples are intended for readers ages nine to thirteen, also known as the "middle grade" (or "MG") market in the children's book industry. While some of these sample pages hit MG expectations in terms of voice, style, and content, there are also some submissions which might be better suited in other categories, and I'll discuss my reasoning in their respective overviews.

SAMPLE 1: MOUNTAIN MISCHIEF
ACTION/ADVENTURE

LUCI BROCKWAY TUMAS

Chapter One: Roommate Woe

Leaves[1] crunched. Lights flashed in the darkness, glinting across the bedroom window.[2]

Brock Billings groaned and rolled over in bed. The humid Papua New Guinea mountain breeze ruffled his hair.[3] He yanked the blanket over his head to block the chill[4] and the flares of light that woke him.[5]

---

1. With chapter headings, I'm always wondering if it's worth basically giving away what the chapter will be about before it unfolds. Something less literal might create more intrigue.
2. One is a very short sentence, the other is much more detailed. Smashing these together might strike a dissonant tone.
3. If they have windows, I'm imagining glass. But it also seems like the wind can freely get in. I'm having a tough time squaring all the details into a cohesive mental picture. (The writer has since clarified that these types of louvered windows are common in the region, though I would argue that too much intricate detail right away can misdirect reader focus.)
4. We have "humid" and "breeze," which connote warmth, even though that's not always the case. The cold comes as a surprise.
5. Need to explain that he wants to block them if he groaned after the flashing lights were described? Let readers piece things together themselves.

Wait a minute. Lights—from where?

Brock jolted awake.[6] [*Why is the window open?*][7] He had made sure the multi-paned window was shut before ~~he dropped~~ [dropping][8] into bed.

More scuffing in the brittle leaves convinced Brock **something or someone prowled outside**.[9]

"Hey Theo," Brock whispered. "Theo!" No answer. Brock sat up. Theo's bed was empty.

Where is my roommate?[10]

Brock cautiously crept ~~to the side of~~ [beside][11] the window, hoping **whatever or whoever**[12] lurked outside[13] wouldn't see him. No movement … no more scuffling … no flickering lights.

Am I dreaming? I know I closed the window.[14] *Theo must have opened it to annoy me.*[15]

Brock glanced at the clock: 2:37 a.m. Crawling back into bed, he thumped his fist into his pillow.[16] Brock rolled over in bed[17] to face

---

6. Good reaction.
7. Verbatim thought uses present tense and should be formatted it in italics. If it's not italicized, it's interiority woven into narration and should be past tense, like the rest of the text.
8. Just a quick tweak to avoid the "he verb" repetition. (This also answers my question about the window. I'm glad the confusion was intentional.)
9. And? So? Does he have an emotional reaction? Fear? A surge of adrenaline?
10. I'll caution this writer against too many verbatim thoughts here. "Where was his roommate?" keeps the action flowing. We also don't need to give most things their own line. This effect draws attention. But if almost everything has its own line, the impact is lost.
11. Why use four words when one will do?
12. This repeats the "something or someone" phrasing above.
13. And this is too close to "prowled outside," above.
14. His surprise and the fact that he closed the window are both already established.
15. I take issue with this, though. Why would he be careful not to be seen if he believes it was Theo? Why would he be scared if he suspects it's a specific person? I'd avoid characters in denial (see the Recurring Notes chapter).
16. The sequencing is off. He wouldn't do this after already getting back in bed because he'd be lying on his pillow. Consider rearranging these details.
17. No need to specify—we had him "crawling back into bed" in the previous

the wall. Sleep [was] ~~now~~ impossible [now], so he replayed yesterday's[18] disastrous greetings with some of the <u>teens</u> living in his assigned dormitory. When he had turned[19] into the large dining room, he stumbled into a towering <u>teenager</u>.

"Hey Billingsley!" Theo[20] had bellowed with a whack to Brock's shoulder.

Brock tilted his head to look at his attacker. "Hi. My name is Brock. Brock Billings."

"Well e-x-c-u-u-s-e me, Mr. Billingsley!" Theo taunted,[21] his black eyebrows pinched together over deep-set brown eyes. "You're kinda feisty for a little shrimp, ain't ya?"

What's his problem? I'm not short—he's a giant.[22]

Now[23] wide awake, Brock kicked himself for trying to joke with Theo.[24] Everything Brock had said or done that afternoon, Theo skillfully twisted to make Brock appear mean and rude.[25]

"Brock, you are insolent and uncouth!"[26] Iris Longmont had scolded him, wrinkling her freckled nose. "You obviously require instructions on courtesy and respect. Besides, don't you know Theo

---

sentence. Once we place a character somewhere, readers will fill in the blanks and keep them there until further notice.

18. Notice we're leaving the present moment. This phrasing also throws me. He was greeting the teens? They were greeting him?

19. I suggest avoiding past perfect tense (see the Recurring Notes chapter).

20. How does he know to call the boy "Theo" here if they haven't met yet and he's referred to as "his attacker" after? Once he has a name, it should be used.

21. Avoid "said" synonyms (see the Recurring Notes chapter).

22. Their size difference is already established.

23. I'm not sure this is a successful transition out of the flashback because the previous scene feels unfinished.

24. But he didn't "joke" with Theo, at least not in the flashback we saw. He corrected Theo.

25. This isn't shown, even though it's told. We see Brock correct Theo, which some might consider rude. What we saw play out didn't take any "skillful twisting" to "appear mean and rude." Readers respond to what they're shown, not told (see the Recurring Notes chapter).

26. This is the flashback again, but going back and forth so quickly at the beginning might give readers whiplash.

is your roommate? I trust you will not prove to be Machiavellian during your stay here."[27]

What in the world is Machiavellian? Theo is my roommate?! How will I survive?[28]

Before Brock could apologize, Theo **folded his arms, scowled,** and **swaggered** out the front door. Iris sniffed, spun around, and flicked her wavy red hair as she strutted away.[29] The other teens disappeared.

How can I change Theo's impression of me?[30] *Maybe he's struggling with the adjustment of living away from his family, too.*[31]

Where is Theo? Is he the prowler outside the <u>window</u>, trying to scare me and freeze me with the open <u>window</u>?[32] *I miss living in the lowland village. I forgot how <u>cold</u> it is here. Crazy how this tropical country gets so <u>cold</u> at the mile-high Karanga Center.*[33]

---

27. I worry about her voice for MG. Is she mocking him by speaking in an overly formal way? Otherwise, I have a hard time imagining a contemporary teenager saying this, unless English isn't her first language or her schooling was very traditional. (The writer later indicated that they hear her with a British accent, though this might be worthwhile to communicate to readers in the text. I'd push the writer to find some more nuance, as a snooty British academic is a bit of a stereotype.)
28. I worry Brock isn't reacting in proportion to events. Sure, he might have anxiety, but there's also been one slightly tense exchange with Theo and Iris. Nothing life-threatening, even if tweens can be dramatic.
29. I suggest limiting lists to three items each (especially with play-by-play action), otherwise, it's a lot for readers to imagine simultaneously. Each of these actions also conveys a similar mood.
30. Why is Brock so invested in this? I like that he has a goal but it's also an irrelevant one. He can't make Theo feel one way or another about him, because this is completely up to Theo. Also, is there still a potentially scary prowler outside his window? He's remembering this while the present-moment threat fades away.
31. This is too obvious a statement of what Brock is going through, even though it's couched in empathy for Theo. How might we show this? Telling about characters and their core experiences is, indeed, the kind of bad telling that "show, don't tell" warns us about.
32. Read this aloud. It strikes me as overly formal, especially for a verbatim thought. We tend to be most colloquial when speaking to ourselves.
33. He also wouldn't think these basic details (which are for the reader's benefit) to himself. This reads like overt exposition.

A long, irritating squeak made him jerk awake[34] when his inconsiderate[35] roommate wildly flung his shoes against the wall.

Theo grumbled, "Stupid little bed!"[36]

"Okay, Jesus, I need Your help to survive living with this jerk. At least we don't share a bunk bed."[37]

---

34. He's already awake in the present.
35. If he thinks Theo is "inconsiderate," why does he want Theo's approval? Though most kids want to be liked, this doesn't quite make emotional or logical sense.
36. I'm confused about the sequencing. Theo threw the shoes and complained about the bed, but I'm guessing the bed made the squeak. The way this is described seems to connect the shoe and bed, but it's unclear what's actually happening and triggering Theo's reaction.
37. If Brock is thinking this, we don't need quotation marks. Also, if Theo has now been located, wouldn't Brock be more urgently trying to figure out who opened the window and where the noise was coming from? This seems like a glaring omission. Isn't there still danger outside, or is it suggested that all is clear now that Theo has snuck back in?

SAMPLE 1 OVERVIEW

This story opening is crowded with detail and could be focused instead on the mysterious opening action—Brock hears something or someone under his window. He's new at this school and struggling to fit in, which is all fine and good, but the acute conflict is the danger he imagines lurking beyond this room. A significant portion of the sample also happens outside the present moment, establishing that Brock cares what Theo thinks because there was apparently a misunderstanding between them. However, if Theo is obviously a bully or has judged Brock wrongly, why is Brock so eager to impress him? Doesn't the flashback show Brock (and readers) that Theo isn't worth the effort? Also, is Brock worried that there's a total stranger beyond the window once he emerges from the flashback, or are we meant to glean that it was, in fact, Theo? The roommate's entrance is confusing. Some of Brock's thoughts and actions speak to the former (which is more dangerous), but then Brock seems to resolve himself to the latter idea (and the stakes vanish). He doesn't overtly address that he's decided to relax, if he has. Overall, there's high tension, but if the writer could go from assumption to assumption with more logic and minimize the flashback, this opening would come together into a more cohesive present-moment scene.

SAMPLE 2: UNTITLED
FANTASY

SUZY FEINE

A PORKY PRANK | Two Days Before the End of Sixth Grade

The[1] <u>sky</u> turned the color of boiled carrots[2] on the day Blaise learned the truth about his mom. And his dad.[3] Outside his bedroom window, the sun looked more like an angry red amoeba than a warm, yellow ball.[4] And beneath it, a strip of soot[, l]~~L~~ike a black marker swiped across the summer <u>sky</u>. Thicker and darker than yesterday['s].[5]

Sitting high atop his platform bed, his brown curls nearly

---

1. Some chapter headings have other data (location, time, POV character), some don't. This immediately sets expectations. Nice.
2. *Love* this description. It's an attention-getter, for sure.
3. Why not combine them (e.g. "about his mom and dad")? The sentence fragment is odd before readers know there's special emphasis on Dad here.
4. I'd cut this, personally, because we already have a great description of the sky. Don't dilute it with other images.
5. I changed this to "yesterday's" because we already have that today's "strip of soot" is darker than "yesterday's strip of soot." Other phrasing could be, e.g., "The soot, like a black marker swiped across the summer sky, was thicker than it was yesterday," but that's clunky.

touching the ceiling,[6] Blaise dipped his chin to get a better view.[7] The sun's fiery rays burned his eyes, but he couldn't turn away.[8] He leaned sideways, touching shoulders[9] with his best friend, Dillon.[10] **"Look,"** Blaise said, **pointing a shaky finger** at the window.[11]

[Instead,] Dillon ~~never looked up. He~~ fiddled with a small gold lock on a rusty tackle box perched on his lap. "Would you *stop* worrying?" ~~The heels of his~~ [He][12] banged his sneakers ~~banged~~ against the three-rung ladder. "The fires are far away. Besides, we've got more important things to deal with. Like your little sister. She can't hear this."[13]

Blaise's sister, Ami, **was a tattletale. Everything that went into her ears came out of her mouth in**[14] **a daily report to their mom. She could never be trusted**, especially with a top-secret mission such[15] as this one.

"She["—][T] ~~"~~the[16] word squeaked. [and] Blaise took a deep

---

6. A good injection of character physical description immediately. Some writers care a lot about setting up this information; others weave it in later.
7. What does tipping his head down have to do with adjusting his view? This level of detail might be distracting.
8. Why, if the sky is doing colors and soot every day? (I know he's seen it multiple times because he compares the levels of soot between today and yesterday.)
9. An instance of play-by-play narration (see the Recurring Notes chapter).
10. Is he on the same bed? This level of detail is so specific that it pulls focus.
11. Pointing a finger is the universal gesture for "look," so there's no need for both.
12. Center Dillon as the character doing the fidgeting, rather than describing the sneakers acting on their own accord. It's more direct.
13. This is a curiosity hook but not a successful one, because we have no idea what "this" refers to. The tackle box? But is it more reasonable to say "see this" instead of "hear this" if it's an object? (We don't have it make noise until later.) Or is he talking about the fires?
14. I like this second description better than the more generic "tattletale," but we only need one.
15. We don't have enough information about the mission to get excited yet. This writer has spent most of their time on the smoke and what it does to the sky, as well as information about Ami, who isn't even technically in the scene.
16. I've corrected a dialogue issue here for formatting an interruption with action (see the Recurring Notes chapter).

breath to slow his pounding heart.[17] But now he smelled smoke,[18] and it sped up again[—]"~~S~~she's in the kitchen. Coloring."

"Perfect." Dillon slipped a string over his head that held a tiny gold key.[19] He unlocked the tackle box.[20] The lid inched <u>open</u> with a loud *screech*[21] as if it hadn't been <u>opened</u> in years.

The sound rattled Blaise. He tore his eyes from the window.[22] Inside the tackle box, he spotted[23] the night-vision goggles they wore last year, their trusty map of the **entire school—showing every classroom, every bathroom, every hiding place**[24]—and something new: a green spyglass.

"Okay. Let 'er rip, tater chip." Dillon yanked out the map and pressed it flat against the mattress. "What's the game plan?"

Outside, tree branches clawed at the house.[25] Blaise snapped his head up. The blue curtains fluttered, making his nerves do the same. [26]A dusty breeze blew through the open window and into his bedroom.[27] *Dillon's right~~, he told himself~~.*[28] The wildfires were burning up near Atlanta, far from Glory.

---

17. A physical cliché (see the Recurring Notes chapter).
18. Why is he having this acute reaction to the smoke if it's already well established that there have been fires for a while?
19. Need to describe it as "tiny" and "gold" if he's already working on a "small gold lock"? Readers will easily connect the two.
20. Would he use the key to unlock the tackle box *after* slipping the key over his head (meaning he has to bend down)? Or *before*? This level of choreography might be distracting.
21. Is this what the sister isn't meant to hear (above)? They need to then say so after it makes this noise.
22. His focus on the window is well established.
23. Some filler on "he spotted" (see the Recurring Notes chapter).
24. We establish it's the "entire school" two ways in this sentence.
25. Sustain the present action without zooming away to the environment. We get that something is going on outside, but this chops up the reader's focus.
26. His nervousness is well established.
27. If there are fires, smoke, and soot outside, why would he have his window open?
28. Who else is he thinking to? Unless this is a book with telepathy, he can only think to himself, so "he told himself" is unnecessary.

But the wind.[29] Wind makes <u>strong</u> fires <u>stronger</u>. Carries flames higher. And closer.

Dillon punched Blaise in the arm. "C'mon, [d]~~D~~ude. Focus! Gimme the details.[30] And this one better beat the chickens. That was the best prank.[31] *Ever*." Dillon giggled and fell back onto the bed.[32] "Remember the picture in the newspaper? Of porky Principal Pinchers[33] chasing after them?"[34]

"Yeah," Blaise said, distracted by the world outside turning angry.[35] Dry leaves swirled.[36] The orange sky darkened, and the wind howled. He slid one hand along the sheets, reaching underneath his pillow. Once his fingertips touched[37] the cool metal of his dad's firefighter[38] badge, his heart softened.[39] It always calmed him. He'd found it right after his dad died, stuffed in a cardboard box of bunker gear. And every night since, for six years, he [has] held it to fall asleep.[40]

---

29. Again, if he's this scared, why is the window open?
30. We already have Dillon urging him on with "Let 'er rip" and "What's the game plan?"
31. This makes it seem like they're on an important mission, so "prank" lowers the stakes. (The chapter title mentions a "Prank" so keep the phrasing cohesive.)
32. He's rather animated, but I'm not sure we need each movement and gesture transcribed.
33. I'm a bit torn on the mean-spirited comment about his body size and shape. This isn't likely something parents/gatekeepers will want to see modeled. Imagine a larger kid reader seeing this, too. It strikes me as unnecessary, especially for this young age group, to showcase name-calling.
34. "Them" who?
35. This is very well established already.
36. Same idea here.
37. Zoom out on this level of play-by-play detail (see the Recurring Notes chapter).
38. This detail needs to be established much sooner.
39. A physical cliché (see the Recurring Notes chapter).
40. I'd say it's important to know that he's especially triggered by the fire due to this history. One thing I'm missing here overall: Is Blaise into this prank, or just Dillon? If Blaise is, he would seem more proactive protagonist and wouldn't be as distracted. However, the fire is much higher stakes than any prank, so notice the split focus.

SAMPLE 2 OVERVIEW

Another opening in action, which is great! A fire is bearing down on the characters, and we get a taste of Blaise's home life and relationship with Dillon. There's also a mysterious box (which, as we know, is always a curiosity hook) and some cool surveillance equipment. Middle grade readers are going to love the shenanigans and the aspirational element of the cool tech. That said, Blaise's emotions could be clearer and more structured here. It's very important to know that his father died fighting a fire sooner—that detail should be front and center. Given this backstory (even though the writer does a good job of not dwelling on it, it's still a timely and salient piece of information), would Blaise be trying to calm himself down? Would Dillon diminish his feelings? Would they focus on a prank instead (which introduces some data about school that we might not need yet)? Rather than lowering tension in this opening, the writer should play it up. When faced with the decision to either turn up the volume on a conflict or smooth that conflict over, especially at the beginning of a narrative, do the former. This writer has created a scenario where real and present danger stands to trigger a character's past wound—all the pieces are in place, so play with them! The prank isn't as immediately engaging unless we also establish timely context for trying it right at that moment.

SAMPLE 3: UNTITLED
CONTEMPORARY

ANONYMOUS

Chapter One

The cafeteria ~~during second lunch~~ was super crowded [during second lunch].[1] **Every single spot** at the long tables where the cheerleaders usually sat **was taken,** and the round tables were **completely filled** with[2] the soccer teams. **The noise was so loud,** with kids waiting in line for their food and **shouting across the room** to save seats for their friends.[3] Everyone was rushing to get a good spot.[4] The kids with packed lunches had the best chance. They'd rush in first and save seats for their friends, making sure the cool kids got the best spots.[5] It was like a daily contest, and the

---

1. Awk. phrasing.
2. I worry that we get three versions of the information "it was crowded" in this sentence, after already getting the same information ("was super crowded") in the previous sentence.
3. One more data point for it being crowded, two expressions of it being loud (they wouldn't be shouting if it wasn't loud).
4. This also restates the previous idea, as we've already seen kids saving seats for one another.
5. This adds a layer of nuance (bagged lunches vs. the kids who have to wait in line) but it's still a meditation on the crowded cafeteria. We don't have a focal character yet, nor context for why today might be noteworthy, since this crowding seems like

winners were the ones who got a hot lunch without worrying about where to sit.[6]

Leah ate nervously, her nose buried[7] in a library <u>book</u>. She had[8] already read two <u>books</u> in the past three days, and a third one[9] was waiting in her <u>backpack</u>. **She needed something to focus on, something to keep her mind busy.**[10] She tightened her grip on her <u>backpack</u> and looked around at the noisy cafeteria.[11] Everyone else seemed to fit in so easily[,] like they all knew a secret code she hadn't figured out yet.[12] She felt like a puzzle piece from a different box.[13] So, she pulled an apple out of her bag and pretended to read[14] while keeping her ears open to the dumb conversations around her.[15] She took a big, crunchy bite and tried to focus on the words in her book, but the chatter from nearby tables kept distracting her.[16]

Across the way, the cheerleaders sat with their colorful ribbons and perfect makeup.[17] Some of them were giggling, their laughter

---

the status quo. I strongly recommend introducing a protagonist. Also, spend less time on generic details that are true for most school cafeteria settings, like the idea that the cool kids want good spots, or that jocks and cheerleaders sit together.

6. More over-explaining.

7. A familiar image for reading.

8. I suggest a contraction here (see the Recurring Notes chapter).

9. Wouldn't her backpack hold the fourth if she's already read two and is holding the third?

10. Avoid the "stutter description" which immediately rephrases the point.

11. This is established.

12. A familiar image for feeling left out, I'm afraid.

13. As is this—a piece from the wrong puzzle, a piece that doesn't fit, etc. Reach beyond the first comparison which comes to mind.

14. We were just told she was reading and has previously read other books. That seems incompatible with "pretending" to read. Which is it?

15. We're also told that she's focusing on the book "to keep her mind busy," and this is another contradiction. Why would she choose the "dumb conversations" over the book, which she clearly prefers?

16. I worry we're getting caught up in clashing details. We're told she's "pretend[ing] to read," then that she "tried to focus on the words in her book." This is a direct contradiction. We're told she's "keeping her ears open" to the conversations around her (which suggests intent to listen to them), but then that the chatter "kept distracting her," which means she doesn't care about it.

17. I worry these details, too, seem generic.

ringing out like little bells,[18] while others were totally focused on their latest TikTok video.[19] Leah wondered why they liked watching themselves so much, replaying the same clips over and over. And why would anyone want to wear ~~that~~ [those] ugly, stupid bow[s]. [?][20]

"Did you see Sophie's TikTok from gym class? It's so funny!"[21] one girl shrieked, her voice cutting through the noise like a knife.[22]

"OMG[,] I saw it. I heard she got suspended for it," another girl responded, giggling.

"Yeah, but it was only in-school suspension. That sucks. If I'm gonna get suspended, it better be out of school," another one said.

Leah rolled her eyes and turned a page, pretending to be deeply engrossed in her book.[23] She couldn't help but listen, though. It was like a bad TV show she couldn't turn off.[24]

"Did you <u>hear</u> about the new kid from Australia? I <u>heard</u> he's

---

18. Laughter is often compared to the pealing of a bell.
19. "Their video" suggests they're all making a video, while "videos" suggests they're all watching separate videos. Clarify which they're doing so readers can make a better mental picture.
20. Unlike the previous sentence, which contains a question but is a statement, this is a question and needs a question mark.
21. Their focus on TikTok is clear.
22. I'd avoid pairing "cutting" with "like a knife" since the image doesn't add much to a reader's understanding of the description (see the Recurring Notes chapter). The noisy environment is clear.
23. Again with the pretending. It's still unclear if she's actually reading or not.
24. Leah seems to be judging the other girls in a way that paints her as superior. However, she also feels left out, so some of her comments (like the one about the bows) feel like sour grapes. Teens who are judgmental bummers are realistic, but I want to give Leah some kind of spark early on, too. What's exciting about her? Otherwise, readers might not want to hitch their wagons to someone who will complain quite so much, especially at the very beginning. What will make young audiences with limited entertainment time (if it's not already taken up by TikTok) want to spend time in her head? Also, if Leah thinks the girls are focused on stupid stuff, why does she want to join them or listen in?

super cute and already has a girlfriend!" a girl from the soccer team said, her voice full of excitement.[25]

"No way! Who is he? Do we know him?" another girl asked, leaning in closer.

Leah sighed and took another bite of her apple. She wished she could tune them out completely, but it was impossible.[26] Every word seemed to worm its way into her brain, making it hard to concentrate on her book.[27]

"OMG, did you see what Ashley was wearing today?" one of the cheerleaders said, flipping her hair dramatically.[28]

"You mean, what she [*wasn't*][29] wearing!" [s]Someone[30] said, laughing.

"I know! She made it to third block before a teacher sent her to the office," her friend replied, laughing.

Leah tried to block out the noise by reading the same sentence over and over again, but it was no use.[31] She felt like she was in a fishbowl, surrounded by people who cared about nothing but gossip and trends.[32] She just wanted to escape into her book and forget about the silly world around her.[33]

---

25. The overall tone of excitement is clear. Let the dialogue speak for itself.
26. This idea is very well established.
27. Same. This restates the previous Leah paragraph. Why doesn't she go to the library or find a quiet corner? Are they all locked into the cafeteria? Watch out for Leah seeming passive. She has a problem, but she's not doing anything about it (other than complaining). Will she strike readers as the kind of protagonist to proactively lead them through a story?
28. Some caricature elements (rather than characterizing ones). See the Recurring Notes chapter.
29. I suggest italics formatting for emphasis.
30. See the Recurring Notes chapter for proper dialogue formatting.
31. Established.
32. Leah isn't accepted but also isn't accepting. This might strike readers as hypocritical behavior, which can reflect poorly on her character. (Especially since we're just meeting her and forming a first impression.)
33. Established.

As she took another bite of her apple,[34] she spotted Jack a few tables away, his hands animated as he described his latest video game win to the football guys.[35] Their heads nodded,[36] and bursts of laughter erupted, making it clear that Jack knew just how to keep them entertained.[37]

---

34. The choreography with the apple pulls a lot of focus.

35. Can she hear what's happening "a few tables away" if there's so much noise?

36. Heads are generally the only parts of a body that "nod," so "They nodded" is all we need.

37. Need to explain that this is what the scene means? Let readers do some of the work. Notice how Leah is also only interpreting rather than interacting. Put her into action rather than making her simply a judgmental observer, especially for the first scene.

SAMPLE 3 OVERVIEW

The setting is very clear in this sample and will be familiar to a lot of middle grade readers. However, the familiarity is also a potential liability, as some of the details here (the cheerleaders, etc.) are a bit generic. How might the writer add some fresh nuance to keep from lapsing into caricature? Also, the protagonist's position is very clear —she wants to distract herself, finds the particulars of the cafeteria beneath her, and mostly observes what's going on. Aside from this, there should be concrete action to really kick off the story and pre-empt some questions. First, why does the story start today? These dynamics seem baked into this slice-of-life school experience. And? So? Now that we have this character who exists on the periphery, what will we do with her that'll get the plot moving? Here, I don't get a clear sense of what the story might be, other than "a day in the life of an underdog." (Careful about the protagonist's judgmental slant on her peers, though. She seems to want to join in but also doesn't seem to want to stoop to their level. If that's the case, why does she want their acceptance? Yes, it's normal for kids to want to fit in, especially at this age, but I had a similar question on Sample 1 in this section.) I suggest a present conflict that's unique to this day (other than a noisy lunch room) which has personal stakes for the character. Add a clear and logical sense of what she wants, why, and what she's proactively doing to get it. Note that an approach objective (where a character actively pursues a goal) is much more powerful than an avoidance one (where a character tries to dodge something undesirable). Leah tries to improve her situation by ignoring it, but this is a passive "action" to play.

SAMPLE 4: UNTITLED
FANTASY

ANONYMOUS

Chapter 1

The sea and the sky were hardly distinguishable[1] from one another. They unfurled along the coast like stained dishrags, forgotten on the clothesline until they faded to the same drab gray.[2] The entire island of Beatha was dull, uniform.[3] Except for me.

The soft glow radiating from my body illuminated the sand wherever I stepped,[4] ~~drenching the grey in~~ gold [overlapping the grey]. I hated overcast days—the gloom[5] made my shining[6] skin

---

1. Awk. with "hardly distinguishable." Sure, "indistinguishable" doesn't have the exact same meaning, but "The sea and the sky were indistinguishable" as a first sentence is quite mysterious. We don't technically need "from one another," either. I wouldn't pay this much attention to any old sentence, but this is the first line!
2. Great image! (Though "the same" idea is already established with "hardly distinguishable.") I also wonder about the verb "unfurled," as the sea and sky are technically already sitting there.
3. Both of these ideas are clear.
4. Not sure about "drenching" here.
5. The weather is very well established. Instead of finding more ways to express this, focus on the new information—the skin.
6. Need to state outright? We already have "soft glow radiating," "illuminated," and "gold".

even more noticeable. **All I wanted was to blend in. But my light made it impossible to hide**.

Despite the weather, I had donned my raincoat[7] and stuffed a satchel with leftovers for Brigid.[8] She was supposed to keep watch at the secluded inlet all day[,] and, though she wouldn't admit it, I knew the old woman would be exhausted by the time lunch rolled around.[9] But kindness wasn't my only motive for trekking to the remote cove under the looming threat of rain ~~clouds~~.[10] I needed to see it for myself: the spectral shape of another land across the sea,[11] haunting the horizon where there was usually nothing at all.

The greenish-brown smudge stood out against the monochrome backdrop like spilled paint on a canvas.[12] It was much less grand than I remembered.[13] Brigid had brought[14] me to the

---

7. I know the writer intends to say the character is *going out* "despite the weather," but the grammar says "I wore my raincoat despite the gloomy weather," which doesn't make sense. The character would wear a raincoat *because of* gloomy weather. Finesse this.

8. I like that we're moving into action but this is a jarring transition. Have the character carrying leftovers, then get into who Brigid is.

9. This sentence is getting a bit long, especially for the age group, so something like "by lunchtime" here would tighten things up nicely.

10. It's the threat of "rain" not "rain clouds," as the clouds are already there.

11. But if the horizon is invisible and everything is cloudy and misty, why would the character expect to see something? This needs more context and a more careful introduction. "They said the spectral island was out, even in this weather, but I wouldn't believe it until I saw it" or something. Otherwise, a good curiosity hook about this mysterious island and what its appearance means.

12. Is this the character already seeing the land, then? Weren't they walking to the inlet/Brigid so they could see it? Have they reached their destination? I'm a little disoriented. Maybe build up to the reveal of the land some more.

13. Play with expectations here, too. Otherwise, this lukewarm reaction is a nothing, just as readers were getting potentially invested. Either build it up and then have the character upset and underwhelmed, or have them complaining about how underwhelming it was the last time and make it funny: "The mysterious portal to the Way better be more impressive this time." As is, we just learned about it … and we're already disappointed. That's not really the experience readers want to have on the first page. Also, if it's so disappointing and if the character has already seen it before, why do they express urgency in the previous paragraph: "I needed to see it for myself"?

14. Notice that we're leaving the present moment.

same spot the last time the Way opened. I was seven, and seeing the fabled "mainland" for myself[15] had been thrilling in the way everything new is when you're a child. Now, at fourteen, the sight[16] still sent a shiver running along my spine.[17]

For as long as anyone can remember, the mainland has been visible from the easternmost point of our island once every seven years, when the Way decides to open.[18] And without fail, exactly seven weeks after each appearance, the connection is severed[,] and our estranged sister continent vanishes along with it.[19]

The Way is how Beatha was settled in the first place. Generations of runaways, ~~and~~ fugitives, and shipwreck survivors landed on the island and—once they discovered that it was infused with magic—decided to stay. The population grew in trickles and spurts as children were born and, every seven years, a fresh batch of travelers was swept across the sea.[20]

I spotted Brigid perched on a flat-topped rock in the shallows. The tiny woman looked childlike despite the cloud of egret-white hair blanketing her shoulders.[21] She reclined on her palms, bony toes skimming the surface of the water, like she was simply enjoying a nice afternoon on the beach. Only the afternoon wasn't nice at

---

15. This also repeats the "I needed to see it for myself" phrasing.
16. Dangling modifier—*the character* is fourteen, not "the sight" (see the Recurring Notes chapter).
17. A physical cliché (see the Recurring Notes chapter). Also, I thought the present view "was much less grand," rather than eliciting a reaction? Which is it?
18. A bit of unintentional dissonance here. Is it "every seven years" (which seems regular) or "when the Way decides to open" (which seems random)? Notice that we're now leaving the present moment for general information again.
19. Some great questions already arising: Has anyone gone there? Can they? Where does it go between appearances? A fun premise so far, and reminds me of *The Hotel Magnifique* by Emily J. Taylor (though that's YA).
20. *From* the Way? So is Beatha the strange oasis that comes and goes (from their perspective)? Or is the other continent the weirdo?
21. A nice, tight description.

all.[22] And her eyes were fixed on the landmass lurking[23] in the distance.

Brigid took her role seriously, even though the once-revered position of Watcher had become little more than a formality over the years.[24] The appointed elder was tasked with keeping watch at the beach while the Way remained open.[25] But no one had expected them to find anything in decades—no islander still living can recall a time when newcomers crossed the Way.[26]

"Brigid!" I had to shout over the sound of the surf.

She turned and waved, a smile wrinkling her already-creased face.[27] I slipped off my shoes and waded toward her, clutching my satchel against my chest to keep the waves from devouring its contents before we could.[28]

My light stained Brigid's skin[29] as I climbed up next to her. It softened the furrows in her forehead and the laugh lines around her

---

22. This is very well established. Trust readers to find this contrast for themselves.
23. The power of a great active verb! This adds a menacing vibe.
24. Is Brigid watching for the land's appearance? They seem to know it happens every seven years. Or is she watching for any breakthrough arrivals in between appearances (seemingly more necessary)? Clarify.
25. Haha. I am impatient. Good instincts! (What does she do the rest of the time, though?)
26. I'm still confused because of the sentence above: "every seven years, a fresh batch of travelers was swept across the sea." It seems that people do cross over. But is "the Way" the body of water or the other continent? Are people coming to or from the island? How do people come every seven years (per the above), but now, no one has come in decades? I think the terms, more than anything, are throwing my understanding.
27. Necessary if we already know she's old?
28. I thought the leftovers were for Brigid? Maybe clarify if they're going to share a lunch.
29. The first few paragraphs are all about the light. Then it has entirely gone away and, truth be told, I almost forgot about it. Put the detail of the glowing skin into action. The character leaves the main drag and can finally pull their gloves off, they adjust their hood to keep from being seen, etc. Otherwise, we're told it's a big deal, then the action unfolds as if it's no deal at all.

eyes,[30] reminding me of bedtime when I was younger.[31] I used to lie awake until she came to blow out the lone candle on my dresser. The light radiating from my shimmering body would encircle the two of us in the darkness,[32] washing out the wrinkles on her face that were deep even then.[33] In those moments, it felt like we were all that existed.[34] As if nothing existed in the universe unless it was touched by my glow.[35]

---

30. Another mention of Brigid's wrinkles.
31. Because Brigid used to do this character's bedtime? Yes, the writing is clear, but this took me several logic leaps.
32. This is also clear, but if there's light, there isn't darkness. "would cushion us against the darkness" or similar would be more precise.
33. Give Brigid more than one attribute (see the Recurring Notes chapter).
34. This also repeats the idea of them "encircled" or "cushioned" (my suggestion). Let the images speak for themselves without explaining them.
35. This seems to take a positive view of the glow, but on the first page, it seemed the character had an adversarial relationship with it. I realize that nuance means both can be true, but for the purpose of the opening pages, this might seem like a contradiction instead, which leaves readers confused rather than compelled.

SAMPLE 4 OVERVIEW

Some great scene-setting, world-building, and mystery here. While the external elements are working well, I suggest clarifying a few details about the character. I got a bit mixed up about the protagonist's existing relationship with and knowledge about the mysterious land. What does seeing it mean to them personally? How might its appearance trigger a change that has significant bearing on *their* day-to-day life? We get a lot of observation here, but less action (other than going to observe). Intrigue abounds about this island and how it connects (or doesn't) to the protagonist's world, but the momentum doesn't quite catch. And? So? What will change for the character now that they have seen it (again)? If the character doesn't know—and that's part of the mystery—let's have them make some clear guesses or develop concrete expectations. The protagonist is the one who understands this world, after all, and readers are just learning about it for the first time. Any context the protagonist is able to add—especially when it comes to how the world-building will make life better or worse—would greatly enhance this opening, which is already nicely stylized and well written.

SAMPLE 5: SOMEDAY

CONTEMPORARY

LISA FREELS

"You're the one who wanted to move here. I wanted to stay in Port Hayes. That was a great place to live. This town is ridiculous. There's nothing to do here!"[1]

I rolled over in bed, listening to my mom yell at Neil. Again.[2] Shifting under the itchy motel sheet, I looked[3] at them through the slit in my eyelids. If they noticed me, I didn't want them to see that I was awake.[4]

"I thought you would get a job. One of us has to work." Neil sighed in frustration,[5] running his fingers through the little bit of hair that he still had on his head.[6]

---

1. A lot of repetition to these ideas. (We also don't have any attachment to the Port Hayes name, so it might not be necessary first thing.) I would discourage this writer from starting with unattributed dialogue, as readers don't know who's speaking (the protagonist or someone else) so there's a bit of initial confusion.
2. Good context with the "Again." This could be a more grounding first line.
3. Maybe "peeked" aligns more with the idea of slitted eyes, and then we don't need the additional description.
4. I like the "If they noticed me," but I'm not sure we need to clarify why she's pretending to be asleep. This is obviously done so she's not pulled into the argument.
5. Need to explain the sigh or the fight? Let the dialogue speak for itself.
6. A bit wordy. Do something like "his remaining hair."

"So why isn't it you? I'm here all day with Angeline."

"Who should be in school. Why haven't you signed her up? It's been months. All you do is sit in this room and do who-knows-what." Neil grabbed his bag from the small closet as he shouted.[7]

My heart began to race.[8] Why was he pulling his clothes from the lopsided dresser?[9] The scarred drawer hit the floor when he yanked too hard. Shirts, pants, underwear, and socks were scooped[10] from the floor and tossed into the bag.

Mom **just sat** in the chair, **staring at him blankly**. I wasn't sure what time she had come home last night.[11] After midnight, I knew. That's when I had put my book away and gone [went] to sleep. [I knew.][12]

The light began to filter through the dingy motel drapes, dust motes flying in the air[13] as Neil tossed his bag on the other bed in the room.[14] He stomped into the bathroom and slammed the door.

"You don't want to go to school, do you[,] Angelbaby? You just want to read your books and hang out with me, right?"[15] **Mom's**

---

7. That they're yelling is already clear. Does Angeline react when she's thrown into the fight? It'd be almost impossible not to when it becomes personal. Just because she's not actively participating doesn't mean she can't react in interiority.
8. A physical cliché (see the Recurring Notes chapter).
9. It seems obvious that he means to leave (or to at least will threaten it). Let the character do some critical thinking instead of asking rhetorical questions with obvious answers (see the Recurring Notes chapter).
10. Passive construction. It's not ideal to start every sentence with "He verb," sure, but I'd rephrase this.
11. I don't know the story, world, or characters yet, but I *do* know that Mom's sin is supposed to be staying in the room all day. So this idea of her out roaming at all hours is a direct contradiction and confuses my image of the conflict.
12. I want to reorganize this a bit to make it sequential.
13. Where else would they be flying?
14. Why would he pack a bag to move into the next room? Is he usually dramatic/ridiculous? Or are we just moving the bag around as he packs? Not sure we need all the play-by-play (see the Recurring Notes chapter).
15. Mom seems checked out, so why does she suddenly come online *and* start talking to Angeline, who is pretending to be asleep? Drunk people have no strategy, so wouldn't she try to rile her daughter?

voice slurred a little bit, her eyes trying to focus on me.[16] I <u>could</u> tell[17] **she <u>couldn't</u> see me, really**.

"I wouldn't mind it," I answered quietly. I learned that speaking quietly when they were arguing was safer.[18]

"Naw, you don't need it. You can read and watch TV all day. **What kid doesn't want to do that? You have the perfect life."**[19]

The bathroom door opened[,] and Neil came out with his toothbrush and razor.[20] I watched him toss them on top of his clothes, and zip his bag closed. The knot that had formed in my stomach grew larger.[21] This couldn't be happening.[22]

"You're not leaving, you know. I won't let you." My mom's eyes were now laser focused on Neil,[23] who was walking to the motel room <u>door</u>.

"I am leaving, and I won't be back. Good luck, the both of you." With that, Neil opened the <u>door</u>[24] and walked out, pulling the door

---

16. Two ways of describing intoxication.

17. This restates the end of the previous sentence. The point is well made. Instead, focus on Angeline's reaction. Has Mom promised to stop getting wasted? Is there betrayal? Or is Angeline too numb from repeated disappointments to hope for better?

18. It seems like this school issue has been going on for *months*. If Angeline feels this way, why hasn't she said so in all that time? Why did she choose today to be honest? Let's get some run-up in interiority—she actually does want to go to school and can't bear Mom's obsession with keeping her home, etc. Why does Angeline speak up in the middle of a fight when Mom is drunk, worked up, and unlikely to be receptive?

19. Both of these statements mean the same thing.

20. Got it. I got tripped up on the play-by-play logistics of what he's doing and where he is with my previous comment about moving into the other room. Maybe zoom out on the spatial descriptions. He's packing, that's all we need to know.

21. Physical cliché for fear / dread here (see the Recurring Notes chapter).

22. Go deeper. We have no sense of who Neil is to Angeline. Would she miss him if he left? Or is he yet another one of Mom's short-term boyfriends? Has he threatened to leave before? If not, what's the worst thing that can happen? Have her think through the stakes.

23. This seems unlikely since so much was made of how she can't focus her eyes because she's under the influence. Yes, drunks can certainly snap to attention, but this is a jarring departure from the established circumstances.

24. We don't need to describe each individual move toward the door, either.

shut behind him. Not a slam, really, but the sound was still deafening.[25]

Mom looked shocked for a minute, then her face completely changed. **Her nostrils flared and her eyebrows met above her nose as she scrunched her face up in anger.**[26] Before I could blink, she was in my face.

"You're the reason he left. If he thinks I'll be stuck with you,[27] he'd better think again." **Her voice became shriller and louder as she carried on. Spittle sprayed as she talked, her anger growing by the second.**[28]

"I'm sor—[—]"[29] Before I could get the words out, her hand connected with my cheek with a resounding *smack*.

I fell back on the bed, the force of her slap pushing me away.[30] Tears began to run down my cheeks. Through them I could see[31] Mom yanking the door open and running after Neil. I wondered if she realized she was still in her robe, [though this]—. Which was nothing new. Unless she was going out, she was always in her robe.[32]

---

25. A familiar image of a sound seeming amplified to convey emotional intensity.
26. One of these descriptions can stand in for Mom's mood. We don't need all of them, especially since we already have the "anger" label.
27. Yes, parents can choose their own happiness over their children's. However, if she was *that* kind of mother, why would she keep Angeline with her all day? That sounds like a drag for a parent who's looking out for herself.
28. Some redundancy here.
29. Use an em-dash for an interruption, rather than an ellipsis (see the Recurring Notes chapter).
30. Need to explain why Angeline falls after being struck?
31. Filler description (see the Recurring Notes chapter).
32. The protagonist is observing quite a bit about the adults in her life, which is fine. However, I'd recommend turning up her own experiences, reactions, and extrapolations about what's happening instead of having her relay the scene in a relatively neutral tone. First-person perspective can go deeper into the protagonist's experience.

SAMPLE 5 OVERVIEW

We get a lot of great action in this opening scene, including a high-stakes departure from Neil, who seems to have offered the character a sense of support and normalcy. I worry that the mom character is too obviously impaired and villainous—this doesn't leave much room for nuance. The overall tension is very interesting: the protagonist wants to interface with the world, but Mom is keeping her in the motel room. The question is even posed in the text: Why wouldn't any kid want to sit around and watch TV all day? Watch out for some logic flaws, though. If Mom doesn't seem invested in parenting the protagonist, wouldn't it be easier for the daughter to go to school, after all, leaving Mom to do whatever she wants all day? Mom even seems to resent the idea of "being stuck" with Angeline, but isn't that the status quo she was just arguing to maintain? The main character could be given a more concrete motivation for her objective. Why does she want to be out in the world? The answer seems obvious—to be a regular kid, to have normal experiences—but this type of objective is difficult to track. What is "regular," anyway? When will she have enough "normality" to be satisfied? Instead, I suggest giving her a passion and a very clear goal which relates back to something she wants to do. For example, the school has a robotics team, and she feels she's wasting away without being able to learn science and engineering. As is, we spend too much time observing and commenting on the adults in the scene, and too little time putting the protagonist front and center. Sure, she's a kid, and that means she's largely powerless in the events shaping her life. Within that framework, though, which exists in most middle grade stories because kids at these ages are not yet fully independent, how can we make the protagonist more proactive? A strong goal, clear motivation, and more participation in this scene would all be good places to start.

SAMPLE 6: SALTY ALICE, THE WOLVES AND THE RAINTREE

HISTORICAL

LINDA J. ROMERO

Six fifty-nine a.m.[1] showed on the timecard as Salty pulled it out of the clock punch machine.[2]

"You're running late! You are to be at your station at 7 a.m. sharp," bellowed[3] a **lumpy round** man in a gray cotton suit. "Bones won't sort and pack themselves, will they?"[4]

"No, Mr. Mason," Salty hollered[5] and shoved the timecard in the rack.[6]

"Get along then," Mr. Mason shouted.[7] His **sausage-like**

---

1. This might look wrong to some (who know to format time using numbers, as is done below) but APA says to spell out all numbers at the beginning of sentences. Nice work!
2. The action and detail are clear right away, but it doesn't turn into a story until we know Salty is late, which comes in the following line. What's more important for an engaging opening?
3. Avoid "said" synonyms (see the Recurring Notes chapter).
4. Good curiosity hook!
5. See above. These do add some color but "said" and "asked" tend to be less showy.
6. Play-by-play choreography (see the Recurring Notes chapter).
7. That they're both yelling is clear. Instead, add some details about how noisy it is on the factory floor, etc.

fingers removed the cigar from his mouth and tapped the ashes on the floor as he **wobbled** away.[8]

One needed to speak loudly to be heard[9] even though heavy doors separated the office from the factory floor.

Salty pushed through the massive double doors. Today would not be just like any other day. No siree. Today[10] she would turn over a new leaf.[11] No matter what, she'd be peaceful as a butterfly.[12] She pushed her slingshot down into the back pocket of her overalls and hurried into the underground cavern of the Bone Novelty Department.[13]

Beneath the Chicago Union Stockyards,[—]the slaughterhouse and meatpacking capital of the country,[—][14] the bones of cows and pigs and sheep were carved into many useful and sometimes peculiar items.[15] The air hung heavy with noxious gases and the smell of ground[-]up bone, which reminded Salty of sweaty, wet hair.[16]

At one end of the floor, men in gray suits manipulated bones through a gargantuan slate-colored machine [that] ~~It~~ clanked and spewed and ground out ear[-] deafening sounds like an iron monster with gnashing jaws.[17] Rib bones, femur bones, [and] clover-shaped vertebrae ~~. The iron monster~~ [were] cut and shaped

---

8. Several similar descriptions of Mr. Mason's physicality.

9. This is good, per the above, but with all the shouting and hollering, readers get it already. I'd avoid outright explaining.

10. There's some word echo on "day" and "today" here but this instance of repetition also suggests Salty is being emphatic.

11. Good pre-empted answer to "Why today?" but it's also not specific. It also seems like she's late a lot, so we are only *told* she'll "turn over a new leaf," not *shown* the same idea in action.

12. Clarify that the "new leaf" isn't in reference to her being late or getting in trouble at work (since we've already seen her do both). Define what she actually means.

13. Ha! More intrigue here.

14. I'd stylistically suggest offsetting this with em-dashes instead.

15. I'm really hoping we get specific examples soon, as this could be anything.

16. Good. This paragraph really starts to paint a picture.

17. I worry that machines are often described as having mouths, and an "iron monster" also strikes me as a familiar image. Reach for something more challenging

~~the bones~~ into buttons and beads, knife handles and combs, trinkets and treasures.[18]

Shiny beige objects paraded on a speeding rubber belt before a long line of girls and young women, each wearing a white apron ~~over their clothing~~. Salty tied her apron[19] as she rushed along the bone[-]dust[-]speckled floor[20] to Station [Five] ~~5~~.[21] Out of breath,[22] she stopped fast, and her elbow struck the tall <u>stack</u> of paperboard <u>boxes</u> piled between her[23] and [her best friend,] Mabel. ~~Salty's best friend.~~ The <u>boxes</u>[24] **swayed, ready to topple over,** but Salty grabbed the <u>stack</u> and steadied it.[25] Mabel gave a quick wink and a wave from Station [Six] ~~6~~.

"Hey, Mabsie," Salty hollered[26] and checked her paperboard box for the item[27] to be counted and packaged for the day.

A two-inch carved wolf with a long snout and tucked tail lay in the box.[28] She picked it up and studied the figure. Wolves were menacing creatures in fairy tales.[29] Eating up little girls and old

---

and surprising, or cut the comparison. Not everything needs an accompanying image.

18. Nice. I did play around with these two sentences to avoid repeating the "iron monster" phrasing in such close proximity.

19. If they're expected to wear an apron, do we need to specify that she's also wearing one? We already know she's rushing to her station from the previous action.

20. This writer is missing some hyphens throughout. I recommend a refresher on their usage.

21. Spell out numbers under 10.

22. Need this if we know she's hurrying?

23. Practice mimetic writing (see the Recurring Notes chapter).

24. Need both?

25. Need to explain her intent? Seems clear.

26. Maybe we can get the idea that they're best friends from their interactions, rather than the above explanation? Also, it's very clear already that it's loud and they have to shout.

27. "items"?

28. It's assumed this is in the box if Salty is shown checking there in the previous sentence.

29. This seems like a generic explanation. We don't know anything about the world or Salty's personal belief system yet. Can we see this more through her unique lens?

ladies. Terrorizing industrious pigs. Hardly worth much in the ways of the world.[30]

"What do you think these are for?" Salty yelled to Mabel over the roaring rhythm of the iron monster.[31]

Mabel shrugged and held up an ordinary pipe stem.

A spindly young supervisor with **tight gelled** curls **plastered to her head** stepped next to Salty and chomped gum in her ear.[32] "**Start packing and stop staring!** Haven't you seen trinkets before?" **Then she shook a [boney], red-polished ~~boney~~ finger in Salty's face.**[33] "**I've got my eyes on you, [m]Missy!**"

Salty clenched her jaw. "And just what do ...!" **Heat crept up her neck** and those little **red welts were rising** to the surface. Dander **blotches**, Pa called them. **Itchy** as mosquito bites.[34]

Mabel looked at her with raised eyebrows and shook her head.[35] Salty swallowed her words. It was never easy for her to hold her tongue,[36] but she had told herself she would not lose her temper

---

30. Not sure I understand, as the writer just described wolves being at the top of their food chain, which seems to convey worth/value/status.
31. Another mention of them yelling due to the ambient noise.
32. Would we be able to hear this if it's so loud?
33. All of the people working here are described as being somewhat ridiculous. That's fine—I'm still learning the tone. However, it's stronger to err on the side of making them more real and therefore menacing. If they're caricatures, the writer loses the ability to use them to threaten the protagonist. If we're meant to fear them, don't make them so cartoonish.
34. A physical cliché (see the Recurring Notes chapter). There are several ways of saying similar things (welts, hives, itching), too.
35. If Salty decided she would be different today, do we need Mabel to remind her to cool it? That takes some of the protagonist power away from Salty (and makes her seem less credible, as she's not the one upholding her own decision to turn over a new leaf). Sure, we can't be perfect all the time, but I think it's important to show her trying.
36. Implied already. Need to explain?

today.[37] Even though nothing positive came from letting people dampen your sparkle. That's what Pa always said.[38]

---

37. Trust readers to retain the idea, even if Salty hasn't shown this yet.
38. I'm not sure about getting Pa into the mix this early. We already have one mention of him and Mabel acting as the voice of reason in scene.

SAMPLE 6 OVERVIEW

Some great world-building details here, as well as obvious conflict for the main character. My biggest issue is the protagonist's inner struggle, which is painted in rather absolute terms without much room to explore any nuance. Salty wants to be one way, but she can't help being herself. That's great internal tension, but her desire to change isn't currently rationalized. Would it make her employment easier? (If so, this begs the question of why she wants to do a good job. She doesn't seem terribly motivated by the work itself.) As is, she tells readers that she wants to do better, then we get several instances of her immediately failing at self-control. This is relatable, but if turning over a new leaf is presented as one of her main conflicts, why doesn't she try harder? This makes one of two impressions: She's either just paying lip service to the idea of self-improvement because she knows it looks good, or she doesn't really care about what she claims to care about. Neither idea is, at face value, very endearing or engaging, especially in a protagonist. The objective is also vague. What does "better" mean, and how will she know if she's achieved it? Will she be judging this, or will her employer? From the way her bosses are described, it's clear she doesn't respect them, so will impressing them be a compelling desire? (This is similar to my comment on Sample 1 and Sample 3 in this section, where I wonder why Brock wants to impress Theo, even though we already know he's a bully, or why Leah wants to fit in with the vapid cheerleaders.) What a character does or wants is only one piece of the puzzle. The *why* is much more interesting, and is an opportunity to generate reader engagement. The tone of this sample is also a bit unclear. Is everyone around Salty (except Mabel, of course) ridiculous? On the one hand, that's funny and introduces good opportunities for voice and humor. On the other hand, the writer loses the ability to generate stakes and tension. If a caricature boss flips out at a character, the protagonist might be less likely to take it seriously or be affected by the consequences, because there's no respect or fear. Making antagonists silly neuters them—and their potential to create true conflict. This is a fine line to walk, but one I'd suggest this writer reexamine.

SAMPLE 7: THE HALF POWERS
ACTION/ADVENTURE

BRANDON JONES

Ramsey Carr knew the streets of New Orleans better than most kids knew their neighborhoods,[1] which was a good thing since he had bad guys following him.[2]

Ramsey crossed St. Phillip Street, ~~and~~ headed for Jazz Park, [and] ~~. He~~ glanced back.[3] The three men were still there.[4] *Who are these dudes?* Ramsey wondered.[5] They'd been with him since he'd snuck out of the home an hour ago.[6]

As a foster kid, Ramsey spent <u>lots</u> [of] time on the streets. He'd

---

1. Good orienting details—we get a character and location right away. (Though I'm not so sure about comparing his knowledge of NOLA streets to kids knowing their neighborhoods—it's an obvious image.)
2. Good humor and a nice sense of action.
3. This change is meant to make the sentence a bit less choppy.
4. Rather static. "were gaining" or similar would keep adding to the action.
5. Italics are used for verbatim thought so there's no need for a "thought" or "wondered" tag (see the Recurring Notes chapter).
6. Hard to imagine them either being in hot pursuit or him running without anyone catching up for a whole hour. Especially if he can see them. What's keeping them from closing the distance? (I'd also be curious about where he's heading, whether he snuck out for a reason or if he's wandering. The decision to go to Jazz Park seems arbitrary, unless the writer clarifies that Ramsey has somewhere to be.)

learned a <u>lot</u> about people[,] and everything about these guys told him they were dangerous. The way they moved as a team, slipping easily through the crowded sidewalks, their expensive clothing, and the sure look in their eyes, like following people is what they do.[7]

Ramsey hurried beneath the Armstrong archway leading into Jazz Park.[8] The morning sun was already beating down on <u>him</u>, while all around <u>him</u>, the French Quarter was coming alive with its unique soundtrack of streetcars,[9] traffic, and the happy chatter of tourists blended with the melodies of jazz floating from clubs and outdoor concerts.[10] Ramsey weaved through a group of women trailing a tour guide and then darted past a couple studying a map of the Quarter.

The park was busy. It should be easy to ditch these guys and make his meeting[11] but when he checked again, <u>the men</u> were closer[,] and Ramsey briefly locked eyes with <u>the man</u> in the middle. He was older than the other two, bald, and wearing a long black coat. *Who wears a coat in New Orleans in the middle of August?*[12]

Ramsey quickly turned[13] away and walked faster. He knew the

---

7. This sentence is trying to do a lot at once and is a bit all over the place. I'd break it up or give it some shape. Limit any lists to three items and make each instance parallel.

8. We've already established him going there. This is all prime real estate, so avoid repeating it. Trust readers to follow. However, I think this writer means Louis Armstrong Park, which is an actual park along Rampart. New Orleans Jazz Historical Park is a tiny triangle along Decatur and one can't really walk into it as if it's a park.

9. The only two streetcar lines surrounding the Quarter run along Canal and the river. But Louis Armstrong Park is all the way on the other side, so we wouldn't hear the trains. I love the sensory details, but if the point is that the kid knows NOLA, these details bounce me. (I've been going to New Orleans since I was a kid and got married there, so I'm a bit more of a stickler.)

10. I'd say "buskers" here because he's more likely to run into a street performer in the morning, when the Quarter is rather sleepy and unlikely to host an outdoor concert/festival. Music would start pouring from the clubs a bit later.

11. Would love a sentence of context about where he's going and why. If he's expected at some kind of meeting/official function, why would he need to sneak out?

12. Good, and good job dropping the "thought" or "wondered" tag.

13. No need to describe people turning (see the Recurring Notes chapter). In this case, he'd obviously turn *away* from the people chasing him. (But also, if they've been chasing him for an hour, and are only now gaining on him, why did it take so long?)

answer.[14] *Bad guys who want to hide weapons, that's who.* And Ramsey would swear Bald Dude was reaching inside his jacket when he'd looked[15] at <u>him</u>. But what did they want with a kid like <u>him</u>?[16] Ramsey believed he knew the answer to that question, too, and as if to confirm it, Ramsey realized he was tapping[17] his jean pocket, making sure <u>the stone</u> was still there. Because from the moment he got[18] <u>the stone,</u> his entire life had changed.

Two months ago,[19] on his fourteenth birthday,[20] Ramsey received a package from a man claiming to be his uncle.[21] Inside the package was a smooth black <u>stone</u> with a note tapped to the bottom and a message written in perfect cursive.

To Ramsey, it said,[22] *Accept this <u>stone</u> and accept its power. I'll be in touch, Uncle Thomas.*[23]

Who's Uncle Thomas?[24] Ramsey had asked himself.[25] Ramsey's a foster kid. He has no family,[26] and he'd almost tossed <u>the stone</u>. Then something crazy happened. Holding <u>the stone</u> in his hand,

---

14. If he does, though, why would he ask? Is he a savvy street kid or not?

15. If they have weapons, why would it take an hour to try and incapacitate or capture Ramsey?

16. Word echoes are especially noticeable when they come at the beginning or end of a sentence.

17. This writer has him "realize" a lot of stuff but I think he'd consciously check his pocket. Make him more sure: "He knew what they were after, and patted his pocket." Otherwise, readers get this strange combination of "Gee, I wonder" and "I know exactly why" and it's a bit uneven.

18. How long has he had it? This piece of data is extremely relevant to figuring out how long he's been on the run, questions of "Why today?," etc.

19. Great, the writer's instincts have pre-empted me!

20. Notice, also, that we're leaving the present moment. I agree this is relevant to the present action, but we're still zooming away to fill in backstory.

21. Is the "claiming" because Ramsey has no family (foster care) or because Ramsey doesn't trust the guy?

22. Necessary if this is formatted as the note's text?

23. This also repeats "claiming to be his uncle"...

24. ... as does this. But here, he seems to accept that the man *is* in his family, and Ramsey just doesn't know him. Which is it?

25. Could omit the "thought" tag.

26. Trust readers to retain this. I'd also stick with consistent past tense, even for a generalization. (These are sometimes done in present tense.)

anything Ramsey <u>touched</u> for more than a second, the color and texture of his skin changed to match what he was <u>touching</u>—like he was a chameleon![27] A tree, a car, a wall—didn't matter— whatever Ramsey <u>touched</u>, his skin would change. Well … most of him[28] would change. There was always a part of his body that wouldn't turn.[29] But how ~~would~~ [did] Bald Dude even know about Ramsey's power—or was it a power?[30] Ramsey didn't know what to call it. Whatever it is, why would these guys be interested?[31] Nothing made sense.[32]

Only way he'd know was to get to his meeting with the mysterious Uncle Thomas.[33] Thomas had kept his word and had sent a second letter promising to explain everything.[34] He told Ramsey to meet him at Jackson Square[35] and warned him **to keep his wits about him, be aware of everyone around him**, which confused Ramsey at first.[36] Now he knew why.

---

27. A common comparison. Reach for something more interesting to match the surprising fantasy element.
28. Awk. The "most of him" doesn't really add anything to a reader's understanding because "his skin" is technically not his entire body. Be more precise with these descriptions.
29. Break this onto a new line. Otherwise it's jarring to go from past generalization to present action in the same paragraph.
30. What does Ramsey think? He's asking a lot of rhetorical questions and seems unsure. But if he's had this thing for two months, it's likely he has already made some decisions and done some critical thinking (see the Recurring Notes chapter).
31. He obviously thinks it's something important if he suspects they're following him for it. If this writer is telling us he's a smart and savvy kid, they can't also have him going "Gee whiz!" He's had two months to consider these angles and experiment with the stone. That's an eternity to a smart kid. Avoid characters in denial, and instead offer buy-in (see the Recurring Notes chapter).
32. Avoid making him clueless for too long. Yes, we're just meeting him and he has room to grow, but he'd theoretically have done more inquiry already.
33. Make this clear sooner, e.g., "He wasn't sure, but all would be revealed today. Uncle Tomas had invited him to his studio … if he didn't get killed first," or similar. Give us a reason to care about the meeting.
34. Don't get lost in the logistics. Include this promise with the first letter. (Notice that we're leaving the present moment again.)
35. He's going the wrong way for Jackson Square if he's at Armstrong Park.
36. That said … why'd it take two months between the note and the meeting?

Ramsey looked again. His heart plunged to his stomach.[37]

Bald Dude *was* holding a weapon, and he was alone,[38] which meant the other two had peeled off and were about to ambush him.[39]

---

37. A physical cliché (see the Recurring Notes chapter).

38. Why'd it take them an hour to spring this trap if they were armed and had a strategy? I'm obviously *really* distracted by this one detail. But the actionable tip here is to narrow down the time scale instead of stretching it out. Make the threat more immediate instead of having this "chase" take an hour.

39. The antecedent for "him" is "Bald Dude," not Ramsey, as intended.

SAMPLE 7 OVERVIEW

This sample features perhaps my most nit-picky notes about New Orleans because I know the French Quarter well. Not all readers will. Part of it could be the sheer amount of logistical and spatial detail involved—if the writer spent less time orienting readers in the neighborhood, there would be fewer opportunities for various discrepancies to snag attention. The time horizon also pulled me out of the action. Ramsey has known about the stone and its powers for two months, yet for all intents and purposes, he's asking basic questions that would've been more likely to pop up the day he got the letter and package. It's like he truly hasn't considered who this person claiming his uncle might be. I like that we skip over the very familiar beginning of "Wow, I got this strange thing, and now I'm going to spend twenty pages learning all about the powers it gives me!" (described in the Common Opening Clichés chapter). However, this means we're also told about it in backstory, which interrupts the present action and makes it seem like Ramsey hasn't done any critical thinking about his situation. Speaking of the present action, the encroaching goons triggered some red flags for me. First of all, why the two-month gap between receiving the stone and going to this meeting to, theoretically, learn more about the object and the powers it seems to grant? Second, would Ramsey really lead them around the French Quarter for an entire hour, with neither party making a move? If the men are armed and dangerous, let's add some urgency. It defies belief that nobody would pounce or try to run, especially once Ramsey knows he's being followed and the goons realize he's on to them. His expectations for the meeting, what he might learn there, critical thinking about the stone, and any reactive or offensive maneuver he might try to shake his pursuers will help keep this scene tight.

YOUNG ADULT FIRST PAGES

The following examples are intended for readers ages fourteen to eighteen, also known as the "young adult" (or "YA") market in the children's book industry. This can sometimes be a misnomer because plenty of adult readers gravitate to the faster pacing and higher emotional register typical of this category, just as younger kids who have "graduated" from middle grade may also explore YA fiction. In each case, as with the MG examples, the writers have indicated their target audience category. While some of these sample pages hit YA expectations in terms of voice, style, and content, there are also some submissions which might be better suited for another age group, and I'll discuss my reasoning in their respective overviews.

SAMPLE 1: HOW TO BUILD A TIME MACHINE

SCIENCE FICTION

DR. STEVEN NOVICK

Category Note: This writer has changed their category from MG to YA, though I would argue that the action/adventure time travel premise aligns more with a younger readership.

Part 1: The Here and Now: Lightstar's Carnival | Lesson 1: Do One Impossible Thing Before Dinner

Cotton candy clung to the back of my throat like sticky cobwebs[1] as I prepared to perform[2] the most dangerous horse jump of my life. The carnival lights[—], a swirl of reds, blues, and yellows,[—][3] threw long, distorted shadows on the dusty ground of the arena.

---

1. The image is stronger without "sticky" because cotton candy and cobwebs already have this in common (which is why the comparison was drawn in the first place). Avoid explaining the image.
2. We don't learn until a bit later that they're not on stage yet. The discussion of the arena in this paragraph might not make this clear. How else might this writer establish that Johnny's still off to the side? Take care with the reader's mental image, especially in the first paragraph or two.
3. I suggest offsetting this with em-dashes instead of commas.

Uni, my magnificent Arabian stallion and best friend, stood patiently beside me, her dark eyes reflecting[4] the churning vortex in my stomach.[5] From behind the gated fence, Uni and I peeked into the horse show field. Inside, [M]~~m~~om and [D]~~d~~ad[6] were checking that the special barricades and gigantic hoops for my show[7] were firmly staked in the ground.

Why ~~does~~ [did][8] being thirteen years old[9] have to be so hectic? Clean your room. Muck out the stable. Jump through fire. Be a big brother. Total [S]~~s~~tress [C]~~c~~ity all the time.

'Worry' should be my middle name. Johnny 'Worry' Winchester.[10]

For weeks, I'd been perfecting[11] this new, heart-stopping stunt. Every move, every turn, practiced until it was carved into my muscle memory.[12] Each successful landing meant another dollar in the collection bucket, another step closer to affording the treatment my six-year-old sister, Lily, desperately needed.[13]

Leukemia. The word slammed into our family like a ten-ton

---

4. Meaning that the eyeballs are literally reflecting this fearful state, or that Uni also seems afraid? How does he know without having access to her POV? Is she acting nervous? Otherwise, this is telling with body language (see the Recurring Notes chapter).

5. A physical cliché (see the Recurring Notes chapter).

6. This manuscript has some wonky capitalization for "Mom" and "Dad." The noun version is lowercase, e.g. "his dad." When used in place of a name, it's capitalized, e.g. "Promise not to kill me, Dad, but you know how I asked to borrow my mom's car…"

7. Implied that they're used in the show. Need?

8. If this was verbatim thought and italicized, use present tense. But since this is woven into the narration, past tense is more appropriate.

9. The protagonist's age is a definite marker for MG instead of YA.

10. Two ways of making this joke. I'm not sure we need both. Do something like, "My name should be Johnny 'Worry' Winchester."

11. If he "perfected" it already, why the fear?

12. This repeats the "perfected" idea.

13. Good. Really nice sense of stakes, and a curiosity hook.

weight[14] [three years ago][15] ~~Three years ago the diagnosis had shattered our world,~~ [and now] Lily, my **shadow**, **following me** everywhere like a **lost puppy**,[16] suddenly needed me more than ever. I made a silent promise to be her hero, which fueled my determination. It also fueled my constant anxiety.[17]

"Stem cell transplant," the doctor had said, a phrase that boomed in my nightmares.[18] A special medical procedure that could save Lily. ~~A procedure~~ [One] we couldn't afford without insurance. Offering my own cells felt like the least I could do, but they weren't a match.

On social media, people leave comments on my videos saying that being the star attraction of Lightstar's Carnival must be amazing. But earning my dinner, performing by day, and cleaning up horse poop by night is not as fun as it sounds.[19] ~~The truth was~~ [The] glitter faded fast when you were staring down the barrel of a super dangerous stunt.[20]

Despite my working long hours at the carnival,[21] my parents loved to tell me how tough it was when they were kids.[22] Mom would launch into stories about surviving on berries while dodging dinosaurs, and Dad droned on about the character-building struggle

---

14. A weight signifying something heavy (emotionally) is a familiar image, I'm afraid.
15. Fold this detail from the next sentence here. Otherwise the following sentence is redundant.
16. Three ways of saying the same thing here.
17. Telling. Do we need this after the aside about anxiety, above?
18. The seriousness of the cancer is quite clear already.
19. It's not about the sound, though. On social media, he's posting photos and videos, so "looks" would be more cohesive.
20. His fear is already established, but the writer hasn't resolved the disconnect between how afraid Johnny says he is and that he has already "perfected" the performance. Yes, both can be true, but these ideas are also close to mutually exclusive.
21. Several mentions of the grueling work already.
22. Notice that we step away from the present moment here to add some backstory. The parents' story can be introduced later (and this writer don't need this data to make the point that Johnny's life *seems* exciting but is actually complicated).

of outdoor toilets and dial-up internet.[23] They couldn't understand why I'd ever complain about having a roof over my head and three meals a day.

"Yes, Mom. Thank you, Dad," I'd mumble through mouthfuls of food while glued to my phone.[24] "Things are different now."

Shaking his head in that way dads do when their kids talk back, ~~he grumbles I~~ [he'd grumble that] I'd ~~would~~ fight the wind if I could. Mom would then patiently explain, for the millionth time, that I was an equestrian prodigy,[25] a fact that somehow justified aerial tricks on horseback instead of homework.[26] Dad would just grunt in response, leaving me to wonder if he secretly wished I'd trade in my riding gear for a math textbook.[27]

In the parking lot, the clatter of the roller coaster wheels mixed with [excited] screams ~~of excitement~~. The Ferris wheel rose above the carnival like a giant, watchful eye, its blinking lights painting the afternoon sky.[28]

---

23. Ha! Some good humor here, but I'm not sure this is the time or place.
24. I get that he's a jaded tween with a hard life and worries. But I wouldn't make him too sarcastic or disconnected. This isn't the most endearing portrait, even if it's realistic. His real spark so far is his determination to help his sister, which should help overshadow his fear.
25. Even though this is a generalization, I'd keep the past tense consistent here.
26. Again, the writer just spent time establishing that Johnny claims to *want* to do these tricks above all else, especially for his sister. Why's he acting like he doesn't?
27. This section is a summary of general conflict, not a specific moment of tension. Also, aren't they fighting about how much Johnny complains rather than him not going to school? This doesn't seem connected to the established topic and the conflict is unclear. (Above all else, though, this entire section is beside the point at the moment.) Focus on the stunt and why Johnny thinks it can solve their problem. Will it bring in revenue to pay for the cancer treatment? Will it boost Lily's morale and make him her hero? Be specific.
28. We're already zoomed out from the stage a bit, then we go back in time to typical family fights and the parents' upbringing, then we return to the present, but now we're in the parking lot. Sure, this adds a bit of local color and "promise of the premise" for a story set in a traveling carnival, but I'd focus on the action at hand—the performance—instead.

SAMPLE 1 OVERVIEW

Notice that we start off nicely in action, though the writer does zoom away to establish some backstory and fill in family context. There's a bit of a disconnect between the protagonist's worries and the notion that he has already worked hard to prepare for the performance. I suggest establishing a sense of stakes for this particular moment and adding logic for why *today* matters. It's clear the family is struggling in the wake of the sister's cancer diagnosis, but why Johnny sees *this* particular stunt on *this* day as the solution needs some bolstering. (It's entirely possible that Johnny is only assuming this is the make-or-break moment and that idea is disproven later, but let's track the logic of his belief.) As I mentioned in the initial note—I'm not so sure this is YA, though that's how the writer has chosen to categorize it. If I was an agent evaluating this, I'd see some markers for MG instead (the character's age is specifically middle grade). This might make me worry about the writer's market knowledge. Of course, the target audience could also emerge more clearly when a gatekeeper evaluates the writing sample alongside the pitch and synopsis. (This could be labeled YA because of how much time passes over the course of the plot, or darker story elements down the line.)

SAMPLE 2: LADY OF HEREAFTER
FANTASY

CAROLINE SCIRIHA

Chapter 1

The green-and-white carriage waiting by the Council Hall rooted me to the side of the road and snapped me out of my dark thoughts.[1] Illian had remembered—and cared enough about the outcome of my testing to fling caution to the wind.[2]

I **increased my pace, hastening** along the crowded thoroughfare towards the carriage.[3] Nelsev, a major in my father's army who'd been Illian's protector since the prince had turned ten,

---

1. This sample starts right in action, which I always applaud, but this is slightly disorienting. We don't know what the thoughts are, aren't privy to them, and now they're over. Why mention it? Simply for vibes? Also, "rooted" is unclear here, as this verb doesn't generally take an object. "Gave me pause"?
2. This seems entirely disconnected from the previous sentence. It also sounds high stakes, but I have no idea what it's referring to. Clarify that Illian is in the carriage and specify what the protagonist makes of his unexpected appearance.
3. I thought the carriage just passed. I have to admit, "rooted," as used, is confusing to imagine. The details are tripping me up here (the character's location relative to the carriage).

met my eye.[4] He swung off the driver's seat. "Mistress Karin, if you'll kindly step inside."

I gave Nelsev a brief nod of greeting and understanding.[5] The major rapped on the carriage door and opened it.[6]

~~In the shadows,~~ Illian leaned ~~forward~~[7] [out of the shadows,] and I gripped his outstretched hand.

"Shouldn't you be at archery practice?" I asked as Nelsev closed the door behind me. "I heard something about clay birds." My twin sister had chattered about it that morning while I braided her hair.[8] She'd put on her new silver-trimmed hunting tunic, her matching[9] silver wrist cuff, and a pair of green leggings—which hugged her figure to perfection, of course.[10]

"Hello, how lovely to see you would have been nice." Illian's eyes crinkled in merriment.[11]

I snorted, reluctantly mirroring his smile,[12] conscious of the warmth and strength of his hand still against my palm. "Thank you," I answered softly,[13] settling on the plush seat across from him. The Prince of Etha[14] had filled out since I'd [last] seen him months

---

4. This also makes it seem like the character is already very close to the carriage, so the "hastening" description doesn't seem to fit.
5. Of what? Unclear what passes between them because we're just being told about the body language (see the Recurring Notes chapter).
6. A lot of logistical play-by-play details so far (see the Recurring Notes chapter).
7. He'd lean "out of the shadows" instead of leaning "in the shadows."
8. Notice we're leaving the present moment here.
9. If it matches the "silver-trimmed" item, do we need to clarify that the wrist cuff is also silver?
10. This strikes me as an odd thing for a teen to say about her twin. It seems more like a writer working to describe something, rather than organic first-person character voice.
11. Need to explain? Eyes crinkling usually suggests smiling. But the dialogue seems more sarcastic, so it doesn't immediately scan as light-hearted.
12. The snorting but struggling to smile also confuses me from a logical and emotional standpoint. I'm not tracking their relationship dynamic.
13. Avoid adverbs in dialogue tags (see the Recurring Notes chapter).
14. Why not name him as such instead of "the prince" above? It'd add more context.

ago. At eighteen, his shoulders[15] now strained the material of his silk shirt[,] and he could no longer stretch his legs in the carriage as he was wont to do.[16]

"And they're called clay *pigeons*"—Illian's words snatched my attention off his fawn leather leggings brushing against the loose cotton of my trousers[17]—"though they don't look like any bird I've ever seen. I'm hoping they'll catch on and replace hunting live game for sport."[18]

"Good." It was the only word I could utter.[19] My tongue and mind seemed to have ~~shrivelled~~[shriveled]. He'd cut his silver hair short, which was very unusual for a noble Hyllethan. Strands brushed his cheekbones, drawing my gaze to the amused curve of his lips.[20]

Nelsev stood outside the carriage door, blocking the light seeping in through the gauze-covered window.[21] Inside, **the air seemed thin, insufficient**,[22] and I consciously **sucked in a breath**. What was Illian doing here?[23] People would recognise the carriage,

---

15. Dangling modifier. All of him is eighteen, not just "his shoulders" (see the Recurring Notes chapter).
16. Same note about the voice striking an odd note. Even if this is a historical or fantasy (or both!), this sample uses first-person POV, and the character is a teenager.
17. Let's get her reaction to seeing him, above, and have her think about her attraction. This is a very roundabout way of suggesting she finds him hot and is conscious that they're touching.
18. They seem to be chatting about random things, but I'm not getting a cohesive narrative from their conversation so far. I'm wondering if we can get a sense of why *this* exchange matters in *this* moment.
19. Make us privy to her thoughts. We're in first-person POV, but there's almost no interiority, which is odd. This writer is still describing her from the outside in.
20. Some third-person-style self-description in first person (see the Recurring Notes chapter).
21. Small nitpick. If he's already blocking the light, it's *not* "seeping in."
22. Thin air to convey nervousness or tension is a familiar image.
23. This seems like a thought to have as soon as she sees the carriage. Define the stakes. What does it mean that he's here? She can think this additional context to give readers a sense of how serious this is. (Also, looking back to the first paragraph, she guesses he's here because of her trial already, so why would she ask this?)

and my sister would hear about this meeting. She'd be furious and blame me.[24]

Illian let go of my hand. The sudden loss drove a spike of disappointment into my chest.[25] He said, "I wanted to see you before …" He waved at the imposing Council Hall doors, partly shielded by Nelsev's bulk. "You can do it, Kari. I know you have the Hyllethan abilities. You just need to want it enough."[26]

"Is that what you think? That I don't want to pass?"[27] I gave a bitter laugh and ran my palms down my short kaftan and wide trousers.[28] Work clothes. But at least they were clean and fitted better than my two-year-old dresses.[29]

The movement drew his gaze down to my hand. He touched the horse-hair bracelet peeping from beneath the sleeve of my undershirt.[30]

"I see you kept that." He sounded pleased.[31]

"I wore it for luck and to remember our"[—]I paused, but no better word came to mind[—]"friendship."[32]

"I hope to be more than just a friend, soon."

---

24. That she'd be mad is already clear, but knowing why would add some logic. Writers *are* allowed to tell certain facts and details. "Show, don't tell" gets in the way of clarity and meaning sometimes (see the Recurring Notes chapter).

25. A physical cliché (see the Recurring Notes chapter).

26. The testing hasn't been mentioned since the first paragraph. If she's nervous or if this is a big deal and happening soon, she'd be thinking about it more. It hasn't crossed her mind, which makes the telling about her fear less credible.

27. Is she attracted to him? Offended by him? Their vibe is tough to pin down, especially since we know almost nothing about them or their relationship yet.

28. External self-description. Go deeper into the first-person POV.

29. This detail seems meant to make her seem shabby, but her twin's outfit was described as rather opulent. Are the twins in separate social hierarchies?

30. Add the below dialogue to this paragraph of narration, as both "belong" to the same character.

31. Avoid describing a character's tone of voice (see the Recurring Notes chapter).

32. I've corrected the dialogue formatting here (see the Recurring Notes chapter).

My heart leapt into my throat, locking my breath in my lungs.[33] "W-What?"

"I'm going to propose to your sister today. Wish me well?"[34]

---

33. Some physical clichés here, especially the heart detail in a romantic context.
34. Ouch! I like seeing this unmet expectation after we've already established her longing for him. I do think their exchange could be clearer to interpret. Adding some context about the trial would be helpful—swap the play-by-play for a sense of plot and stakes.

SAMPLE 2 OVERVIEW

There's a lot going on in this opening, and I'd actually suggest the writer trim some of the action and detail. Why? The context of the characters' relationship gets lost. First, clearly establish why Karin is doing what she's doing and why the trial she's heading to matters. Even if things are about to take a surprising turn, she can have expectations for what her day is going to look like, her goal, and the stakes driving her. Second, throw an obstacle into her path—she gets pulled into a carriage. Her reaction to this unexpected development can be used to contextualize who Illian is to her. As is, we see them interacting, and there's a lot of interpretation of their flirtatious banter, but I felt on the outside of it as a reader, since I had no sense of who they were to one another (other than the length of their relationship), why they were meeting here and now, what either of them wanted from the bond (macro) or the current exchange (micro). There's absolutely a sense of emotional tension, but without context, it has an alienating effect on the reader. Plus, longing without a clear reason—including a sense of their past romantic connection, if any, and the current reason they can't be together—is not a concrete hook. When he announces that he's going to propose to Karin's sister, it's a twist, sure, but it comes out of nowhere, as Karin was just salivating over him. Instead of compelling readers, it might read more as a cheap trick. How could she have misread their interaction so profoundly? If he has designs for her twin, how would she not know this already? It's suggested the sisters interacted earlier that day. Wouldn't Karin have clocked something going on?

SAMPLE 3: UNTITLED
DYSTOPIAN

ANONYMOUS

I stare at the wall across the room.[1] White tally marks from past prisoners taint[2] the jagged cement. I counted them yesterday. Six hundred and forty-seven.[3] I wonder who stayed in this prison before me, but more importantly, I wonder what happened to them. I don't belong here.[4]

I'm perched with my legs hanging off the edge of the top bunk of a **steel bed**. The mattress doesn't cover the whole frame, so the **cold from the metal** sinks[5] through my orange jumpsuit.

---

1. I'm going to push this writer on their first line. The tally marks are more specific and immediately interesting than a character staring at a wall.
2. If the cement is jagged, it's already "tainted," so this, while a strong verb, is maybe too dramatic and unnecessary.
3. How do we know this is a cumulative tally if the marks were made by multiple people? The total number could be meaningless.
4. This seems like the thing to lead with, rather than counting the tally marks. This is a great set-up. The character is in prison. Readers will have tons of questions. Highlight the emotionally resonant parts immediately.
5. I like the level of detail, though notice how clear it is that the bed is metal. I also wonder if it's worth zooming out a bit on the minutiae. This writer has the reader's curiosity, but it won't last forever.

I want to leave. I want to find my family, to know they're safe.[6] I want to know what's going on.[7]

"We should get out of here," I say. I slide off the bed and land in a crouching position on the hard floor. My tan canvas shoes are bent at the toe. I stand and turn[8] to face Libby, who is sitting on the lower bunk.

She glares at me. "We can't leave, Evelyn."

"Why not?" I ask. "It's not like we're locked in here."[9] I start pacing the concrete toward the back wall, but I can only take a few steps before I'm inches from the steel toilet[10] and have to turn around.

"Shh! Someone might hear you." Libby folds her arms tight to her chest.[11]

"What? We're not. It's not like we're the only ones who know that." I take two more steps to the front of the cell where the heavy metal door is propped open. I turn on my toes and face Libby again.[12] A tinge of fear cuts through my stomach.[13] I ignore it. I have to make a point.[14] I step backward through the doorway, keeping my eyes locked on Libby's, silently praying I won't be blown up or shot.[15]

---

6. Good statement of objective, but is this available to the character? Do they have a plan to make this happen? Or is it wishful thinking?

7. Well, the character is in prison. Do they have a memory issue? Did they just come to? By the time one gets to jail, they usually have a sense of what brought them there.

8. Some play-by-play and description of turning (see the Recurring Notes chapter).

9. I like the surprise angle here, but it also drains the tension and mystery from the situation. Proceed with caution here.

10. A lot of detail to convey that it's a small room.

11. Her whole vibe is clear. Maybe walk it back a bit with the glaring and arm-crossing.

12. See above. The physical logistics are the least engaging part of what's happening.

13. A physical cliché here (see the Recurring Notes chapter).

14. Does she want to leave and find her family (altruistic)? Or does she want to make a point (ego-driven)? Also, it undermines her a bit that she has all of these desires but is currently not pursuing any of them.

15. If this is a risk, she should be weighing her choices (which also raises the stakes) and thinking about possible outcomes before she acts. This will increase tension.

"Evelyn! No!" She lunges forward, clamps clammy fingers around my wrist, and pulls me back inside the cell.[16]

Did I go far enough to prove my point? I wonder. But I'm just glad I didn't die.[17]

"Libby, look at me." I stretch out my arms to the side and step one foot behind me in a slight bow.[18] "I'm totally fine." I straighten. "Nothing's going to hurt us if we leave."[19] My stomach twists.[20] I don't know if that's true.[21]

"You didn't go that far." She turns away.[22]

"We're in a prison!"

"Be quiet!"

I drop my clenched fists to my sides.[23] "The doors are open[,] and there are no guards! This is ridiculous," I **whisper, fighting to keep my voice low**. "We'll die!"

"But it's safer!"

"Than what?" I fold my arms. "It's been two months. The soldiers haven't come back for us yet, and we're going to run out of food eventually."[24]

---

16. I suggest some mimetic writing for this quick action (see the Recurring Notes chapter). Especially if Evelyn's life is in danger—that should be the focus.

17. Her priorities seem reversed (and don't cast her in the best light).

18. "I bow" is really all we need. Every reader's imagination can fill in the logistical blanks.

19. Darting out the door for a second is different from actually walking out, though. What makes her so sure?

20. Physical cliché here as well.

21. I like that this writer has planted the seed of internal tension, but the source is unclear. Are these characters in danger, or aren't they? What does Evelyn actually believe? If she claims they're safe and someone gets hurt, she'll be responsible. Is that a risk she wants to take?

22. See earlier note about turning. Lots of turning in this sample.

23. Some third-person-style self-description here (see the Recurring Notes chapter).

24. So they're hanging out in an abandoned prison? For two months? That seems a really long time to wait before anybody thinks to leave. To help this make more

"One month and 21 days. And there's plenty of food in the kitchen." She yanks the sleeves of her jumpsuit over her hands and balls the extra two inches in her fists.[25]

"How do you know? You've never been there."

"Neither have you."[26]

I let out a quick breath of air through my nose.[27] "The cooks only bring us one meal a day as it is. It's being rationed for a reason."

"Well, then I don't think I can complain. I'm happy to be eating at all. Anyway, I'm sure something will happen, and we'll get out of here before the food is gone."[28]

"And if nothing does happen?"

She bites her lip and loosens her folded arms.[29] "I guess we'll have to figure that out when the time comes.[30] Besides, we can't

---

sense, add some context earlier about what's outside and why it's potentially worse than what's inside.

25. The writer can likely picture these gestures very clearly and wants to be faithful to what's in their head, but I'm just not sure this choreography is important enough on a story level. Also, Evelyn was just clenching her fists. I worry this sample is working too hard to convey an edgy mood.

26. They both seem so certain of their positions, but with every new line, I'm getting the impression that they have no idea what they're talking about. This could be an issue because readers like protagonists who are—or at least seem, especially at first— credible. Even if they're not rational, readers should be privy to their rationale. Here, there's no rationale yet, and it doesn't seem rational, either.

27. Do we need to know this? Nose or mouth, it really doesn't matter. (The huffy vibes are already established.)

28. The idea that she wants to find her family is less credible if they *can* leave ... but it's been two months and they haven't. This conversation also seems odd to be having two months in. Surely they would've discussed their options on the first day.

29. I worry that the play-by-play distracts from the dialogue and getting the story off the ground, especially in terms of pacing.

30. This is confusing to me. When is that time going to come? They've been in a holding pattern for two months. A word of warning here—this writer risks these characters seeming passive, rather than proactive. Sure, they're trapped (I think?), but it's tough to make a protagonist compelling when they're unable (or unwilling) to act.

leave. There are guards walking around, and you heard them when we got here. We'll be killed if we leave the cells."[31]

---

31. Some obvious telling in dialogue for the reader's benefit (see the Recurring Notes chapter). I'm still struggling to square why Evelyn seems convinced she can leave if there *are* guards.

SAMPLE 3 OVERVIEW

This is a vivid scene that offers a clear sense of the world the characters find themselves in. That said, it's also quite confusing. Can they leave or not? The time horizon is an issue here, as it was in Sample 7 in the Middle Grade section. Prison has been the day-to-day reality for these characters for two months. Why does the story start today? Why have they never tried to leave, despite no direct evidence that danger will befall them? Where are they getting their information (that they will be killed)? Have they seen this happen to anyone else? It'd be most active if they watch someone make a run for it and get shot out of nowhere. Yes, there are psychological reasons, like learned helplessness, that someone might stay in a bad situation without realizing the cage door has been open all along, so to speak, but it's unclear if this is happening here. As with the previous sample, the writer would do well to clearly establish expectations, including logic for how the characters are sure of the rules. Otherwise, it's unclear why they didn't leave sooner, and why they seem interested in testing boundaries today. What do they think is out there, and how will leaving get them closer to their goals? It's suggested that Evelyn's family is beyond the walls, but does she know this for sure? They were separated two months ago. A lot could've happened since. I'm not sure I find the information given here credible, because it seems that nobody knows much about the situation. This is, perhaps, an issue of starting in the wrong place. A clear prison break scenario, like the one described above, would offer indisputable stakes. Then we can have the characters decide whether or not to leave, given the obvious risks. Or maybe we don't need the prison at all. If this is a place they're leaving behind, will it factor into the rest of the story? If not, maybe introduce readers to the world they'll be living in, rather than offering a peek at an ultimately irrelevant situation. A prison escape makes for a dramatic opening, but this actual event could also be temporary in the grand scheme of things.

SAMPLE 4: THE TESTING OF TERRABON
SCIENCE FANTASY

EILEEN LARKIN WILKIN

Category Note: This writer says she's still struggling with her target audience. The primary POVs are teen siblings, but there are also adult perspectives, which is considered unusual (and is not recommended) in MG or YA. The writer says: "I understand the importance of using language more in line with teens when I'm in their heads, but at the same time I want the writing to be a step or two above that, with a more timeless feel, similar in scope to Madeline L'Engle's *A Wrinkle in Time* series." It's noteworthy that *A Wrinkle in Time* is widely considered middle grade.

Prologue

Gwithus took the form of an eagle and soared over Lakton.[1] The

---

1. An interesting first line, as "took the form of" suggests magic, and this orients readers immediately in a fantasy environment.

shadow of his great wingspan swept across patchwork farmland,[2] tree <u>homes</u>, and hill <u>homes</u>. He flew over the rippling lake and flowery field, swooped upward along Mount Mechtild's incline, and alit on a high mountain spruce.[3] The branch, thick though it was, swayed with the sudden extra weight. The sun warmed Gwithus[,] and the breeze preened his feathers as he looked down on his people.[4]

Next to Gwithus, on the very same branch, a lappet-faced vulture appeared, its mottled scalp, scrawny neck, and ugly feathers like a blot of black on a colorful canvas.[5] The air around the birds turned suddenly cold, and a putrid smell snaked through it, squelching[6] the scent of evergreens. The vulture eyed the Laktonians jealously,[7] while from its beak a forked tongue darted in and out.[8]

Lakton was waking up. Chimney smoke curled scents of sweet bread into the air, laughter leapt from pane-less windows and song sprang through doorless entrances. Laktonians emerged to go about the day's work, calling out to one another in greeting.[9]

---

2. This is subtle, but this writer really did a nice job of imagining what it'd be like to view the land from the vista of a soaring bird.

3. I really appreciate the dedication to not repeating words (choosing new verbs for "fly" each time, calling it Mount instead of Mountain to avoid word echo). There is a repeat on "homes," though.

4. Maybe put the crowd in the scene so it doesn't come as a surprise. And what kinds of creatures are they? Human people? Or is this a figurative "his people" meaning "his kingdom"?

5. Nice image.

6. That said, I do think it's possible to overdo it on the descriptive language. Clean, clear, and simple writing is nice, too. We don't have to prove ourselves as a Writer (with a Capital W), even if we're feeling the inherent pressure of the first pages.

7. Telling via body language (see the Recurring Notes chapter).

8. Awk. phrasing here, too. This writer wouldn't speak with this type of Victorian syntax, so they don't need to write with it. People tend to have a fixed idea of what Fantasy Voice sounds like, and I always ask them to interrogate this notion and find their own style.

9. Do this while Gwithus is flying, as we've already had the overview description. Now that we've zoomed in on the birds, let's get some interaction between them instead of zooming out again.

"Such noble children," the vulture hissed.

Gwithus nodded but did not turn his head.

~~The vulture continued,~~[10] "[And w]~~W~~hy shouldn't they be good?[11] They've never known hardship. You've done nothing but smile upon the work of their hands for century upon century. None but the First Ones have been tried. Given an opportunity, their progeny may choose differently."

The eagle remained silent ~~deigning not to engage with this lesser adversary~~.[12]

"There's no virtue in their goodness. **They don't love you; they love what you've given to them and what you do for them.**[13] Let me test your treasured Terrabonians.[14] Let them prove their fidelity in the face of trial. They must be given a choice, as the First Ones were."[15]

Now the eagle turned his head, and the scavenger recoiled under his fixed gaze, cowering as Gwithus spoke.[16] "It is time. You may test them."[17]

Not until the eagle turned his face away did the vulture resume

---

10. Unnecessary.

11. I'm adding "And" here to indicate that this is a continuation of the previous point. Otherwise it risks being confusing. He just called them "noble," now he can be taken to suggest they're "not good," and this is a mismatch. I had to read it a few times to get this meaning.

12. This is unnecessary. Him not turning his head and remaining silent speaks volumes in and of itself.

13. He's repeating his earlier points and these new ideas, too.

14. One of my fantasy pet peeves is that everything is jargon. This sample has called them Laktonians, now they're Terrabonians. I get that one might be a city/state/land, another might be a planet, but without any additional context, it's unclear why distinct terms are used.

15. He's already said the First Ones were tried.

16. Since both characters get narration here, keep this line separate. Put the reaction dialogue on its own line.

17. The third-person omniscient POV is fine and expected in fantasy, but I'm missing a connection to Gwithus. It's implied that a trial is rare and that he might not want to grant one, but he does. I'd like to be privy to the interiority of that decision.

its prideful stance.[18] It cackled, spread its wings, and readied for flight. "Watch your sweet lambs turn into wolves!" With a screech, the vulture lunged down the mountainside and flew over Lakton, casting inky shadow, cold, and stench [over the town].[19] Babies cried, children fled to their parents, and bewildered Laktonians **looked up and searched the sky,**[20] but the vulture had disappeared into the forest, taking the darkness, chill, and reek[21] with it.

CHAPTER 1: THE SHADOW OF DEATH | EARTH: 2,000 years later

Kalin[22] had always thought[23] it was a beautiful place, with its colorful gardens and spring-fresh grass, its pleasant balance of sun and shade, level ground and low hillocks.[24] It was well-kept, too—flowers and shrubs were nurtured and pruned, the summer grass regularly mowed, the winter snowfalls quickly cleared from the drive. Kalin knew all of this because the [they passed it twice a day] route going to and from New Minden High School meant they had to pass it twice a day.[25]

---

18. No need to describe so much turning (see the Recurring Notes chapter). This writer did the same successfully when Gwithus refused to turn, but otherwise, it's too much focus on the mechanics.
19. Usually we're "casting" "over" something.
20. One can only "search the sky" while looking up, so this is an unnecessary bit of stage direction.
21. Third mention of the vulture bringing darkness, cold, and smell with it in the prologue, second in this paragraph. This detail is overdone.
22. Good use of a chapter heading.
23. This sample is about to reveal that this place is now a sad one for Kalin. That said, this sentence doesn't make clear what we're getting at. It could be that she no longer thinks it's beautiful, or the writer might be using the past perfect tense ("had thought") and being a grammar stickler. Go for clarity. "Kalin used to think" would mean it's still beautiful, but Kalin has a new perspective now.
24. Even though this is fantasy and we're making some allowances for Fantasy Voice, think about the target audience and character age. This term does not scream kid or teen. Even though we're in close third-person POV, which could technically be inflected with a narrator's voice, I still suggest using language that'd fit the lexicon of that young person.
25. I ironed out this sentence to address a bit of wordiness.

It was a quiet place. The occupants never made noise, not even at night (Kalin didn't believe such claims).[26] The only sound came from visitors and was usually subdued.

Expansion was steady. Sometimes people arrived too early but, <u>Kalin knew</u>, accommodation was still made for them.[27]

It was a peaceful place—for most visitors, anyway—tinged with sadness.[28] The only prerequisite for becoming an occupant was death, a condition all on Earth eventually meet.

Until a year ago, it was a place to which Kalin had never given much thought.[29] Until a year ago, she'd never had reason to.

---

26. Formal voice here as well.

27. Same.

28. By this point, most people will realize we're talking about a cemetery. But this writer is being clever about it and will "reveal" it soon. My question is: Why? What's the storytelling point of tricking the reader? This might put them on the defensive right away. To me, twists and reveals work really well in thrillers, or later in a narrative. Here, this writer trying to talk about a kid's dead parent (or similar). Are they being clever? Sure. Do they *need* to be *this kind* of clever *here*? It doesn't really fit the tone.

29. This also doesn't ring true because this sample just spent a page talking about how minutely Kalin has observed it throughout the seasons, including its visitors, while passing it two times a day. I get what the writer is saying—she didn't have a reason to care before—but they're are also contradicting themselves with the overly detailed description readers just got.

SAMPLE 4 OVERVIEW

The prologue reads like classic high fantasy, with a mysterious encounter between the sage protagonist and an antagonist. We do a literal flyover of the world, but it's tough for a reader to become invested in any one focal character, as the villagers are all lumped together. If Gwithus doesn't respect the vulture, why does he almost immediately agree to "test" his subjects? This seems like a sudden 180. My incredibly astute colleague (and fellow editor), Amy Wilson, noted that the exchange between Gwithus and the vulture is identical, beat by beat, to the interaction between God and Satan in the book of Job. This seems intentionally done on the writer's part, as the "First Ones" bring in Adam/Eve and Edenic themes. Madeline L'Engle, who the writer admires, also used strong Biblical allusions. There are two options here. If the writer is relying on reader familiarity with the dynamics in the Bible to pre-empt the answers to some of my story logic questions about the situation and character motivation, that's one strategy. On the other hand, without adding a bit more logic to the scene, the writer might lose those readers (like me!) who didn't immediately make the connection. As a craft purist, I suggest putting the dynamics on the page more overtly. This reminded me of Sample 6 in the Middle Grade section. If Salty doesn't care about her bosses, why would she want to impress them? Gwithus clearly holds this vulture in contempt. And what does "testing" the people mean, in practical terms? Yes, some readers might find this intriguing, or use the Bible to enhance their understanding. But at face value, the exchange doesn't have a lot of concrete meaning, as the stakes aren't clear. Maybe define the test so readers can start imagining the ensuing action. When we switch to the contemporary teen character, I worry that the theme-heavy focus on death is too overt. We're likely being set up for some backstory, but I'd throw in a word of caution. A past tragedy can, of course, be formative, especially to a young character. But dead is dead. There's nothing Kalin can do in the present to change the past (unless this is setting up to be a time travel story). Focusing too much on the past and her current grief might stymie the character in the present. Though backstory is important in a novel, it should provide the foundation for a character (or characters) to move forward and act. What is Kalin's current objective, need, etc.? Going back to the past and having needs met there is a starting point, but it doesn't suggest present action. I'd like a clearer sense of the tension and plot that might unfold, even though this is a tall order in two pages which showcase two different worlds, times, and casts of characters. For anyone writing in multiple POVs, timelines, or narrative threads, this is a great reminder to try and showcase at least two of your storytelling voices and perspectives in the first few pages. If you pitch multiple POVs (or similar), you will want to show a gatekeeper that you can differentiate your voice and writing style in the first ten pages (the usual length of a writing sample). One of the first things an agent or acquisitions editor will want to know is if you can pull off distinct characters, worlds, etc., to justify this more advanced storytelling choice.

SAMPLE 5: UNTITLED
ROMANCE/ROMANTIC COMEDY

LISA BRADLEY

Chapter One

The white puffer coat slung over my arm threatens to come alive[1] after being squeezed in the airplane overhead bin for nearly two hours.[2] It wouldn't surprise me if the downy fabric expands just enough to block my view as I exit the Uber.[3] I'll probably trip on the curb and break my leg in the process—and not in the super encouraging way Mrs. Fitz trills[4] before the curtain rises. *"Go break a leg, kiddos!"* Not that I'd know firsthand the adrenaline rush of show time.[5] I'm the one waiting in the wings, headset on, ready for my

---

1. Literally or figuratively? This is quite distracting in a first sentence.
2. Letting air into a compressed jacket doesn't take that long. How did it stay compressed between the overhead bin and the Uber (through the whole airport)? The specificity of this odd detail really pulls focus. We've placed the jacket in the overhead bin *and* on her arm *and* offered a timeframe. That's a lot of data—for a coat.
3. Let's get past the jacket. We have no sense of the character, where they're going, why, etc. I'd cut this transportation sequence.
4. Stick to simple dialogue tags (see the Recurring Notes chapter).
5. A lot going on. We're now out of the present moment and in a generalization about the character's situation, which has to do with theatre. We also get her feelings about her desire to be on stage, as well as a snippet of dialogue from her teacher, but we're not in the actual theatre or currently meeting these people in action.

cue to hand the lead her prop suitcase as she reaches backstage and yanks it from me[6] just before her opening number.

I nudge the ~~car~~ passenger door closed with my hip[7] and maneuver my suitcase over the slush and onto the <u>sidewalk</u>. All this, while balancing my backpack and ginormous coat over my arm.[8] Juggling things seems to be a metaphor for my life. From the <u>sidewalk</u>,[9] I catch my breath, blow a stray curl out of my face, and re-focus.[10] A wind gust chills my bones[11] through my sweater, and I'm rudely reminded I'm in the northeast in the dead of winter.[12] A trip every sixteen-year-old girl fantasizes about.[13] Seriously, who comes to middle-of-nowhere Maine to visit their eighty-something-year-old great aunt so that aunt doesn't spend Christmas alone?[14]

Me.

Emmaline Phillips.

That's who.

I remember my great aunt's house being big. Honestly, I remember everything about Aunt Lorna as larger-than-life.[15] But I

---

6. Overly detailed on the suitcase mechanics. Maybe end on "to hand the lead her prop suitcase" without losing any of the sentence's meaning. (I still suggest cutting this digression, though.)
7. Some play-by-play (see the Recurring Notes chapter).
8. The coat has had a lot of air time.
9. We've already placed her there, so there's no need to specify unless she moves (and unless that movement is important).
10. On what? The most important part—where she's going, why—hasn't been clarified yet.
11. A familiar image for cold ("bone-chilling").
12. "reminded" doesn't fit here because she didn't forget … hence the jacket.
13. The sarcasm isn't the best entry point. Bummer teens are realistic, but I want some kind of spark early on, something about the character that's exciting. (We learn about her passion for theatre, but even there, she's complaining about being in the wings.) Otherwise, readers might not want to hitch their wagons to someone who complains so much right away. We know nothing else about the trip, so her attitude is the focus … and it doesn't reflect well.
14. This seems like a nice thing to do, so to know she's upset about something so decent strikes a mean tone.
15. This writer tells about the character here, which is the bad kind of telling that "show, don't tell" warns us about (see the Recurring Notes chapter). I'd much rather

was six years old when I was last here. And when you're small, everything is big.[16] I roll my suitcase toward the black wrought iron gates that block my entry to a long, winding drive. Attached to one of the massive brick pillars that adorns either side of the gate[17] is a brass plaque that reads:

Heartkeepe

I check my phone, confirming the address Dad gave me. It's true. Aunt Lorna's house has a name and ~~an engraved~~ plaque ~~out front~~.[18] Releasing my suitcase for a moment, I tap out a text to my parents.

> u didn't say aunt lorna was rich

Mom immediately texts back.

> You landed early!
>
> All good with a cab?
>
> Tell Aunt Lorna hello!

Dad joins our chat.

> Don't forget to wear your coat and gloves
>
> Weatherman says 5 below there
>
> Brrr

---

meet her and allow readers to get this impression themselves through action. Unless the twist is, of course, that the aunt isn't home. Instead, focus on Emmaline's feelings about coming here (and add a bit of spark to her, so she's not so fixated on what a drag this is).

16. Love this insight!

17. Trim some of the spatial details.

18. Same.

Mom again.[19]

> Twins say hi.

> Gotta run. Covered in cookie dough.

> Miss you already, Em.

My heart sinks.[20] When[21] my parents ~~sprung~~[sprang] this solo trip on me (not the original plan[,] by the way),[22] my best friend, Renee, had words. "Your folks must really trust you. My parents would never let me travel alone.[," she said.] I admit, I felt worldly navigating the airport and my connection through New York's LaGuardia all on my own.[23] Like a grown up, but in a good way. Still, the subtle[24] reminder of spending Christmas away[25] from my parents and the twins for the first time ever quickly makes me feel like a kid again.

Snowflakes shake loose from evergreens overhead, bringing me back to the reality of the gray pavement.[26] I'm in Stillwater now. Aunt Lorna is expecting me. I ring the buzzer mounted on a post next to the gate. Here goes nothing.

I rock on my heels a few times, trying to maintain what little warmth remains in my body from the car ride. I press <u>the buzzer</u> again, longer this time.

---

19. Would she take the time to type all of the below in such detail if she was literally baking with young twins? This seems elaborate. It would also contribute to showing Emmaline's loneliness if Mom abruptly dropped out of the chat.
20. A physical cliché (see the Recurring Notes chapter).
21. Notice we're leaving the present moment here.
22. Was it going to be the whole family? Specify, because if she wasn't originally going to be alone, that explains some of her resentment.
23. Good insight, but then let's see some of this pride when we see her at the airport earlier, instead of focusing on the coat. (I still suggest cutting the run-up to her arrival, though.)
24. Is it subtle? She's been fixating on this.
25. This context would be important to establish earlier.
26. Good example of a transition into the present.

Still no response.

I stab the buzzer several more times in a row. The gate doesn't budge.[27]

I poke at a numbered keypad below ~~the buzzer~~. It beeps at me.[28]

"Hello." I call into a tiny speaker ~~next to the keypad~~. "Is anyone home?[29] ~~Hello?~~"

---

27. I suggest omitting a few instances of this. The point is clear. Move on to poking the keyboard.
28. Ha! I like the comedic timing here.
29. Good. I really like that we're mostly in present action, with both external and internal conflict.

SAMPLE 5 OVERVIEW

There's great action and mystery in this opening. Emmaline shows up alone to this house, and her expectations are immediately challenged. We also get the text chat with her family, which only goes to underscore how much she misses them and how disconnected she feels from her real life. That said, I'd trim the business with the jacket and the transition from the plane to the Uber to the front gate. This is all logistical, and it doesn't get at the heart of the opening set-up, which is this mysterious house and no answer at the door. Overall, logistical transitions are boring (see the Common Opening Clichés chapter section on waking up at the beginning of a story). We don't need them. Start when the scene starts, not in the taxi or on the plane. The theatre information will likely be relevant later but is out of place here—and gives Emmaline one more thing to complain about. It can feel difficult to trim words or sections or even entire scenes and chapters because the work has already been done and those passages already exist. But this is a cognitive bias—the Sunk Cost Fallacy. Just because those words exist doesn't mean they're doing the writer or story any favors. Otherwise, some engaging voice and immediately relevant conflict!

SAMPLE 6: BLACKTHORN
FANTASY

EMILY EVE

The assassin watched the man breathe.[1]

In, out. In, out.

It would be easy to kill him, she thought. *Too easy. He really should reevaluate the security in this place.*[2]

Her job tonight wasn't to kill him, though. In order to suffer, he needed to live.[3]

Her mark, Lord Frederick Stonewood,[4] looked peaceful as he slept.[5] Beautiful, even. Dark brown hair curled over his forehead, stirred by the gentle breeze coming from the open window. A cup of

---

1. I'm immediately at attention with this opening line!
2. This is pretty sassy. Why not say it to him? "You really should've gotten a Ring cam, huh," or something, would be funny and unexpected. (It's not clear he's asleep yet, or that this is a historical setting.)
3. Love this phrasing!
4. I'd maybe do, "The assassin watched Lord Frederick Stonewood breathe" or something. It's a touch more specific, which makes it more arresting. We'd also learn that he's asleep sooner.
5. Okay, so I'd actually do, "The assassin watched Lord Frederick Stonewood breathe in his sleep." It's perfect. That he's asleep makes the whole thing feel more dangerous and vulnerable.

tea sat steaming[6] on the bedside table beside a large, leather-bound book.

The ~~room was quiet, the~~ silence [in the room] was broken[7] only by the sound of his breathing.

Shifting his head on the pillow, he snored loudly.[8] Very undignified, for a lord—the son of the king's advisor, no less.

Across the room, lurking in the shadows,[9] the assassin wore a stolen servant's uniform. She tensed where she stood, hand reaching for the knife sheathed at her hip, and relaxed only when he settled down once more.

She shook her head, angry at herself for lingering.[10] She had a job to do.

Dodging ~~around~~[11] several leaning book towers, some stacked as high as her waist, she crept towards the desk in the middle of the room. Her feet, clad in black silk slippers, made no sound on the plush carpet.

Papers covered almost every inch of his desk, apart from a lantern that sat in one corner.[12] Nothing on the desk was unexpected[13] from the man known for his love of libraries.

---

6. He fell into a deep sleep before his tea could cool? Another distracting logistic. Unless this writer is suggesting she just drugged him and that's why he dropped off, or that he didn't actually drink the tea.

7. Nitpick: The sample says it's "silent" only to contradict itself.

8. Odd to have another noise described so soon after the focus on the silence.

9. I disagree with this. She's been describing things in pretty sharp detail, so if it's dark and she's across the room, the level of minutiae she'd see doesn't match the description given so far. (Sure, one could make the argument that assassins are observant, but steam needs light to be visible, etc.)

10. Naming emotions (see the Recurring Notes chapter). We're able to access her thoughts even in third-person POV, so go deeper. Why does she think she's lingering?

11. Going "around" something is technically part of the definition of "dodging."

12. Clarify that there's a light source sooner so readers can add it to their mental image.

13. Awk. phrasing with the double negative. Saying something simple in a complicated way.

Nothing unexpected—for now.[14]

The assassin removed the materials she had[15] hidden underneath her clothes. Leaflets from vocal citizens, criticizing the king's unwarranted use of power. A small notebook, written in an easily breakable cipher. A wanted poster for a member of the rebellion, complete with a scribbled note in its margin that looked suspiciously like the lord's handwriting. Several ledgers accounting for supplies not found within the castle walls. She tucked each of these in random spots on the desk,[16] **careful to hide them from view**.[17]

Nothing too obvious — nothing that would stand out in the chaos on the desk. But, if someone were to claim that the Lord of Navian was associated with the feared rebel group, the Amlucen. . .[18]

Questions would be raised. Questions that the lord could not answer. Questions that might sow doubt among the king's inner circle, even if Lord Stonewood were to protest his innocence.

Doubt was a powerful weapon. Doubt could topple entire kingdoms.[19]

Job done, she turned back to the door to make her escape. And stopped in her tracks.

Lord Stonewood wasn't sleeping anymore.[20]

He stood in front of the door, dressed in a pair of loose-fitting

---

14. Good spike of tension!
15. Use contractions for voice, even in a historical context (see the Recurring Notes chapter).
16. It's clear she's planting them on the desk from the previous paragraph.
17. Saying the same thing two ways here. To "hide" is to obscure from view.
18. On the one hand, I like this sneaky plan. On the other hand, what happens when he wakes up tomorrow, looks at his desk, and removes the stuff? Who's going to see this material and start spreading rumors overnight? This elaborate scheme could easily be undone.
19. Avoid this stutter description of saying one thing, then immediately restating it. The repetition can be cut without losing meaning.
20. Good! I was just wondering if her rifling around was making noise.

nightclothes, hands in tight fists by his side[s]. He towered over her.[21]

"Who are you?" His voice came out in a low growl.

She cursed internally. How was he awake? She had been told his nightly tea would be laced with enough sleeping potion to knock him out for hours.[22]

She weighed her options. She really, *really* didn't want to kill him — he was worth more to the cause alive. Killing him would complicate too much.

Maybe she could bluff her way out of it.[23]

---

21. This suggests very close proximity, but he's over by the door.
22. Good. I did wonder about the tea. This suggests she has a person on the inside the household, though. Why not ask them to place the materials? Why does she need to incriminate the lord if her accomplice could start some rumors instead?
23. I'm hooked! I want to know how she gets out of it.

SAMPLE 6 OVERVIEW

Some really great opening action with an assassin lurking in the shadows. This level of intrigue is tough to beat! A few things the writer could add to flesh it out: Why are this mission and target important to her *personally*? Is this just another assignment or is it something that matters beyond the nature of the work? For example, it could be her last bounty before she's able to quit doing dangerous work that no longer fulfills her. Or the target did something to her family, which would suggest she's also partially motivated by revenge? On a logical note, the poison in the tea detail snagged me. If the tea was still steaming, did the lord drink any? If he did, the speed at which the poison took hold also threw me. I was unclear whether he woke up because he didn't actually drink it, or if he simply woke up because he heard her rifling around. A reaction from her—if these details are indeed relevant—would help, e.g., "How did she fail to notice he'd skipped his tea?" In addition to all that, the tea introduces the idea that she has someone else in the household who's working alongside her (or can at least be bought temporarily). If so, why not have them slip the materials onto the desk? Why not take a more direct route to sabotaging the lord and have the staff start spreading rumors? What happens when the target wakes up, notices his desk is in disarray, and removes the incriminating material? The action, descriptions, and pacing are working really well, but I want to make sure the big-picture reasoning behind the mission is juicy and engaging, too. Otherwise, all the narrative craft in the world—which exists here in spades—won't turn this opening into an engaging story beginning.

SAMPLE 7: UNTITLED
FANTASY

ANONYMOUS

The wild sweet chorus of robin song was a welcome indication[1] that not everything in Saga's world was falling apart.[2] Her footfalls tamped down the dewy grass of the field[3] as she crossed to the tree line with her sisters in the early morning chill.[4] The sharp smell of vegetation and damp earth mingled on the breeze. Another unfamiliar scent threaded through the air[: a]A **foul odor** that **stung her nose** and sent an ominous chill through her veins.[5]

As they entered the dense forest at the edge[6] of their sprawling family farm, Saga saw[7] Freya **shiver** and **wrap her arms tight around her body**.[8] Her youngest sister wore light, loose pants and a

---

1. Immediately, I worry about this voice for YA. Even if it's historical, or there's a reason for such phrasing, it's overly formal.
2. But we get to a nice curiosity hook here. Good work!
3. Fields are usually covered in grass, so I'm not sure we need to clarify.
4. The "dewy grass" suggests morning. We might not need this level of scene-setting detail before we introduce who the girls are, where they're going, why, etc. Readers might have these more relevant questions first.
5. Avoid describing "vibes" or atmosphere (see the Recurring Notes chapter).
6. It wouldn't be in the middle. I'd zoom out on the logistical and spatial details here.
7. Filler description (see the Recurring Notes chapter).
8. The cold is established.

thin blue tunic. An odd choice for a fall hunt. Saga caught Ena rolling her eyes in Freya's direction. She, like Saga, was dressed more sensibly.[9]

Together, the three of them moved through the forest along a well worn trail [, which].~~It~~ was wide enough for them to walk side by side. Saga **sidled closer** to Freya, **letting their shoulders brush** in an offer of warmth.[10] The sickly sweet stench of rotting meat and ripe compost was getting stronger.[11] Saga noticed her sisters' curious glances at the trees around them[12] as she covered her mouth in an effort to block the stench.[13]

"What is that?" Freya asked, nose scrunched up in distaste.[14]

"I don't know ... but something isn't right,"[15] Saga answered.

"**Look at this**~~,~~[.]" Ena **pointed** to a large pine <u>tree</u> on her left.

Bulging out of the gnarled bark was a gelatinous mound. A thick pale yellow syrup ran in slow rivulets down the trunk. Saga **leaned toward** the <u>tree</u> **to get a closer look.**[16] **Up close**, the **smell was far worse.** She gagged on the **foul reek** of **putrid decay.**[17]

---

9. The girls' personalities are coming through, but they start off on a mean note toward their sister. Is that realistic? Sure. But what does it say about them?

10. This redeems Saga a bit, since she sees Freya shivering and helps, even if she thinks it's a preventable issue.

11. Why not describe the scent with this much detail sooner, instead of starting off with simply "a foul odor"? The more specific the better, so we're not asking readers to revise their mental picture once more details are introduced. Be precise the first time.

12. And? So? What does she make of these glances? Are the girls meant to be looking for the source of the smell? Or is there something else to notice? Better yet, does Saga maybe do some critical thinking about what she thinks the smell is and look for it herself (rather than watching her sisters do it)? Center her in the action.

13. A lot of information to convey there's a bad smell. Yes, this is important to the story, but trust that it's well established.

14. Necessary to play out the bad smell detail?

15. This repeats the idea that something "ominous" is happening, but that's already clear.

16. Need to explain why someone might lean closer?

17. The type of smell has already been well established.

Ena was by her side, reaching out a finger to catch a drop of the **sappy syrup**.[18] Saga **slapped her sister's hand away**.

"Don't touch it!" She **admonished**.[19] "We have no idea what that is."

Ena ignored her and snatched a glob before Saga could stop her again. She rubbed it between two fingers. "It's grainy," she reported.

On Saga's other side, Freya's head[20] was tipped back, her chestnut braid falling down the center of her back. She squinted up[21] into the tree canopy. Saga followed her gaze. Apart from the strange, gaping wound in its trunk, the tree appeared[22] perfectly normal. Nothing else indicated[23] disease.

Saga looked at the trees around them.[24] No others played host to whatever this was. It could ~~be~~ [have been] a random plight[25] that none of them had encountered before. Maybe it was nothing to worry about. Still, the fact that one tree could exude such a strong stink was more than a little concerning.[26] Her whole body shuddered as a terrible sense of foreboding washed over her.[27] She took a deep breath and forced her worry away on an exhale.[28]

---

18. Is "sappy" necessary given the definition of "syrup" and that it's coming from a tree?

19. Avoid "said" synonyms (see the Recurring Notes chapter). Furthermore, don't have a character do something (slapping the hand away), then repeat the point in dialogue ("Don't touch it!").

20. Awk. "Freya's head" isn't on the other side, it's all of Freya. "On Saga's other side, Freya had her head tipped back" could be a fix, though I'd argue these spatial details aren't necessary to begin with.

21. Implied if she has her head "tipped back."

22. Overly formal word choice for the target audience.

23. Same.

24. The previous paragraph is focused on them doing this already.

25. "blight"? "Plight" could work, but "blight" is more precise.

26. Saying something simple in a complicated way.

27. This repeats the "ominous" idea and is a physical cliché (see the Recurring Notes chapter).

28. Make the worry more concrete. This is new and unnerving, but what does it mean for Sage? What are the *personal* stakes for the family? If the trees get sick, does their farm fail? Let her think critically about what could be happening to give this event urgency.

"We'll have to tell f[F]ather when we get home,"[29] Saga said with as much assurance as she could muster.[30] Her father had been hunting in these woods longer than she and her younger sisters had been alive.[31] He would know if this was truly something unusual. She turned away from the tree and its offensive odor[32] and returned her attention to the task at hand. She needed to focus on the hunt.[33] They left the ailing tree[34] behind and continued along the path.

As they drew deeper into the woods, Saga cautiously[35] scanned for more traces of the nauseating scent. She smelled nothing but pine-scented forest air.[36] Normal.

"Did you guys think Mother looked a little better last night?" Freya asked.

"Yeah, a little," Saga responded. But she knew there was no real conviction behind her words, only hope.[37]

---

29. Need to explain that they have to return home first? They can't well tell him now unless they have cell phones.
30. See note below about Mother ...
31. A familiar expression.
32. Need to explain which tree and what's wrong with it again?
33. Ramp up the stakes here, too. Or else what? Let this hunt have more importance than just daily chores to add some tension. Is winter coming? Did their previous hunt fail?
34. Restates "turned away from the tree and its offensive odor."
35. The foreboding is clear.
36. But didn't she also smell it out in the field, meaning the stink is pervasive?
37. ... the second moment in a few paragraphs that she has faked something. Why does she do this? If she has secret worries, define them, even if she doesn't voice anything. I worry the target audience might resonate more with a character who doesn't subvert herself to make others comfortable. (This also tamps down tension because it's denial.) Finally, I suggest avoiding describing the tone of voice (see the Recurring Notes chapter).

SAMPLE 7 OVERVIEW

This sample features many successful opening ingredients. We have characters in action who encounter something unusual—a smell in their forest which points to a diseased tree. We get a few characterizing details for the sisters, and an ominous tone which pulls readers in. My biggest suggestion is for the writer to insert some context, which would allow the stakes to grow. The characters are clearly familiar with the forest and might even rely on it. Take this further—the forest needs to be healthy, or their family will starve. Or there's a sense of lore around sick trees that the sisters have grown up fearing. Now the threat has come to their backyard, literally. As is, they're relying on Father to know what's going on, but if they're already aware of the risk a sick tree represents, readers will be able to appreciate the potential conflict sooner. Also, why does the story start today? Yes, the smell has appeared, but let's tie that into the plot in a more overt way. They're on their last forage of the season, there's pressure not to come home empty-handed, etc. On a sentence level, I strongly suggest this writer pare back the play-by-play and logistical/spatial details and focus on the bigger picture of why this unsavory discovery matters on this particular day.

FIRST PAGES FOR ADULT READERS

The following examples are intended for general adult readers. (Though calling it "adult fiction" is industry standard to differentiate it from MG or YA, this term can have romance/erotica connotations for lay readers, which is why I've selected the clunkier "for adult readers" descriptor.) It's important to note that some readers younger than eighteen regularly read adult fiction, whether for school assignments or pleasure, if they feel they have "aged out" of the content and style of MG and YA. (There is also a "new adult" or "NA" category which deals with characters in their early twenties and attracts both adult and teen readers.) A young protagonist doesn't automatically equal a children's book, though.

Notable examples of adult-marketed books which feature younger characters but are still intended for adults are *The Brief, Wondrous Life of Oscar Wao* by Junot Díaz, *The Curious Incident of the Dog in the Night-time* by Mark Haddon, *The Book Thief* by Markus Zusak, and *All the Light We Cannot See* by Anthony Doerr. Some of these "crossover" titles are packaged and marketed to adult and kidlit readers separately. While many adult readers gravitate to adult characters, the division between these categories has more to do with style, content, and tone than simply with character age.

SAMPLE 1: THE MAKE-UP ARTIST
MYSTERY/THRILLER/SUSPENSE

MARCUS BREWSTER

Regional Note: This project is set in Cape Town, South Africa, and uses local terms and British English spelling and dialogue formatting. My advice in these situations is to have the writer create a version with standardized U.S. spelling and formatting conventions if they're going to pitch to the U.S. market.

Chapter 1 | Cape Town

My fingers **patter** the steering wheel, the kind of **rhythmic flutter** that's supposedly going to cause a hurricane halfway across the world.[1] Today[,] of all days[,][2] there's no parking anywhere around the agency, the East City's[3] gridlocked. Normally I'd be flaring with

---

1. The butterfly theory is interesting but is also often invoked in an offhand way. Does this hint at the novel's theme? Is this the first thing this writer wants readers thinking about? (The idea of the butterfly is yet another instance of something fluttering, which makes these initial descriptions redundant.)
2. Consider offsetting with commas or em-dashes for pacing.
3. Normally, cardinal directions don't need capitalization, but the writer tells me this is the name of a Cape Town neighborhood.

aggravation[4]– banging the steering wheel, flinging my head[5] in search of a quicker, better lane – but this morning[6] I have to say it[7] feels **like arousal, like foreplay, my senses languorously heightened with delicious anticipation.**[8]

After last night's **downpour,**[9] the roads are **puddled**, gutters **awash.**[10] Posters, crenelating from the **sodden** cardboard, tug against their streetpole[11] ties. **I shiver involuntarily, shoulders raised**[12] into the cocoon of my cashmere coat. Cape winter – gotta love it.

The delivery van ahead inches in stop motion,[13] a hundred cars in front of him hunting, too, no doubt. We're good – I've got this.[14] I turn up the volume so Shania and I can belt out the best part of being a woman.[15] ~~"Oh, oh, oh "~~[16] A bit off key, but hey, my heart's in it.

---

4. So far we have a lot of patter, flutter, flaring, etc. But these are all external markers of what the character is doing. There's no interiority yet, which is odd, given the choice of first-person present tense POV.
5. Some self-conscious third-person-style self-description (see the Recurring Notes chapter).
6. Instead of giving us so many details about what *isn't* happening (her usual agitation), focus on what *is*. It's still tough to tell exactly what's going on.
7. Does this stand for "the way I feel" or does it stand for the "no parking" situation? Unclear.
8. These images are all quite similar.
9. This doesn't seem to connect to the previous paragraph. A bit of a jarring transition.
10. Need all of this?
11. Another regional term.
12. Two similar actions to convey that someone is cold.
13. I had initially corrected this to "slow motion," but the writer intended to reference the "stop motion" filmmaking style.
14. Why is she so eager to reassure herself if it seems today is a big deal ("today of all days") *and* she would normally be agitated? Heighten the tension, don't flatten it. What does she make of her unusual frame of mind?
15. This song has entered the realm of cliché. It seems a bit reductive to have a female character blasting it seemingly unironically.
16. Not sure we need this in addition to the song title, as it's not really a discernible lyric. (Though I'd caution any writer about relying on lyrics, as they are very expensive to license.)

I chance my luck down a narrow side street,[17] hemmed in by dark brick buildings. Nope. Just a huddle of dodgy guys [in]~~,~~ baggy ~~denims~~ and hoodies, outside the takeaway, fluorescents bright through its steamed-up windows. We[18] used to get Coke and slap chips there at four in the morning, after the club. And Grandpa headache powders. I used to climb out my bedroom window. God, twenty years ago, more. Don't ask, don't tell.[19]

Next street. [*Nada*]. [*Nyet.*][20] No. Very odd.[21] I roll forward in automatic. A gym, black glass frontage with a yellow barbell logo.[22] Over the road, where Bangers used to be, a fancy, no-plastic grocery store for the yoga moms. I chant along with Miss Shania – "Men's shirts, short skirts[,]"~~,~~ flipping my shoulders to the beat.[23]

I let another driver in. Glance at the dashboard clock. Lots of time still. The lesson [learned] from a million shoots: come early and be prepared.[24] The punchline to my story when strangers ask who's the most famous person I've ever worked on.[25]

---

17. The action of searching for parking (a mundane task) would be more engaging if we knew why the character needed to arrive on time today, what the importance of the moment was, and whether there are any stakes. This writer has made a point to say the protagonist is in an unusually good mood. And? So? Why should this parking problem matter to anyone else but her? Why does the story start today?
18. Who? A generic "we" for a group of friends? Anyone more specific? A missed opportunity to learn something about her, though I wonder how relevant it is. I'd prefer it if we stuck in the present moment instead of zooming away for potentially irrelevant past context. These are the first things we're learning about her. We want them to carry some weight and meaning.
19. The choppy sentence fragments may get grating after a while, especially since there's no apparent plot- or tension-based reason for this syntactical choice. Inserting a bunch of sentence fragments doesn't automatically translate to voice, tone, or style.
20. Italicize foreign words.
21. Missed opportunity to deliver a bit more context. Why's it so odd? Why does it matter today? Is she late? (Again, avoid flattening the tension.)
22. It's an urban landscape. Do we need generic details like this on the first page or two? We already got the takeaway shop to fill in some local color.
23. Still not sure about this, as it's a bit of a caricature. There's no tension or intrigue yet as there isn't enough information outside of parking logistics. Consider toning down some of this play-by-play (see the Recurring Notes chapter).
24. This is the first bit of context we get for what she might be doing.
25. What's the punchline? This doesn't follow from the discussion of coming prepared to shoots.

Somebody hoots[26] behind me. I roll forward a car length.

Must be the weather. The mountain's completely covered with pumice-coloured clouds ~~with~~ [and] more rain forecast.

The traffic trickles, hourglass slow.[27] My favourite line – "Colour my hair, do what I dare."~~.~~ Going to be such a great day. Can't wait for Steph to deliver the news.[28] The finish line to a years-long entrepreneurial journey[29] that started when? Could say it started with Tina.[30]

She loved her glow-up. So gaga about the metallic sheen on her lids, she asked what I'd used. My own formulation, G Eyes #1, I told her.[31] She tilted her face back and forth admiring the glimmer, before seeking my reflection. Goldeneye, she chuckled[32]—natch— then begged the tub off me. That's when I realised my products had commercial potential.

The line of traffic idles past Mavericks.[33] Gentleman's club – huh![34] Same posters, obviously still working; the girls – Spanish, Portuguese, Russian – in peek-a-boo lingerie. I used Heidi Klum-era

---

26. This is apparently regional dialect for "honks."
27. I like this image, but the overall pace of the action is already established. There would be tension if she was late, but it's already clear she's not. What's going to get a reader engaged in this scene?
28. Another small bit of context. Build on this. Offer some factual statements. Not all "telling" is created equal, nor is it all bad.
29. Spend more time and care here rather than resorting to the same choppy sentences.
30. If today is a big culmination, she'd be able to reflect more precisely on everything it took to get here. I worry this seems wishy-washy and doesn't mesh with the idea that today is important.
31. We don't know the protagonist yet, so I'm not sure about taking readers to an unspecified time to learn about Tina. This person has no significance yet. I'd have more happen in the present moment and save the reflection for later.
32. Is this meant to be dialogue? Then format it as such. Also, actions that accompany speech (smiling, nodding, etc.) do not produce speech themselves, yet this is formatted like a speech tag. Consider "said with a chuckle" instead.
33. A real place in Cape Town. Otherwise I'd add an apostrophe to make "Maverick" possessive.
34. Consider using mimetic writing here (see the Recurring Notes chapter). If traffic is dragging, the choppy sentences don't fit the context.

Victoria's Secret as the reference,[35] all wide-lashed and moist-lipped. [The] cClient wanted something more overt ("sexy, gimme sexy") but I had a different vision. I argued the girls would find it easier to project sensuality if they felt beautiful rather than hookerish. Told him about Ziegfeld putting his showgirls in silk panties;[36] the guy had no idea what I was on about. Ne-vah heard of the Follies—dumbfuck.[37] Those poor Mavericks dancers[. F], fortunately I had my concealer #4 for the bruises.[38]

Even here there's no parking and it's not even nine fifteen.[39] Curiouser and curiouser, Alice.

[*Bam*][40]—and there's the problem. A shoot: orange cones, striped tape, <u>production</u> trucks. A traffic marshal in a neon yellow waterproof. Two whole blocks of parked vehicles. That's a big <u>production</u>. What the hell—at this time of year?[41]

---

35. For … the eyeshadow? For models to sell the eyeshadow? We're only getting snippets of what's going on, so it's tough to parse her meaning. She's sitting and thinking about (seemingly) random stuff, which isn't as dynamic as it could be.
36. If this scene is important to the origin story, play it out in full narration, with dialogue. But do that in a few pages, once the present-moment action is up and running
37. Sometimes the voice is a bit overdone, but it comes and goes, so the overall impression is uneven. I'd rather have consistency.
38. Her bruises when she stood up to the client? The bruises of the working girls? The jumping between ideas adds a certain manic energy but can be tough to follow.
39. I'm surprised that she's surprised, as there hasn't been parking anywhere. But instead of repeating the same idea, let her do some critical thinking or consider what might be happening. (Of course, this is only relevant if the search for parking and the layout of the neighborhood are important to the story. Otherwise, I'd tone down the focus on them.)
40. Italicize onomatopoeia as well.
41. There's surprise here, but why does this matter? She didn't know about the production, but things happen beyond our awareness all the time. Does this play into the plot later?

SAMPLE 1 OVERVIEW

This writing sample absolutely has voice—which is largely conveyed through choppy syntax. We're pulled right into the character's world and search for a parking space. Lots of details are thrown at readers which *could* represent salient context about the character and what she's currently doing, but I worry the connections aren't made explicit. From the title, we can guess the protagonist is a make-up artist. Where is she going? Why? There are mentions of clients and other elements which sound like they belong in her professional world, but I'd push the writer to be a bit more explicit. For example, she has finally gotten a lucrative contract to launch her own make-up line. A celebrity has agreed to model the product, and this is a high-stakes photoshoot, etc., but there's traffic everywhere, and she's worried she'll miss her appointment with some very expensive studio space. People are waiting for her, including a business partner, the talent, photographers, etc. Otherwise, many of the details we get—setting, production vans, the local strip club, etc.—don't seem connected to the present action. Notice how the character works to relax, also. I wouldn't recommend flattening tension, especially in an opening scene. Instead, clarify why this particular search for parking is a make-or-break moment. Otherwise, we're just running an errand, and the stakes will sink accordingly. To that end, I suggest the writer pare back some of the details and digressions which don't serve the present-moment action.

SAMPLE 2: UNTITLED

CONTEMPORARY

ANONYMOUS

I shot up in bed and **gasped for air that wouldn't reach my lungs**.[1] The lightning sounded as if it had struck my cottage. My heart was beating like a hummingbird trapped within my rib cage.[2] I <u>threw off</u> the covers and jumped out of bed, hoping to <u>throw off</u>[3] the traumatic memories that had overtaken my body. [*Breathe*],[4] I reminded myself in an effort to gain my equilibrium.[5] The memories were more than words and mental images. They were locked[6] somewhere deep within my neurological system.[7]

---

1. "Gasping" already suggests the character isn't getting enough air. Notice that we're starting with waking up (see the Common Opening Clichés chapter) but the character is ripped from sleep by an event, so this isn't an ordinary morning scene.
2. A physical cliché (see the Recurring Notes chapter). Unfortunately, the hummingbird image is a very popular description for a rapidly beating heart. I'd push this writer beyond what comes to mind immediately.
3. This repetition might be intentional to make a point.
4. If this is a verbatim thought, consider formatting it in italics (see the Recurring Notes chapter).
5. It's clear the character is worked up and attempting to calm down. Need to explain?
6. Maybe "they were triggers" or "they were sensations" in order to differentiate them from "words and mental images"?
7. Is the character in medicine? Would they say this or the more colloquial "nervous system"?

When lightning cracked like that three years earlier,[8] at precisely 11:17 [p.m.]~~pm~~, it was as if some otherworldly consciousness had taken control of me. In that brief moment, I heard a voice say, "He's gone," as I felt Will's life force leave his body.[9] It was a disgustingly objective awareness.[10] It had taken a moment for my mind to catch up. But when it did, terror[11] ripped through every ounce of my being. I hadn't allowed myself to break down. Instead, I'd spent the next two hours trying to slow my racing heart and stop the ravaging tremors.[12] All I could do was pace and try to convince myself it wasn't true.[13] Over and over I told myself I'd just been frightened by the storm[,]~~;~~ that I was being irrational[,]~~;~~ that my son couldn't be dead. But deep inside, I knew.[14] I hated that there was no emotion associated with the awareness when it occurred.[15] It seemed as if the universe had been indifferent to Will's death, and therefore, his life. How could that have been true?[16]

It was still dark, but I couldn't return to my bed. I moved through the cottage and settled on the porch overlooking the back

---

8. We're leaving the present moment here. This interrupts the tension building in the current timeline.

9. Maybe "It was as if I felt" so we know it's meant figuratively, not literally. (Readers could start looking for hints of a fantasy or magical realism element and be confused.)

10. I want to know more about "disgustingly objective," as if the character was outside themselves, observing? As if it came from elsewhere? An emotionless statement of fact?

11. Avoid naming emotions outright (see the Recurring Notes chapter).

12. I worry that we're getting a ton of very intense and emotional description and language, but without it being grounded in a clearer sense of character or context (e.g., who's Will?). It's all panic so far and could veer toward melodrama.

13. This restates the idea of trying to calm down.

14. Did the character have a way to check? It seems like the lightning corresponded with the insight, but in the chain of events, above, it could also be read as the lightning killing Will. Correlation doesn't imply causation, but the narrative sequencing is a bit disorienting right now.

15. This goes back to "disgustingly objective," but then the character spends two hours shaking. So I'd say the mention of "no emotion" doesn't entirely ring true about the episode as a whole.

16. I like getting a concrete sense of why this "objective" remove bothered her. This issue could be clarified sooner.

bay. **My heart rate slowed**[17] and **my body relaxed** as **the sky lightened. Sunlight** was the only thing that calmed me after these incidents. Within a few minutes, I saw[18] **slivers of the sun peeking** through the oaks and slash pines on the mainland. The bay was narrow here, making it easy to witness the wildlife awakening on both shores. It would've been nice to sit a while longer, but the lightning had struck close by, and I wanted to check in with Becca and Dave.[19]

As I walked along the short path through the mangroves, I picked up branches the storm had ripped from their host trees. When I reached the clearing,[20] I found myself gasping for air again. But this time it wasn't terrifying memories taking my breath. It was the tree that had crashed onto the deck of our studio[21]—our lovely studio due to open in just eight days. This ~~can't~~ [couldn't] be real.[22]

I heard Becca before I made my way to the back of the building, where I found her crumpled on the floor, sobbing. [*This isn't right. Becca doesn't cry.*] When I sat down and wrapped her in my arms, she convulsed against me, and her pain coursed through my body.[23] It was mine now, too. I learned in my trauma healing courses to take slow, rhythmic breaths to calm both of us.[24] As I did so, my

---

17. This is the third mention of her heart rate slowing. Once in this timeline, once in the past, and now in the present again.
18. Some filler description (see the Recurring Notes chapter).
19. Her memory of Will's death is triggered, but now it seems she's shifting gears. What's the focus of the present moment—reacting to the current lightning, remembering Will and the past lightning, or getting on with her day?
20. Does she have any cause for alarm? Add some tension to this walk, otherwise it's purely logistical. This writer says "the lightning sounded as if it had struck my cottage" in the second sentence, but the Will flashback quickly overshadows this. Wouldn't the character at least check her home?
21. Focus on what it is, rather than defining it first by what it isn't. The former is more straightforward.
22. If we're weaving her thoughts into narration, use past tense. If it's a verbatim thought, present tense is better, but the phrase should be italicized.
23. We just saw the character completely undone. Now she slips into the role of comforting Becca. That's a bit of emotional whiplash. How does she manage to be so strong here and so ruffled a moment ago?
24. I wonder if we're seeing the mechanics of calming down play out too often in a

thoughts slipped back to that night when she was holding me. It was the only other time I'd seen her cry. I caught myself and shoved those memories back in the box where they belonged.[25] This was about Becca, and I needed to stay present with her.[26]

As her breathing began to mirror mine,[27] I wondered if the permafrost that had locked up her emotions was finally melting. When I felt her relax, I whispered, "You're crying."[28] She sniffled and nodded. "It'll be okay. We'll fix it," I said. But when I looked over her shoulder and took in the full spectacle of what I'd only seen from outside, I understood why she was crying.[29] We'd spent thirty years planning ~~this~~ [to open a business together] and now, a week away from the ~~opening~~ [realization of our dream], a tree was sprawled across the back of our studio.[30]

Becca pulled back and looked at me with her big blue eyes and burst into laughter. I assumed it was the shocked look on my face that made her laugh harder.[31] She gasped[32] repeatedly to [re]gain her voice. "I'm not worried about the building. Dave will fix it. It's the tree! We lost the tree, Drew!"

I should've known. This was so Becca. She never got riled by

---

page and a half. The story seems like it'll be about healing, but we don't want to hit the reader over the head with theme.

25. This contradicts her allowing memories to overtake her so viscerally earlier.

26. Unclear why Becca is the only one who needs solace here if "*our* lovely studio" (emphasis mine) was destroyed. Does the protagonist have any stake in it? Allow this to affect her, too, or the scene won't be as resonant.

27. Odd that they haven't spoken to one another. Sure, it could be one of those "we don't need words to talk" friendships, but this misses an opportunity for readers to get to know their relationship through interaction.

28. The character already indicated that this was notable in her thoughts. Do one or the other.

29. I'm confused from a spatial perspective. Aren't they still outside in front of the cottage? How does her vista change here?

30. She already described the damage, yet this is phrased as if it's fresh information.

31. Some roundabout description of the POV's reaction (see the Recurring Notes chapter).

32. I worry there's a lot of gasping so far from both characters. This sample doesn't want to tip over into melodrama (strong emotion without grounding logic).

petty things like building damage.[33] I found myself caught in the irony[34] and burst into laughter with her. In a matter of seconds, we were clutching our sides and rolling on our backs in a fit of inappropriate, uncontrollable laughter.[35]

---

33. Can this be finessed? Natural disasters being what they are, people routinely lose everything, especially down in this part of the United States. This might come across as diminishing those losses. Maybe something like "She never got riled by things, saving her concern for trees and animals." This way we capitalize on Becca's unique perspective while not laughing off building damage as "petty," which might rub some readers as callous.

34. Is it irony? Or is it more like her unique priorities?

35. The laughter is surprising and catches reader attention, but it's also overstated by this point.

SAMPLE 2 OVERVIEW

This sample features clean writing and a great sense of place. We're thrust into dramatic action with the lightning strike, which threatens the friends' dream business. The biggest issue so far is the Will flashback. Is his death a cornerstone event in the character's life? Yes. Is it tied to the current lightning storm? Yes. But do we need the trigger and flashback in the first pages? I'm not so sure, as it stirs up such dramatic feelings and keeps the character in a sense of panic for a few paragraphs, pulling a lot of focus. Meanwhile, the drama of the current storm takes a backseat and is even diminished —a child's death makes anything else seem insignificant. Unfortunately, this takes the wind out of the present conflict's sails. I'd focus instead of the destruction of the studio and how Becca and the protagonist start reacting, coping, or rebounding. Save the Will stuff for later. The sample also makes it seem like Becca is the most invested in the business, though the POV character is affected, too. Clarify her *personal* stakes and how this obstacle stirs up her own emotions (separate from her grief). This writer has started off with a bang, literally. Now let's get the most emotional juice from it.

SAMPLE 3: UNTITLED
CONTEMPORARY

LIZ LYDIC

My ex-husband, Sean, was waiting for me when I got home from work the week before the S[s]pring time change[1] in 2018.[2]

"Do you have a spare key ring?" he asked. "Oh, and did you ask the HOA if they have an extra garage door clicker?"[3]

I breathed in. "Dude, Sean, I'm not giving you a garage door clicker. It's weird enough for you to have a key to my home."[4]

Sean shifted in his seat, and I noticed he had[5] poured himself a glass of wine. My brain toggled between two burdens: on the one hand, being down one glass of wine;[6] on the other, that the man

---

1. No need to capitalize the seasons. The more specific term for this is "daylight savings time."
2. This is a rather straightforward statement of fact, orienting us in time and place but not really offering any intrigue (except the ex-husband's presence).
3. This trips me up because he's talking and acting like they're still married. Maybe say something like "My now-ex-husband" in the first sentence.
4. Ha! Good. At least I'm not the only one thrown by his attitude.
5. Consider a contraction here.
6. Ha!

who said he no longer wanted to be in our marriage was ~~across from me~~ [sitting in my kitchen].[7] Drinking my wine.[8]

"Becca, we can go over it again if you want. I pick up Austin every day so you can work until 5 p.m.[9] [Me having a] ~~A~~ key to the place that you love to label as Austin's 'actual home' is something you should be cool with,[10] not something to analyze or hold over my head." Sean took a sip and glared at me over the rim of the glass. I was grateful he wasn't raising his voice, but still, his words left little aches everywhere.[11]

"You don't live here. You didn't want to live with me. Don't you think that means you give up the right to access my home?"[12]

"Becca."

Sean held my gaze and placed both hands flat on my white tiled counter that felt both mine and also unfamiliar.[13] I couldn't help ~~but look~~ [looking] at his left hand, purposefully torturing myself to acknowledge ~~the bareness of~~ his [bare] ring finger.[14]

"If we're going to do this—be the best parents for Austin—~~it includes this~~ [we need to make sacrifices].[15] You were chill before you bought this place—"[16]

---

7. To me, the issue is his invasion of her space, but the grammar suggests the problem is him sitting across from her.
8. The character has her priorities!
9. I worry this veers into expository dialogue, especially when he explains her work schedule *to* her (see the Recurring Notes chapter).
10. The key itself isn't the problem, it's him having one, so I've rephrased.
11. Which part? Be specific. He has touched upon several things, and if we know what bruises her, we learn more about the character and what makes her tick.
12. Good.
13. This detail seems neither here nor there. The entire conversation is about this being her home, so the "unfamiliar[ity]" introduces a confusing emotional layer.
14. I took a stab at streamlining this a bit.
15. I rephrased this because otherwise he was saying, "If we're going to do this, it includes this" which is a bit muddy.
16. Ah, I thought this was the marital home, not that she'd moved since they separated. "Unfamiliar" makes more sense, but only after the fact. Consider rearranging the information. We could say something earlier like, "Did you ask the HOA for a spare clicker? You've been here three months already, and I'm getting tired

"What does that mean? I *was* chill?" I opened the fridge, looking first for the bottle of wine. I didn't even want any, but I pulled it out and put it pointedly on the counter in front of Sean.[17] My work badge from the U̶[u]niversity got caught i̶n̶ [on] the drawer [pull] under the kitchen counter.[18]

"Let me finish.[19] Not you, but we were. We were actually doing great, as a newly divorced couple for the past six months.[20] I mean, I hadn't missed any of my days with Austin—don't roll your eyes[21]—you know that wasn't easy with my work schedule—"

"No one said you should have taken that copywriting gig—"

"Don't interrupt![22] It was steady, and I could work remotely. Not the point. God! We've been getting along, right? We've been respecting each other's … new lives. Now you're deciding to be difficult. That's on you, by the way. Your choice."[23] Sean took a substantial sip.

"I don't think we were necessarily 'getting along[,]'‚[24] as you say." Sean opened his mouth to talk,[25] but I continued, crossing the

---

of waiting." Yes, that's expository dialogue, but I think offering this data sooner rather than later will help to ground the reader.

17. This gesture confuses me. It could easily be misconstrued as an invitation to stay a while and have some more.

18. I think this writer means it snagged on the handle, as she didn't open the drawer to get the wine, unless she has one of those drawer fridges. Again, these very specific logistical details tend to distract.

19. She interrupted him, sure, but then she stopped talking. It's not like she's presently shouting over him.

20. Some more expository dialogue (see the Recurring Notes chapter). Have her think about the stats, how long she's been there, how long they've been divorced, etc. It's not "bad telling" to sprinkle in some factual context.

21. A roundabout description of the character's reaction (see the Recurring Notes chapter).

22. Now *this* makes more sense as a comment from him because things are getting heated.

23. I can really hear his voice coming through (and would like to throttle him on her behalf).

24. In this case, the punctuation goes inside the quotation mark.

25. Need to explain why he'd do this during a heated argument? It's not to eat a corn dog.

two whole steps from the counter to the cabinets above the dishwasher[26] to extract a wine glass. "It's business. I guess we've handled the Austin … duties well, but don't say we were getting along like besties or something, and don't say I became an ogre once I bought this condo.[27] By the way, you have not once acknowledged that I'm ensuring a stable, permanent home in Carmelito so we can keep our kid ~~going to~~ [in] a good school district—"

"You guys?"

Sean and I turned toward the hallway to see our ~~10~~ [ten]-year[-]old[28] marshmallow of a boy, Austin,[29] standing, holding both sides of the doorway. He was crying.[30]

"What is it?" Sean asked. We exchanged a swift glance, and Sean shook his head as if to say, in infuriating code, ~~in an infuriating code that said,~~[31] *Don't assume our fight is why our son is upset.*

---

26. Not sure we need the spatial logistics of their kitchen layout. She didn't want a glass of wine, now she does. That's the relevant detail of this action.

27. If it has a garage, is it a condo or a townhouse? I think I want to know what she bought and when sooner so we can visualize what they're fighting about.

28. Spell out all ages and note the hyphenation pattern here.

29. They've talked about him enough that I'm not sure we need to connect the name to the son when he shows up.

30. And? So? Does she react inwardly or outwardly to this?

31. They know one another well, but we technically can't be 100% sure what his body language is saying if we're not in his head. I've added some hedging language to clarify this as her interpretation. She also still hasn't reacted to Austin and seems more fixated on being annoyed with Sean. Is this the sense this sample wants to convey?

SAMPLE 3 OVERVIEW

A great scene with engaging dialogue which kicks off with immediate intrigue—why's the ex-husband in her home, acting like he owns the place? To really make the most of this opening, consider rearranging some details to clarify that she has moved into her own condo/apartment/townhouse, etc. Furthermore, this writer can trim some of the spatial logistics and choreography. The first two pages end with Austin, their son, walking in on them fighting. Depending on the family dynamic in play, this could be seen as a big deal. It's lightly suggested that she doesn't want him to see his parents in conflict. If that's the case, let the protagonist react in a bigger way (internally or externally) when Austin appears. Right now, she seems more invested in venting about Sean, but the sample leaves some potential conflict and emotion on the table.

SAMPLE 4: SAVE THE DATE
ROMANCE/ROMANTIC COMEDY

TAMMY SUTHERLAND

"That's your thumb!" I cry out in frustration[1] at the customer's back as he yanks open the door to Lee's Photos, letting in a whoosh of frigid air, and stalks away, leaving me with a pile of photos on the counter, each one marred by a fuzzy moon in the corner.[2] He saw the flaw on all his images, but still hit print and then refused to pay for them.[3]

I pick up the garbage bin and shove them all to the bottom, worrying about how[4] my boss, Mrs. Lee, is making enough money to keep this place open and take care of her ailing husband at

---

1. Telling using dialogue tags (see the Recurring Notes chapter).
2. I worry this is far too detailed for an opening sentence. We get dialogue, emotion, setting, action, and the reveal of the thumb issue. Also, that the protagonist is right and the customer is being unreasonable. Play this out for several sentences. The humor will get readers invested, so we don't need everything all at once.
3. Is this a self-serve print shop where he could preview the images on a machine? (It's possible he uploaded them at home.) I think the point is that the customer is an idiot and the character is having a bad day, so the exact logistics don't matter, and some of these details could be trimmed. Do something like, "He saw what he'd get in the preview and still ordered prints" or similar.
4. Awk. phrasing. "wondering how" or "worrying whether"?

home[.]?[5] People are so used to shopping at big corporations now that they don't recognize the impact ~~they~~ [their actions][6] have on an independent business owner. My cell phone pings in the back pocket of my jeans. Looking over my shoulder to make sure Mrs. Lee is still [distracted] in the back room[,];[7] I pull it out to check[,] and my stomach twists like a pretzel.[8] It's a Google review about the business I've been trying to get off the ground.[9] My first Google review.

Jules took random pictures, like the backs of people's heads, instead of the photos I specifically asked for. Wedding photos should remind you of the happiest day of your life, but mine remind me of how frustrating she was to work with. Brides beware! - @influentialison[10]

The heat crawls up my chest and neck steadily[11] until the potent combination of anger and shame[12] pulsing in my veins is written all over my flaming cheeks. The comment and one-star rating sit next to a gorgeous profile picture of radiant bride. A photo I took. It's been three months since I shot @influentialison's wedding, my first solo wedding, and the burgeoning lifestyle influencer is still finding new ways to tell the world that I sucked.[13]

---

5. This sentence contains an implied question but doesn't actually require a question mark. It is a statement and needs a period instead.

6. More specific?

7. Semi-colons are used in lists and to string together somewhat related sentences which could stand alone. This was used incorrectly.

8. A physical cliché (see the Recurring Notes chapter).

9. I have an idea, but this writer doesn't have to take it. When Jules is looking at the irate customer's thumb photos, she should think something along the lines of, "He obviously didn't know anything about composition anyway," or similar, which suggests her interest in photography sooner.

10. Love the handle, conveys that Alison has a following.

11. Give us her thoughts instead of relying only on the physical body.

12. Naming emotions (see the Recurring Notes chapter).

13. If it's been three months, wouldn't a negative review blast be one of the first things Alison did? That's usually the best way to put public pressure on a business, then the campaign tends to spread out to other venues. Or, if the wedding was this past weekend, Jules could be bracing for the review and would dread any phone notification, which could be established *before* she gets the alert. This would give the present moment more immediate tension.

Except that photo she's talking about? I love it. It's [of] the guests watching the groom wipe his tears away during the vows. Yes, it is the backs of their heads, but if you look closely, you can see what they were all feeling in that moment. It's in the tilt of one woman's head, and in the way a man is turned to kiss his partner on the temple. It's in the mother of the bride resting her cheek on her husband's shoulder.[14]

At least, that's what I see. But if there's one thing I've learned from Mrs. Lee, it's that the customer is always right.[15]

The decision hits me like a bolt of lightning,[16] even though the bolt shatters my fragile heart:[17] I'm done. I need to sell my camera and the equipment and find something else to do with my life.[18] It's been three months of bad reviews.[19] Three months with zero interest from other brides. Three months of barely scraping by on my paycheck from Lee's Photos. It was ridiculous to think I could build a successful business without my sister, anyway.[20]

I swipe away the review and click open the buy and sell app I downloaded when I first moved to Toronto,[21] letting my frustration fuel this brilliant idea.[22] I wonder how much I might be able to get for everything? Since my bank account is more of a way[ ]station for

---

14. Some very nice, warm imagery. We can really tell Jules loves what she does.

15. This is maybe an unintentional contradiction, but we open with Jules correcting a customer and shouting them out the door. This is a complete 180. I wouldn't undermine the protagonist's credibility by telling and showing opposite ideas (see the Recurring Notes chapter).

16. A familiar image, I'm afraid.

17. A bit too much heart imagery for one page.

18. Why is this the realization *here*? After one review and one major wedding? Obviously, this knee-jerk reaction makes sense, but it's very clear she loves photography. How Jules got from there to here is unclear unless her creeping sense of failure has been building for a while.

19. She says it's her first Google review. There are only a few other places she could be reviewed, and Alison spamming them with this bad review wouldn't take months. (I'm caught up in the logistics because they're very detailed.)

20. First mention of the sister, which is an immediate curiosity hook. Maybe seed this sooner: "And Amy isn't here to see it" when the review comes in, or whatever.

21. Good grounding detail.

22. If this has been ongoing for three months, why didn't she think of quitting

my paycheck to pass through briefly before being spread thinly across my expenses,[23] I chant *big money* in my head like a ~~[*Price is Right*]~~[24] contestant. But my search for DSLR cameras brings up a list of available items that seems to scroll forever.[25] How do I create an ad that will stand out? I can't say *used*. That sounds unappealing. Maybe *secondhand*? But I'm the second owner, so does that make it thirdhand? Is thirdhand a thing?

"Jules."

Mrs. Lee's no-nonsense voice cuts through my spiral[26] and I stash my phone. "Someone needs your assistance with the machine," she says, pointing to the only customer in the store, a senior sitting at the self-serve photo printer in the front window.

This decision, to cut off a limb to save myself—at least, that's what the idea of selling my camera feels like—will have to wait a little longer.[27]

[The f] Fluorescent lights overhead can't counteract the weighty March gloom outside,[28] making the display cases of cameras and shelves of frames that I weave through look like relics of another time. Which they kind of are.[29]

The smell of hot chocolate emanates from the takeout cup in the

---

before? Especially if there were other reviews? I'm not sure I buy this idea hitting her like a bolt from the blue today.

23. Ha!

24. Format show titles in italics.

25. Good. This writer did a great job of setting up her expectations and then knocking them down.

26. Ha! Good voice.

27. Again, I'm not sure this is a new idea if Alison has been waging a campaign for months. Second, the sample shows a frenzy of activity that's cut off abruptly. It is, indeed, a quick spiral, but since she abandons it right away, her intention to sell her camera and quit doesn't read as credible. "Methinks the lady doth protest too much." She's probably going to stick with photography in this story, but how seriously does the writer want to sell readers on the idea of her giving up?

28. Already got the cold burst from outside in the first sentence.

29. I'm surprised that she doesn't make this connection right away. Photo stores are dying, if not already dead.

man's hand as I help him crop shots of tidy garden beds. I consider showing him the backs-of-peoples-heads wedding photo, to get another opinion,[30] but judging from the way he's cutting grandkids jumping on a trampoline out of the horticulture snaps,[31] I worry that he'd side with the bride.

---

30. The three-month time horizon is really killing me. Even if Jules is new in town, she'd have a friend or two to try and get validation from once the first review hit. If she has no friends in town, she has friends from her old town. She wouldn't be showing the photo to random strangers three months later, she would've gone validation-seeking from her nearest and dearest immediately after.

31. Ha! Some nice voice. This opening does a great job of sustaining present action with a dose of conflict and only a few necessary bits of context about the past.

SAMPLE 4 OVERVIEW

This is an immediately engaging scene with great voice. Notice how the writer *shows* Jules's passion for photography rather than explaining it. Top marks for that! We're also presented with a protagonist who must make a high-stakes decision—whether to give up on her passion. But the *why* and *why today* need some bolstering, and I think both can be addressed by compressing the timeframe between the influencer wedding, review, and reaction from Jules. For example, if this was Jules's make-or-break wedding which might've allowed her to quit her retail job, and it happened the previous weekend, there would be more tension. She'd be dreading the Google review and flinching whenever her phone pinged because maybe the bride had ended the day on an ominous note. Then the review comes in, and that's it. Jules was barely making it work, and now she can't justify continuing. The wedding was recent, the review happens in real time, and Jules is forced into a tough choice. The set-up is great, but I want to push this writer to generate maximum tension from the pieces already in play.

SAMPLE 5: UNTITLED

MEMOIR

MAE CORBIN

The weather wasn't perfect for a graduation, even with the beach view.[1] Then again, down on the grass, ~~our~~ [the graduates'] seats were protected by the stage from the icy Pacific **wind** whilst[2] all of our beloved friends and family in the stadiums got the full brunt of the **gale**.[3]

The sun reflected off the bleachers, and my sunglasses were the only thing keeping its intensity from frying my hungover brain.[4] Just remembering my sister, Lauren, and all that booze made me want to vomit.[5] I smiled against the ache. I hadn't realized how

---

1. It's unclear what the writer wants us to pay attention to right away: the graduation, the beach, or the bad weather. These all play a role in setting the scene, but how much weight should each detail be given? (The weather as an objective correlative for mood is also a familiar way to introduce tension, though, in the case of memoir, we're tied to what actually happened.)
2. Overly formal for a contemporary memoir.
3. I get the broad strokes—the auditorium's stage was protected while the bleachers got hit—but I'm also a bit lost in the logistical details.
4. I feel like we need the POV character/writer in the scene right away, rather than doing the setting flyover first. Not only were they hungover, but the weather sucked, etc.
5. Maybe "my sister, Lauren, showing up with all that booze" or similar? Right now, the grammar is saying that remembering the sister made the character want to vomit,

dark ~~my~~ her humor was. Turns out we did have some things in common.[6]

I tuned back into the student speaker. He had[7] been assigned one seat over from me[8] and was giving one hell of a speech.[9] I remembered him trying to hit on me during our freshman year in our library's computer lab. I should have gone for him. Aside from ~~being the head of~~ [leading] the [*a cappella*][10] choir group, [being elected] president of speech and debate, graduating summa cum laude, double majoring, and [earning][11] an onslaught of other honors, he was extremely good-looking and very well built. Oh to go back in time and tell my freshman-year self, "Go for the ~~hot,~~ black[12] guy!"

The short grass fluffed out around my sandals. It would have been useless advice.[13] I'd had no idea how to flirt, which I blamed on going to an all-girls Catholic high school, though it probably had more to do with my broken brain.[14]

"We are a class of honor and unity ..." Amare[15] continued.

HA! I didn't feel all that honorable. The only thing on my

---

which might be true, but I want to make sure the language is crystal clear. Notice us leaving the present moment, too.

6. This is neither here nor there right now. Let's see them in action together and show the humor playing out. Or hold this for later, as Laura isn't active in the present scene, nor are we focused on this relationship. Maybe open with the night before, if it's important. They don't necessarily have to start on stage.

7. Use contractions for more colloquial voice (see the Recurring Notes chapter).

8. Does this detail matter if he's at the podium?

9. Maybe a bit more information about this if it is, indeed, necessary. "one hell of a speech" doesn't really tell me much, or even if this is a serious or sarcastic comment.

10. This is often italicized as it's Italian.

11. Notice how I've made the verbs in this sentence parallel.

12. Some people capitalize "Black" while others don't. Maybe read up on the current cultural commentary about this issue.

13. These ideas don't seem to flow. The second sentence continues where the previous paragraph left off. The grass seems neither here nor there.

14. In what way? This is intriguing but also not really specific, so if this matters enough to mention now, maybe supply another line of context. Is the writer alluding to being neurodivergent? Or just making fun of themselves?

15. If we know his name, why not use it right away? That could help with clarity.

gown[16] was a taped piece of paper that read: *Kent Student-Athlete.* I hadn't even remembered my real tag and only noticed once I was surrounded by people with cords and pins.[17]

It represented my only other achievement apart from getting a diploma. Janky or not, I was going to wear it.

Why hadn't I remembered it? I had even put it by the bathroom sink to remind me to put it on! Then again, if something that simple worked for me, I would have as many honors as my friends.[18]

"Congratulations, class of 2010! As was God's will, we made it!"

The crowd stood and roared at his declaration.

Ugh. I squinted against the pain in my head.[19] I stepped in the line to the stadium, my classmates buzzing in excitement.[20] I pretended to celebrate with them when all I really thought about were my half-assed accomplishments:[21] not swimming during summer vacations; adopting a "Cs get degrees" mentality my senior year; losing the respect of my classmates and teachers by slacking;[22] and spending most of my senior-year weekends depressed in my

---

16. Explain that people are wearing all kinds of sashes and badges, but the character isn't, sooner.

17. Good. Maybe reorder this paragraph to relay what everyone else was doing, and what the writer ended up doing (to underscore the feeling of blowing it).

18. This could all be rolled into one paragraph. Instead of asking rhetorical questions (see the Recurring Notes chapter), speculate about the reason. And the tone is a bit unclear. At times, it seems like the writer is being funny and self-deprecating. Here, though, the tone changes to actual frustration. Maybe drill a bit deeper into what the writer believes is below the surface here and how it made them feel.

19. A bit conflicting because the last time the glare was mentioned, we read, "I smiled against the ache." I'm guessing that smile was for Laura, but since it was also connected to the description of the sun, I want to make sure I'm following the emotional logic.

20. This echoes the crowd standing and roaring. The mood is clearly lively.

21. This restates the same idea from the previous few paragraphs, just in more detail. I wonder if there's a way to streamline. Was it the visible representation of everyone else's achievements that triggered this?

22. This sort of restates the same idea as "Cs get degrees."

room reading manga, watching Korean dramas, masturbating, and binge eating. My cocktail of temporary success.[23]

"Mae Corbin!" I took a deep breath,[24] trying to be present. It was over anyhow, nothing to be done about it now.

"Congratulations! You did it," said our school's president, handing me an empty box that represented my time at Kent.

He was right for the most part. "Yes! Yes, I did," I said, feeling more relieved than proud.[25] I'd have a fresh start once this was all over. I turned to the crowd, thrust my cap into the air, and screamed my mother's war cry before my peers, who echoed with cheers of their own. Letting my voice go gave me the first moment of respite[26] since waking up.

At least my inner wildling existed regardless of the state of my education.[27]

---

23. Is it even temporary "success," though? The theme seems to center on how far the writer feels they've fallen from their potential, and that "success" has eluded them.
24. Putting the dialogue on the same line as the character's reaction makes it seem like they're saying their own name and taking a deep breath. The dialogue calling the writer to the stage needs to be on a separate line.
25. I worry the writer is contradicting themselves. If it *is* over, and there *isn't* anything to be done, that's all fine and good, but then why fixate on it? Instead of dismissing themselves, they might explore why these feelings came up in this moment.
26. Is this a respite, or is this a jolt of energy and freedom?
27. I like the contrast of the inner self and the institution. I do wonder how the writer feels about themselves, though, since it seems they're judging their worth according to the standards of the institution, after all. Is this a "me vs. the man" narrative, thematically, or a "me vs. self" narrative? This has have the seeds of both.

SAMPLE 5 OVERVIEW

Graduation ceremonies are very symbolic, putting the break between "past" and "future" into concrete action. As such, this is a fitting setting for the beginning of a memoir about identity, meaning, and the writer's relationship to self. However, that relationship isn't presented as clearly here, which comes down to an issue of tone. The pins are called out as significant—and make the writer feel "less than" her peers. At times, though, she pokes fun at herself and hand-waves the fact that she didn't strive as much as she believes she should've. On the other hand, she seems bothered by the same ideas. Take a stronger stand about the internal struggle and iron out some of these contradictions. Keep the graduation motif in mind as well. Is there a sense of "now what"? Of being left to her own devices as the rest of her life unfolds before her, but feeling unprepared? Some details and logistics can be trimmed, including the mention of Laura (unless the hangover is going to really impact the scene). The writer's relationship with the sister could be woven in when Laura's actually on the page and all of the associated feelings are more relevant to the present moment.

SAMPLE 6: ANGELUS CUSTOS - BOOK ONE OF THE ANGELUS TRILOGY
FANTASY

H.G.MARSH

Delania, Angelus Custos, Guardian Angel of the Alder Grove, scowled at the blank paper in front of her.[1] The Archangel Michael cleared his throat and waited until Delania looked up at him.[2]

"You need to do this, Delania."

She frowned[3] and shook her head. "Why? I don't even know what happened[.][4] ~~when~~ I wasn't there, so how can I[—]"[5]

The Archangel raised one hand, and Delania pressed her lips together. "I have explained this to you[," he said.][6] "You have mixed feelings about your worth as a Guardian Angel.[7] You have come to

---

1. An engaging opening that contrasts the mysterious names with the rather pedestrian conflict of a blank page.
2. Are we in Michael's POV or Delania's? It's subtle, but we get a POV shift from hers to his. We can't conclusively know what he's waiting for unless we're in his head, and we were just in hers (see the Recurring Notes chapter).
3. Already got a scowl, so her emotional tone is clear.
4. I'd break up this sentence. Dialogue tends to move more quickly.
5. Use an em-dash to convey an interruption (see the Recurring Notes chapter).
6. I'm adding this to clarify who's speaking, since the narration in this paragraph refers to actions by both characters.
7. Make no mistake, this is outright telling. Putting quotation marks around the information isn't a workaround.

me in tears more than once.[8] You even believed[9] that you had killed your 'lost soul[.]'.[10] For your own sake, you must do this,[11] and the Lord will help."

Delania sighed unhappily.[12] "Alright[All right]. I suppose so. But how—"

The Archangel interrupted her again.[13] "You must learn to put your trust wholly in God."

His lips twitched as he realised what he had [he'd][14] said. "Pun unintended."

Delania leaned back in her chair and ran her fingers through her unruly hair, trying to conceal her smile.[15] Then she sat up alertly[16] and picked up her pen. "Right. So, I start writing whatever God tells me to?"[17]

---

8. Some expository dialogue (see the Recurring Notes chapter). She seems to be asking about a specific incident, then he explains her own general situation to her. I don't see this response as connected to the previous line of dialogue.

9. Does she still believe it? "Believed" makes it seem like she once believed it but doesn't anymore, yet Michael's dialogue hints at current doubt, so I'd use present tense.

10. Punctuation goes inside quotation marks (with a few exceptions).

11. Do what? Sign the paper? Continue to be a Guardian Angel? Answer questions about "what happened"? Be more precise.

12. She is already scowling and frowning. Necessary?

13. No need to narrate this if the previous line ends on an em-dash again.

14. A contraction is more colloquial.

15. This is a sudden change of mood. She was just very unhappy. Is it the pun that turned things around? Has she made some kind of decision? I'd challenge this writer to filter this scene through the close-third POV of either character so we can get deeper into someone's head and offer reaction or context, rather than sticking to body language cues. This is one of the ways in which writers are hampered by the well-meaning advice of "show, don't tell."

16. This doesn't seem to follow the secret smile. Her mood feels all over the place, but readers can't relate to her on a deeper level because the physical body can only tell us so much.

17. Unclear what Michael is asking her to do, how it connects to her crisis of faith (which seems more like backstory), and what they were talking about initially (some event she wasn't privy to). I'd add a few sentences of context. It's okay to tell certain pieces of information or re-imagine the opening scene so it makes sense without

The Archangel nodded. "Start at the beginning[,][18] and God will provide what you need, as He has done so many times before.[19] This exercise will help you to come to terms with what you did. Or didn't do.[20] Use this time to absorb your story and learn from it. Pray first, write next, and then read to learn and grow from what you have written." He smiled compassionately.[21] "I shall pray for you, Delania."

She watched as the figure of the Archangel Michael faded from view, leaving her sitting alone at the desk with the blank paper on it.[22] She sighed again, put down her pen, and knelt by the chair.

She was still for quite a while, praying for help, for the words she would need and for the wisdom to understand and learn from them.[23] Then she rose again, sat down, picked up her pen, took a deep breath and started to write.[24] Her eyes widened as she saw the words appear, and she sat back in amazement. "What the … I never knew this!"

She smiled in delight. "This might just work after all!"

She put pen to paper again, excited to see what came next.[25]

---

backstory (and we don't need to understand so many past events). How might the writer start in the present moment with action that's unfolding in real time?

18. Of what? It seems like they're having a whole conversation around a hollow core. I worry this will be disorienting to readers who have no idea what's being alluded to.

19. This idea is well established, and Michael's position is clear.

20. If we were in her close-third perspective, we'd have more data. Otherwise, it's unclear what they're talking about and if she was even involved. Why does she need to write about it? Too many open questions might distract the reader, rather than tantalizing them with mystery.

21. Avoid ascribing emotional adverbs to his actions. (See the Recurring Notes chapter for why this is an issue in dialogue tags as well.)

22. Where she is and what she's looking at are already established.

23. Why not have her pray aloud or put us into her thought process? Summarizing the contents is passive.

24. Getting into the weeds of some play-by-play here (see the Recurring Notes chapter).

25. All of this conveys the same idea—she's surprised by what she's writing and wants to know more. But what does she write? That could help add context. As is, too much is omitted (with the intention of stirring up intrigue, I'm guessing), and readers might not have enough concrete information to really engage.

———

BEN ROBERTSON WAS CELEBRATING HIS EIGHTY-FOURTH BIRTHDAY [alone—] ~~in~~ the same way he had[26] celebrated his ~~last three~~ [three previous birthdays]~~: on his own~~. His life had been bleak[27] since his wife died. His only comfort in the silence that surrounded him was the sound of his own voice but, rather than speak to his departed wife, which he found disconcerting and a little unsettling, he had started speaking to his Lord.[28] He never expected an answer, of course, but Ben felt closer to Him ~~when he talked to Him~~ [this way],[29] and it had become a familiar habit.

Now, he closed his well-read copy of [*Second Foundation*][30] by Isaac Asimov and carefully placed it on the small table beside him. Leaning back,[31] Ben closed his eyes and sighed in satisfaction. "They don't write them like that ~~any more~~ [anymore], Lord."

He opened his eyes wide and chuckled.[32] "Yes, yes, I know, there are two more books in the series after this, but the first three were the ones. They were the story.[33] Yes, Lord, there's something very satisfying about a well-written trilogy."

He levered himself out of his comfortable armchair, picked up the book and slowly walked over to the bookcase. Reaching up, he carefully put it away.[34] "There you go, Isaac mate, back in your rightful place. On the top shelf."

---

26. Could use a contraction to loosen up the voice.
27. Need to explain? The idea of him celebrating his birthdays alone suggests this.
28. Awk. phrasing. Read this aloud and see if it can be streamlined.
29. I'd avoid repeating "when he talked to Him" because it repeats "to Him" from the same sentence, and reminds readers that this paragraph is about Ben talking to God, which is already clear.
30. Format book titles in italics.
31. A lot of granular detail. Focus instead of the action of the scene.
32. This minutiae will negatively impact the pacing.
33. Unclear phrasing at first. "the ones" what? Only the first three books matter?
34. This is also an unnecessary level of detail, especially after the careful description of him putting the book on the table only to get up and put it on the shelf. Too much physical business throughout.

SAMPLE 6 OVERVIEW

This is an ambitious opening because we're introduced to two different worlds, sets of characters, and timelines (potentially). I like that we can evaluate both threads in the first two pages, and we saw a similar division in Sample 4 from the Young Adult section. That said, there's an imbalance between the two narratives. The first is full of mystery, with two characters seemingly unpacking a key event. But it's unclear why Delania must complete this assignment or what it means to her, exactly. The notion of her losing her faith is floated, and from the prayer in the second section, it's clear that faith might be central to the theme or conflict for several characters. However, Michael seems to have information, while Delania has little, yet she's expected to add clarity to the current situation. Per the Common Opening Clichés and Action and Conflict chapters, I strongly suggest this writer reconsider how little actual data they're providing. Yes, it's a fine line to walk between withholding everything to generate intrigue and telling too much. This example runs into both issues, one after the other, in the two narratives. However, for readers to get personally invested in Delania's experience, they should know more about the set-up—what she's doing, why, and why it matters to her *personally*. I'd also suggest the author tighten their POV so we're in Delania's close-third experience, rather than head-hopping into Michael's perspective as well. Otherwise, the logistical details and play-by-play choreography overshadow the substance of the opening scene. This writing style is also present in the second part of the sample, as we shift focus to Ben. While the Delania section is mysterious and intense (though readers aren't quite grounded in the logic and context yet), the Ben passage represents an energetic comedown. This is a slow-moving sequence, spotlighting a retiring gentleman, and immediately strikes a low-stakes tone. When these two are taken together, it might be tough for readers to characterize the overall pacing, scope, and potential forward plot thrust of the story.

SAMPLE 7: JASPER, AL
HORROR

CADE LOTT

Chapter One | Something Beckons

This[1] isn't a town that demands attention.[2] It's a place worn smooth by time and circumstance, content to settle into the quiet hum of its own existence.[3] Traveling east on ~~18th~~ [Eighteenth] Street toward Alabama Avenue, on the left, the Jasper Public Library[4] stands sentinel, its brick exterior, dignified but weary, its windows like watchful eyes holding the stories of generations.[5]

Across the street, a faded Coca-Cola sign advertises

---

1. Very horror-appropriate chapter heading!
2. Nice opening line. Sure, this is telling about the character of the town, but "demands" is a strong verb, and readers will be curious.
3. Love this writing!
4. A dangling modifier (see the Recurring Notes chapter). I know that "Traveling … (one sees) the Jasper Public Library" is phrasing someone might use. However, the writer is also technically saying "the Jasper Public Library" is "traveling east" and I'd hate for them to trip over some muddy grammar right out of the gate.
5. Windows are often compared to eyes, and I worry this image is a bit obvious, given that libraries hold stories as a matter of course. Though there's some strong writing, let me come in and relieve this creator from the pressure of having to come up with an image for everything. Only use an image when it can offer something fresh and enhance reader understanding.

refreshment[6] from its perch atop a one-story diner, [whose] chrome gleams [have] long succumbed to the relentless humidity. The[7] woman rolls her Electra 225 to a stop—top down, drinking the last rays of the setting sun.[8] She and the car,[—]a sleek, black machine, pretty to look at, and hiding a powerful engine inside,[—]have traveled thousands of miles together.[9]

Thick air, scented with honeysuckle and exhaust fumes, carries the **distant** rumble of a train and the rhythmic hammering from a construction site **on the outskirts**. A stray dog, ribs showing beneath matted fur, trots down the sidewalk and casts a wary glance at a rusted pickup truck as it sputters by.[10] A pedestrian crosses the street in no particular hurry. The woman's eyes move over him like a connoisseur appraising a fine sculpture[11]—each detail absorbed, cataloged, and stored away in the vault of her memory.[12] She'll see him again, but for now she'll savor the anticipation.[13]

---

6. A bit wordy. Maybe "swings from its perch" or similar.

7. Maybe "A woman," since we don't have our eye on a specific one yet?

8. Dangling modifier again. The "top down" modifies the Electra, but "drinking the last rays" suggests the woman is performing this action, not the car.

9. We get a flyover of the town from a seeming omniscient narrator. Now we zoom in on the woman and offer context only she would know. I suggest clarifying the POV from the get-go. Are we seeing this town through her eyes? Or is there going to be a narrator hanging back and viewing everything (including the woman) at a distance?

10. I feel like we're hitting all of the vintage Americana clichés (down to the Coke sign) at this point. Move along with the action. Show a few select details instead of emptying the entire imagination arsenal, at least for the opening.

11. An odd choice of image given the surroundings, unless this is meant to convey that she's very fashionable and sophisticated while the town … is not. Is this dissonance intentional?

12. Need to clarify if there's also the image of the "connoisseur apprising"? Let the chosen description stand alone.

13. And? So? What was the result of her appraisal? What draws her to him? Otherwise, notice we're zooming out in time to this hazy "If only I knew then what I know now" type of teasing. Tension should come from the present moment. Jumping into an undefined future to comment on the present is cheating. Stick to this instant and what the character knows now (see the Common Opening Clichés chapter). If there isn't enough tension, and the writer finds they're tempted to tease, they should work on creating more conflict in *this* scene. In many of the first page samples in this

A siren wails in the distance.[14] The woman shifts the Electra into drive, its engine purrs like a contented cat.[15] Her gaze sweeps across the scene once more, taking in unassuming facades. Ordinary people, going about their ordinary lives.[16]

In Jasper, the past hangs heavy in the air, and the future unfolds at its own slow pace.[17]

---

guide, the writers go backward in time. Here, we're going forward, which is less common, but also pulls us out of the current action.

14. We've already covered distant sounds. Unless the siren is coming for her and this is a hint of danger, omit it.

15. Not sure we need to define "purrs like a cat." Leave it at "purrs," though this is a common description for a well-oiled engine.

16. All of this is well established, which is a credit to the writing and storytelling. Trust that these ideas are coming across and do less.

17. The slow pace and backward-looking culture are both established as well. The writer might like this turn of phrase but it's not needed. Instead, give us more present action. The woman observing—in addition to the narrator observing—add up to a relatively passive present moment.

SAMPLE 7 OVERVIEW

This is an atmospheric opening full of strong and evocative writing. There's actually a conversation currently happening in publishing about the role overall "vibes" play in plot and storytelling. Some readers, especially in the romance and fantasy spheres, don't want high-stakes plot or conflict, and select their next book based on promised vibes, tone, and style. However, I'd argue that we need some kind of action to underpin those vibes in a horror project, and the writer shouldn't try to get by on mood alone. Horror also plays a lot with suspense and tension. I don't want to be told that something ominous is happening, I want to feel it from the details the writer chooses to describe, an edge to the syntax, or the presence of something overtly creepy or disturbing. Someone is watching the intersection from a high window, their face shrouded in shadow. The car rolls away and there's a hand dangling out of the trunk, for example (though that's a pretty familiar image). The scene-setting itself can be left to its own devices without quite so much repetition or explanation. Once the environment is established, do something with it that'll hint at the larger plot. For example, the omniscient POV holds readers at a distance. Is the woman going to be important to the story, or are we merely doing a flyover? The writing and setting will pull audiences in, but it's also important to offer a clear perspective and character focus. Horror is all about the dark side of human nature as it plays out in a dangerous situation, and offering a character who'll act as the reader's proxy for empathy and relatability might add to the tension and conflict this writer will create down the line. The reader's potential engagement with the woman will swing one way if they suspect she's a future victim, and go in a very different direction if they sense they're watching a potential perpetrator.

SAMPLE 8: SANDALWOOD AND ROSE
HISTORICAL

VANITHA SANKARAN

Chapter 1 | August 1953 | The French colony of Pondicherry, India

The[1] future of colonial India, Chandana's mother had always told her, was never going to lie in the dancing arts of their ancestors.[2] The British looked on classical dance forms with disgust, deeming ~~their styles~~ [them] **too sensual, too provocative**. The French, who had wrested control of several territories across the country, didn't disagree.[3]

---

1. Great data points in the header to orient readers right away.
2. Awk. phrasing here. We're getting a lot of information: telescoping into the future; meeting a character's mother; and learning about ancestral dancing … except the dancing is being dismissed. I worry this opening asks readers to juggle a lot of material (some factual, some emotional), and this can be a difficult entry into the story.
3. There are very few circumstances where a double negative is clear and effective. This could be more straightforward.

"Have faith," her mother had assured.[4] "One day, when we are free, the entire world will see the beauty of what we do."

One day…

Fisting her hands, Chandana sped up her morning constitutional along Serenity Beach. Her mother had lived[5] <u>long enough to see</u> India win independence but hadn't <u>seen</u> true freedom. Chandana had continued teaching at her late mother's school <u>long enough to see</u> students through the term but hadn't been able to parlay that into the apprenticeship she needed.[6] Enrolling at the new Franco <u>dance school</u> wasn't the only <u>way</u> forward[,] but it was the best <u>way</u> to advance[7] and stay close to her grieving father.

"It should have been different, Amma."[8] It should have been her and her mother <u>dancing</u> together, at their <u>dance school</u> and beyond. Not her fighting for a spot on a stage paid for by the French.[9]

Despite India securing her freedom from the British,[10] French rule in this colony still lingered, out of a love for all things Indian,

---

4. Notice that we're not in the present moment yet. The past perfect ("had verb") suggests we're in a flashback to the past. Meanwhile, readers are in limbo. Also, avoid "said" synonyms (see the Recurring Notes chapter).
5. If we start with the distant past, clarify when we are now relative to the memory once we're post-transition and in the story's present. (Also, since we begin in the past, is the conversation with Mom in 1953, or is the morning constitutional in 1953? The history of Indian independence suggests the latter, but some readers might not know the context.) Consider grounding the reader more firmly (see the Recurring Notes chapter).
6. If she's teaching at her family's school, why does she need an apprenticeship? Or does she then have to go apprentice elsewhere?
7. In her career? In her craft? I'm still missing how Chandana feels about the style of dance they do. We know Mom's feelings and cultural attitudes, but what about the POV protagonist's relationship to it?
8. Is she taking to Mom's memory while walking? And did Mom die suddenly and unexpectedly? It seems like Chandana regrets the recent past, but readers don't yet know enough about Mom's death to understand the emotional nuance.
9. "Franco" could be a name or it could mean "French," but it's unclear what the conflict is until this line.
10. This has already been recently mentioned in the "lived long enough" paragraph.

their Franco leaders claimed.[11] Only, Pondicherry's once-and-still overlords[12] kept to themselves, living their lives in the stately houses and **quiet streets** of White Town, as the French Quarter was popularly known. Named for the Franco architectural style that involved white columns, white walls, even whitewashed roads, the big pastel villas here **set a sleepy mood**.[13] Large leafy trees added shade along the roads, but like the many potted plants gracing the front walkways of every house, they seemed more for decoration than appreciation.[14] Most of these homes were guarded by tall gates, often closed, so different than the Indian-style verandas in Heritage Town that encouraged idle visits, reading breaks, a space to have hot coffee and fried snacks while watching the world.[15]

The French might live here[,] but they seemed oblivious to the town around them, uncaring about the arguments against them.[16] Even now, just as the sun peeked over the ocean horizon, the daily protests were audible.[17]

"*L'Inde sans les Britanniques, L'Inde sans les Français!* India without the British, India without the French!"

If these protestors actually aimed to disrupt this unnatural quiet that somehow existed despite the surrounding cacophony of bleating goats and lowing cows, bells and church knells, they would be greatly disappointed.[18] All of India had been sliced into pieces

---

11. A lot of references to the French, too. This writer doesn't have to spell out every detail of India's post-colonial history right away. Is there a way to streamline the progression from British to "independent" to "lingering French" without mentioning it in several places and in several ways in such close proximity?
12. I can really appreciate the difference between "technically independent" and "free," but I worry this phrasing only confuses the above issue.
13. This echoes the "quiet streets" description.
14. Good scene-setting, but I worry we're losing the character and present action.
15. Nice. I like this contrast but I also think we're spending too much time on a historical setting flyover.
16. The split between the two cultures is clear.
17. Put this into action. Maybe Chandana has to cut through a throng of protestors, etc.
18. Saying something simple in a complicated way. I like the sensory details, though.

between Independence and Partition, and yet the French simply carried on as usual.[19]

By the time she reached *Le Pensionnat de Jeunes Filles*, sweaty and out of breath, the muggy weather had grown insolent.[20] An ugly storm had been brewing on the ocean horizon for days, kicking up the humidity.[21] Every breath she sucked in was wet and salty. It was the monsoon, threatening from afar but till now only spouting in short tantrums.[22]

Its looming vexation built in the space between her ribs.[23]

---

19. This restates the idea of the French keeping themselves separate.
20. Nice.
21. Need to restate if we already saw the muggy weather intensifying in the previous sentence?
22. Similar to "An ugly storm had been brewing on the ocean horizon for days." The sense of place is great, but the character, action, and context could be stronger and more anchored in the present.
23. The weather as objective correlative is a common gambit. I worry it's perhaps too familiar, especially in a story opening (see the Common Opening Clichés chapter).

SAMPLE 8 OVERVIEW

The writing captures the sense of place, and we get a lot of deep historical information and description right away. However, this can be a double-edged sword, as it also seems like the writer might feel too much pressure to get complicated history, setting, the Mom's backstory, and the character's personal and familial relationship to dance established. While there are some mentions of what Chandana is doing in the current moment, the reader's sense of why her movements matter, and who she really is (aside from her contrast with Mom) is peripheral to other information. What's the event that triggers this opening scene? Can it have to do with finding out something about Mom (if this relationship will be central to the story) or show Chandana interfacing with dance in some way? What's presently going on for her regardless of Mom, the French, or Indian history? To be clear, all of these elements are important to the plot, setting, and character development, and this historical novel cannot be written without them. I'm not asking the writer to divorce the character from her context. However, this context can be established as we go, and without a strong character acting in a present moment, I worry we won't get far enough into the story itself to see these elements play out on the page.

SAMPLE 9: UNTITLED
HISTORICAL ACTION/ADVENTURE

E. ROBERTS

October 20, 1714 | Boston

Samuel[1] counted thirty-six newly-[ ]arrived[2] slaves, nearly all women, as they disembarked from the ship.[3] The bulk of the men and children, he knew, had [already][4] been brought to one or more islands in the West Indies—probably Jamaica, New Providence or Nevis—and forced to work on plantations. As the [remaining][5] unwilling arrivals marched [along the wharf] in front of Samuel along the wharf, the[ir] **iron shackles created a dissonant symphony**—obscuring the rhythmic sound of waves lapping against the ships' hulls and gentle sea breezes luffing the sails—**as the chains clanged and groaned like untuned instruments**.

Everyone on the dock—sailors, longshoremen and fishermen— had been pushed back by the crew of the slave ship to prevent any interference from the public. Samuel snarled at the man who nailed

---

1. A good use of a chapter heading, especially in a historical work.
2. Nitpick: Never hyphenate words with an "-ly" suffix.
3. Nice description, though the context is disturbing.
4. Inserted this to convey that they've previously disembarked.
5. My effort to shore up the same bit of clarification.

a poster to the piling next to him announcing the upcoming slave auction. Turning his gaze toward the unfortunates, he met the eyes of any slave ~~that~~ [who] looked his way, hoping to impart some sort of message like an apology or, at least, an explanation ~~as to~~ [for] why he had been spared ~~enslavement~~.[6] Instead, he was sure that his eyes transmitted only a sense of hopelessness or pity. He wondered what they thought of him. On the outside, they would see a Black man, whose freedom they could resent, but could they tell he was not an African by birth?[7]

Sapped of all strength and infested with sores, the fettered captives[8] **appeared unhealthy, as if the elements of disease clung to them**.[9] Many walked naked through the cold, autumn air, reeking of sweat, feces, and vomit—the pain of loss and separation visible on their faces.[10] For a few fortunate slaves, the remains of tattered clothing hung from their thin frames.

As a younger, naive person, Samuel would stand on the harbor's embankment and stare out over the horizon, wondering what ~~lie~~ [lay] beyond Boston. For the colonists who were escaping religious persecution, the sea ~~was an agent of~~ [signified][11] freedom,

---

6. Taken to mean he's Black himself? I'm torn on whether to introduce this detail sooner, or if this reveal adds to the reader's experience. Also, if he's Black in this time and place, would he be punished for snarling at a presumably white person? Would he be afraid to act out with such a stark reminder of what's possible right in front of him? Even if he's not currently enslaved, he's still near the bottom of the social hierarchy in this historical period.

7. This is implied in the set-up. Maybe cut right to the idea that he's not African-born.

8. I'm not sure this writer needs to find so many ways around saying they're slaves (though the current terminology is "enslaved people," this would not be historically accurate). Sure, we want to avoid word echo, but we also don't want to burn through the entire thesaurus coming up with increasingly obscure words.

9. Not everything needs an image to make it more meaningful. If they're "infested with sores" and "appeared unhealthy," then "as if the elements of disease clung to them" doesn't add much (see the Recurring Notes chapter).

10. This seems like an understatement. This writer has obviously chosen a tremendously painful part of history to work with. I worry this doesn't do justice to the horror these characters have witnessed and what real people experienced.

11. Why use four words when one will do?

a means to liberation[12] and a formidable boundary offering protection from distant tyrannies.[13]

Samuel, now twenty-five, judged the sea more harshly with each passing year, having watched similar scenes replay week after week. To him, the sea was a means to enslave, an instrument of death and the odious link that united the subjugated ~~to~~ [and] their oppressors.[14] The recent completion of Long Wharf[15] hastened the ritual by bringing hundreds of captured souls a half mile closer to their brutal enslavement.

As the last of the slaves entered the warehouse to await the next horror, the onlookers became active workers once again, sending Long Wharf[16] into a bustle of activity. Samuel ripped the poster from the piling and tossed it into the harbor.[17]

Arriving at the Lotus, Samuel found six barrels of rum ~~still waited to be loaded~~ [waiting to be loaded][18] into the ship's hold. He mentally prepared himself for the task ahead. Unfortunately, the loading boom, having collapsed under the exhaustive weight of some previously loaded cargo, resisted all attempts at repair.[19] A crippled block and tackle was a **setback—a minor complication— not a catastrophe.**[20] The barrels would be loaded onto the ship even if they ~~have~~ [had] to be brought on board[21] the hard way. Samuel,

---

12. Necessary if "freedom" was just used?
13. This also goes back to the idea of "freedom." Freedom from what? Tyranny, especially given this historical context. But the point is well made.
14. I worry the imagery is too obvious—it explains the theme instead of letting it arise naturally in the reader's mind. I'd avoid this kind of overt explanation, especially when it comes to big ideas like freedom vs. enslavement.
15. Good historical detail.
16. Maybe "the pier" to avoid the word echo? (Though I confess I don't know the difference between a pier, wharf, or dock!)
17. He's technically free, but in this society, I do wonder again if he'd be this bold. White onlookers could see this and "put him in his place" for his skin color alone.
18. I've rephrased as the original was a bit awkward, but this is a small tweak.
19. Saying something simple in a complicated way.
20. Three ways of saying the same thing.
21. Repeat of "loaded onto the ship." Try and streamline this sentence.

committing to the difficult task,[22] rolled the barrels up the gangplank—made steep by the high tide—and ignored the disadvantage gravity provided.[23] He preferred to complete a strenuous task rather than leave a job unfinished. He would do everything in his power to ensure the *Lotus* would be ready to leave tomorrow night.[24]

---

22. Repeats "He mentally prepared himself for the task ahead" from earlier in this paragraph.
23. This is also a very simple idea but phrased in a complex way.
24. Is he a dockworker? Does he work on the ship? Is he just helping out around town? I'm asking because we have a statement of objective here (to get the ship on its way) but I'm not sure if he has any personal investment in the task or if he's just doing his job. What are the *personal* stakes here? Maybe clarify his role sooner.

SAMPLE 9 OVERVIEW

This historical project establishes some stark contrasts right away, between African-born Black enslaved people and a free American-born Black man, and between freedom and captivity. But notice that Samuel doesn't actually interface with the unfolding scene much. He's observing. On the one hand, this is appropriate in a historical project, as the writer faces some pressure to outline information about the period and describe the time setting *and* physical location. But other than observing and interacting with a dock worker, what does Samuel do in the present moment? We get plenty of nods to theme, lots of data, and some clear and proficient writing. And? So? The tension seems to come from Samuel wanting to get the boat unloaded, but is this because he's eager to do his job, to get it over with so he can leave, or to get away from the horrific reminder of another slave ship docking? Why does the story start today? Why is Samuel our focal character? How is he personally invested in the scene at hand? The story elements are clear. Now I'd love to take them all a step further and make some meaning from them for the protagonist (and, by extension, the reader).

SAMPLE 10: SALLY'S STORY
CONTEMPORARY

ANONYMOUS

Just when I thought I was going to scream from the pain, the server approached our table and asked Malcolm if we needed anything else.[1] He immediately lifted the fork he'd been pressing into my thumb[2] and asked for another beer[3] and the check. I headed for the restroom. Thankfully, it was empty. As I held my throbbing hand under ~~the~~ cold water, a woman came in.[4] She stood beside me, her

---

1. The intensity of the emotion really doesn't match the apparent setting, so I'm immediately intrigued!
2. My expectations shift again! Now I'm interested, though it's unclear if there's danger here or it's maybe two frat boys goofing around. (Obviously the title and pitch would set expectations correctly, but other interpretations are possible based solely on the pages.)
3. This detail turns the screw again. Notice how readers have to keep correcting their mental image of what's happening. These descriptions could be resequenced slightly.
4. I'm surprised the narrator is a woman (though the title sends this message), which suddenly turns this scene dark. Maybe have her react to the pain in interiority (and offer a bit more context) instead of simply naming it ("the pain") to start.

concerned look reflected in the mirror.[5] I could feel myself blushing as I looked away.[6]

She wasn't much taller than five feet, at least six inches shorter than me, and probably close to the same age, perhaps a year older, maybe about twenty-six.[7]

"~~You know~~ [You] don't have to tolerate that sort of treatment, ~~you know?~~" she said.[8]

"You don't understand." I had hoped[9] no one had noticed. Only someone who had been in an abusive relationship ~~can~~ could understand what ~~it's~~ [it was] like, and how difficult it was to get out.[10]

"I <u>understand</u>. <u>I know what it's like</u>. You don't deserve to be treated like that. I know you think you've[11] no choice, but I'm going to give you one." She handed me a small piece of paper. "If you decide to leave him, I can help you."

"Caitlin's Nail Salon?" I stared at the sticker[12] in my hand. There was also a phone number and nothing else.

"Keep that in your purse. If he sees it, he won't consider it ~~to be~~

---

5. This clause doesn't make sense with the semi-colon. I read this as description attached to the first clause, rather than "reflected" as the verb and "look" as the subject. (That'd be the incorrect use of "reflected.")
6. This is rather external, yet we're in first-person POV. Also, does she need to feel herself blushing when she can see herself in the mirror?
7. I'm not sure this is done as well as it could be. It's too obviously a physical description of the protagonist, but the oddly specific data feels shoehorned (plus this makes readers do some math to figure out her demographic details).
8. This read better as a statement than a question to me.
9. Consider avoiding the past perfect tense (see the Recurring Notes chapter).
10. Maintain the past tense throughout, even for generalizations. It tends to be cleaner when the rest of the narration is already in the past.
11. Technically correct, but this isn't commonly said outside of certain regional dialects.
12. Nitpick: A sticker isn't usually paper but vinyl. If the character can tell it's a sticker here, she'd be unlikely to mistake it for a piece of paper one line above.

threatening.[13] **Call me if you need help. I'll help you**; it's what I do. You can get out of this situation safely if you want to. We operate an escape route for victims of domestic violence."[14]

Realizing I must['ve] look[ed] like a fish, opening and closing my mouth but making no sound,[15] I **shut my mouth and said nothing; I didn't know what to say**. I put the sticker in my purse and hurried out. Malcolm was already in a bad mood. I didn't want to give him anything more to be angry about. He still had an almost full glass of beer in front of him. I sat down and sipped my water, watching the woman from the restroom leave. I guessed her name was Caitlin.

Malcolm waved to the server, gulped down his beer and stood up. As soon as the bill arrived,[16] he grabbed it with one hand and my wrist with the other, and almost dragged me towards the cashier. As we drove home, the silence was deafening.[17] I stared out the window, trying not to make a sound that might trigger his temper.[18] Just before we turned the corner onto our street, I spotted Caitlin. She was going into a duplex set ~~a little~~ back from the road. I guess it shouldn't have surprised me, considering she'd been at the restaurant, [a local joint].[19] ~~It made sense that she lived close by.~~ As we got out of the car and went into our apartment,[20] I prayed Malcolm had calmed down. He hadn't.[21]

---

13. Some of this writing is grammatically correct but also sounds more formal than organic speech. Read this aloud and rephrase.
14. While it's not clear exactly what she does, it's becoming clear that she helps abused women and wants the protagonist to get out of the relationship. Here, she's starting to repeat these same ideas.
15. Again, why does she have to imagine what she looks like if she can easily see her own reflection? The mouth agape/fish description to indicate surprise is also a familiar image.
16. Why does he wave down the server for the bill when he already asked for "a beer and a check" in the first paragraph? Pin down the logistics.
17. A familiar image, I'm afraid.
18. That she's scared of him and doesn't want to make him angry is already clear.
19. Trust readers to catch on.
20. Getting into some play-by-play here (see the Recurring Notes chapter).
21. Does the writer want to show the abuse in action? There are two schools of thought on showing gratuitous violence or abuse. On the one hand, we don't want to

Two hours later, I was banging on what I hoped was Caitlin's back door. Although I still had her sticker ~~with the phone number on~~ [and number], I no longer had my phone. Malcolm had smashed it. I hammered on the door again and heard footsteps and ~~the~~ [a] key turning. As the door opened,[22] I almost fell into the small kitchen. Caitlin caught my arm, preventing me from hitting the floor.[23]

"Help me, please!"[24]

Caitlin guided me to a chair and turned on the lights.

"He did this to you?"[25]

"Yes, my boyfriend Malcolm."

"What's your name?"

"Sally."

"Hi[,] Sally, I'm a nurse[,] and I need to make sure you don't have any serious injuries, other than what we can see."

I hadn't <u>looked</u> in the mirror, but guessed from how much it hurt, and the blood all over my clothes, I must have <u>looked</u> bad. She examined my entire body and concluded that there were no broken bones or apparent internal damage.[26]

---

glorify his actions or trigger readers. On the other, if someone is going to write about domestic abuse, they can't really keep the violence "off screen" and sanitize it, since that's not true to a victim's experience. I find it odd that we completely skip over this in a seemingly serious portrait of domestic assault.

22. Need to explain? It's clear someone is coming to open the door.

23. Need to spell out that being caught while falling prevents the fall?

24. Let's get into the protagonist's head a bit more. What prompted her to decide she'd had enough? That she would, in fact, seek help, when she initially didn't want to? That this episode was the breaking point (another argument for actually showing part of it)? What's going on in her head as she asks for help for possibly the first time? All of this is the juice of this kind of narrative but is missing here.

25. Narration of a character's action and the same character's dialogue go in the same paragraph. Put this with Caitlin's line, above.

26. This is suggested by Caitlin's dialogue, which tells Sally what's about to happen. I worry we're not getting deeply enough into Sally's experience, though. If she was just violently beaten, would she tolerate a physical exam without recoiling? Etc.

"Do you want me to take you to the hospital just to be certain?"[27]

----

27. I hardly ever give this note about a story opening, but I feel like the story is moving too quickly. Slow down and spend more time in Sally's experience and on the decision to escape. I'm afraid one can't really tell a narrative about this kind of situation without "going there," at least in part. There's a certain expectation of vulnerability and authenticity that readers might find missing in this version.

SAMPLE 10 OVERVIEW

My primary note relates to implied reader expectations. This is a contemporary realistic story about a woman in an abusive relationship who decides to save herself with the help of an ally. Readers drawn to this subject matter will be expecting deep access to the protagonist's perspective because the minute-by-minute emotions she's experiencing as she navigates her situation are extremely relevant to this target audience. A story about surviving abuse usually hinges on the protagonist's courage, redemption, growth, and change. As such, we need access to the main character's interiority throughout. That it's almost entirely missing is an issue, and a lot of the other notes stem directly from the lack of POV access. (This also contradicts the writer's choice to use first-person narration, which is meant to offer readers the closest possible psychic distance to a character's experience.) Since we're not inhabiting the character's head too much, the plot also moves very quickly. Sally's decision to take Caitlin up on her offer and seek help reads like the inciting incident of the novel (a one-way door through which the character chooses to pass, which ends up truly kicking off the plot). In a women's fiction project with an anticipated word count of 60,000 to 80,000, it's very unusual to have the first major plot beat on the second page. Sally has theoretically wanted to escape many times before, and she's always talked herself out of it. She was even resistant to the idea when Caitlin offered her card. Why does she decide to finally do it today? A victim of domestic violence is never more endangered than they are as they attempt to leave. This is probably the most high-stakes choice Sally has made in her life, but readers aren't privy to a single thought, consideration, question, or emotion (other than fear, which almost goes without saying) as she takes this enormously consequential step. This will not satisfy the type of audience who's drawn to this type of narrative. Similarly, it's a very personal decision to show an instance of abuse on the page, for the reasons I detailed in the sample comments. However, implied reader expectations come into play here as well. If we're going to go into the perspective of a character who has these experiences, are we telling the full story by completely glossing over them? This writer might decide not to, and that's valid. But if we're not showing the conflict on the page, and we're not providing interiority about the character's experiences, what will make up the bulk of this manuscript?

SAMPLE 11: THE SEAGULL'S NEST
CONTEMPORARY

BUXTON MANNING

Dust Bunnies Reproduce Faster in Winter

Eve hadn't been in the house for more than a minute;[1] barely enough time for her to say, "Hi," give him a quick peck on the cheek, and hang up her coat.[2] Yet **Leo could feel his stomach clench already**.[3] He knew what was coming.[4]

His daughter[5] disappeared into the kitchen, where she always began, though no room in the house would be safe.[6] He wondered if he should wait for her to say something[7] before confronting her,

---

1. Awk. phrasing here, a bit wordy for what this writer wants to express, especially given the note, below, about matching phrasing to action.
2. Consider mimetic writing here (see the Recurring Notes chapter). The movement is quick, but the sentence describing it drags.
3. A physical cliché (see the Recurring Notes chapter).
4. We start on Eve then switch to Leo, who seems to be the primary POV character. Make it clearer whose lens we're seeing the action through, especially to start, so readers have their expectations set.
5. Shouldn't she be defined as such when we first get her name? Avoid needless imprecision.
6. Good tension! This raises some questions.
7. But she did. She technically already said "hi," per the previous paragraph, so this is a bit inconsistent.

drawing out his stomach agony, or [if he should][8] just go out there and get it over with.[9]

He had barely completed his thought[10] before her voice rang out. "What are all these containers in here?"

Nuts. Better deal with it and try to cut her off before—[11]

"And why do you have so many pints of ice cream? You know the doctor said you need to watch your cholesterol."

It was only going to get worse.[12] Leo pulled the lever of his recliner, shot himself upright,[13] and headed for the kitchen. "Just sit still until I get there,"[14] he called, knowing she would neither sit nor stay still as he could hear her heels ~~click~~ [clicking] on the tile floor, no doubt headed for the pantry.[15]

Sure enough, ~~the next two sounds~~ [he heard] ~~were~~ the door opening, then Eve.[16] "What the hell?"

He quickened his pace and got to <u>the pantry</u> just as she bent over, dropping to her knees[17] and pawing through his wine bottles

---

8. I'd remind readers what the set-up to the question is since this is a longer sentence.

9. Good spike of tension!

10. This doesn't ring true, as we've been privy to many of his thoughts already.

11. There's a bit of pacing dissonance here. He keeps insisting that he wants to confront her, that everything is happening so quickly, and he wants to cut her off— yet he doesn't, and she's already ahead of him. This would be more legible if we knew the stakes of him speaking up. Why doesn't he say something? (We don't even need to know what their conflict is about yet.)

12. That he dreads this is already clear. Instead, give us the stakes. What's the worst thing he worries will happen? (And if this is so fraught, why is she over there? Did he try to keep her from coming and she insisted?)

13. Great action! I would've liked to know he was here when I first pictured him, though. Maybe spend another sentence on the lay of the land initially.

14. But she's not sitting or still, so this doesn't make much sense.

15. Avoid the awk. synecdoche of "her heels ... headed for the pantry."

16. Trim this up a bit.

17. Need both indicators of her lowering herself? Readers can fill in these details if we see her kneel (or similar).

lined up along the bottom of <u>the pantry</u>. He braced himself for the onslaught when she stood up.[18]

"Honestly," she barked,[19] "is *this* how you plan to spend your off[-] time next week?"

It was a slap that he felt didn't deserve a response,[20] and he knew it wouldn't do a bit of good anyway, but the words were out before he could stop himself.[21] "Grocery Outlet has a [monthly wine] sale ~~on wine once a month~~. You save ten percent, so I stocked up, but **I won't have time for that next week. I've got stuff to do** before the end of the year."[22]

She harrumphed, then turned and headed for his bedroom.[23] He considered following her, then realized it would only give her an audience to play to,[24] so he stayed by the still-open pantry door.

Eve didn't let that bother her.[25] He could hear[26] her rifle through his drawers, then the closet. There was silence, which he initially took as a good sign. But the longer it went on, the more worried he got, anticipating some sort of blowup or blowout any minute.[27] Eventually, he stopped listening for it and headed back to

---

18. He has been bracing himself since the beginning. This is well established.
19. Some "said" synonyms (see the Recurring Notes chapter).
20. He was expecting this, so why does it still land like a slap? Also, if he's an active alcoholic, instead of being stung by this implication, he might become defensive, downplay it, or turn the mirror back on her. To become upset about it would mean he's admitting to having an issue, which is tough to do from the throes of addiction.
21. Even if he's playing out a defense mechanism, make this a choice, rather than an automatic action. The former teaches readers more about the character than the latter (see the Recurring Notes chapter).
22. Two ways of getting at the same idea. Need both?
23. Was he dreading Eve discovering the wine the most? For how much he worried, it seems she was very easy to disarm.
24. Where was this rational thinking when he rushed after her into the kitchen, though?
25. This technically goes into her POV. We can only know what bothers her or not if we're her head, and so far, we've only had close third-person POV access to Leo. Avoid head-hopping, as it signals potential POV issues (see the Recurring Notes chapter).
26. Some filler description (see the Recurring Notes chapter).
27. This is the source of tension so far, so the repetition doesn't add much.

his recliner,[28] but Eve was in hot pursuit,[29] holding a brown and white sweater from the closet in front of his face.

"Dad, just <u>look</u> at this nice cardigan I made for you two <u>Christmases</u> ago. It <u>looks</u> barely worn. You could wear it on <u>Christmas</u>. It'll <u>look</u> nice on you."[30]

"But the wool makes me itch. I told you that."

"And I saw dust bunnies under the bed. When was the last time you vacuumed?"[31]

Leo shook his head in disbelief. "I did it last Sunday like I always do," he said, gritting his teeth. "The dust bunnies reproduce faster in winter because I can't open the windows. Seems counterintuitive, but there they are."

Eve made a face and crossed her arms tightly to her chest, then pointed a finger at him. *Crap, here it comes*, he thought. *She's been on the warpath a lot lately, and she needn't be worried.* He braced himself for the next volley.

---

28. And? So? Has he decided anything? Did anything change?
29. She seems to be taking her time rifling around, so why does she immediately storm out? I'd suggest less choreography and more actual conflict. His shame? Their relationship? Dig a little bit deeper and plant some seeds.
30. This dialogue doesn't quite ring true between two people who know one another well. If she's mad that he hasn't worn it, let that come to the forefront. She might spend a few lines acting frustrated, rather than putting on the charm offensive right away.
31. The dynamic is very well established—she's invading his space and making him feel ashamed or criticized. And? So? It seems as if this type of interaction has happened many times before. What makes *today* noteworthy? Why does the story start with this particular visit? The writer might want to suggest the answer to this question, even if it's just a hint.

SAMPLE 11 OVERVIEW

Why today? Amp up Leo's specific dread or expectations about Eve's visit, then weave in a sense of any bigger ramifications. The conflict between the two characters is very present on the page, but the context for said conflict is missing. Does she regularly come over and pick his life apart? Is he getting sick of it? That's implied, but it could be framed up more clearly. If this is the first time she's visiting after not seeing him for three years and if he has some secrets which bring up a lot of shame, contextualize that on the page. But if this is their usual routine, why does the story start the way it does, and with the current instance? Bickering is not necessarily conflict because it's low stakes. Siblings ribbing one another, spouses sniping back and forth, adult children and parents grating together —these are all static situations, even if they feel contentious. Something about this visit needs to represent a shift in the characters' dynamic, and to change the status quo. From there, we can get a sense of what Leo truly values, what he wants (other than to be left alone), and what the ramifications of Eve's intrusion into his space might mean for the larger plot.

SAMPLE 12: UNTITLED

UPMARKET/HIGH-CONCEPT

ANNIE ASHDOWN

Chapter One

At 10 a.m., I stomp onto ~~the~~ [a] set that looks like a tornado hit it.[1] My Chanel suit is squeezing me in all the wrong places, making me feel like a stuffed sausage.[2] The polished floor echoes with the clatter of my expensive heels,[3] trying to drown out the growling protests of my bloated stomach from last night's ~~binge on pasta~~ [pasta binge].[4]

Everyone stops what they're doing to gawk at me, probably

---

1. To tighten things up, I'd do "a set that looks like …" rather than "the set" here, or "onto the set, which looks like …" Otherwise, an intriguing opening line!
2. These two descriptions convey the same thing. This is prime real estate so avoid repetition.
3. The "Chanel suit" mention does a lot of this work already. I wonder if the first person POV is clashing with the way this writer is choosing to have the character describe herself (see the Recurring Notes chapter).
4. Changed slightly to make this description snappier.

wondering if I'm here to save the day or just to add more drama[5] to their mess.[6]

My trusted team of stylists buzz around me, adjusting every inch of my appearance to perfection.[7] Nick, my talented hair and makeup artist,[8] delicately touches up my already flawless look.[9]

This[10] is my destiny, apparently. Surrounded by a swarm of stylists who could probably dissect the latest fashion trends in their sleep,[11] and Nick, the wizard of hair and makeup,[12] meticulously perfects every detail on my face.[13] Despite their confidence in me, a seed of uncertainty[14] sprouts within me. Can I truly measure up to the pedestal they've placed me on? The weight of these doubts bounces around my mind like a pinball,[15] ready to crack the facade of calm I'm desperately trying to maintain.[16]

---

5. "save the day" and "add more drama" are both vague. This is a missed opportunity to add context about what's going on in the scene, and the character's relationship to the crew (I'm guessing actor/producer/director but that's just a first assumption).

6. "more drama" suggests there's already some conflict going on. Need to clarify "to their mess"?

7. This description is a bit generic for what one might imagine stylists do. That said, stylists (clothes), MUAs (make-up artists), and hair stylists (hair) are all different and many of these functions would take place in a separate trailer rather than on set, with the exception of touch-ups. Small details like this can really make or break the reader's first impression.

8. Depending on the set, these are different disciplines.

9. This restates "adjusting every inch of my appearance to perfection."

10. Which part? Being styled? Unclear what "this" means.

11. The multiple stylists are mentioned in the previous paragraph already, though we only name Nick.

12. Established.

13. Third mention of people tweaking her appearance.

14. Dangling modifier (see the Recurring Notes chapter).

15. A familiar image that doesn't add much to the notion of "bounces around."

16. This establishes the same idea that there's inner tension, but instead of repeating that notion, make it specific. Why is the character experiencing doubt? Is it about this role? Her acting abilities? Something else entirely in her personal life?

Eyes ablaze with a stubborn resolve,[17] I brace myself for the day ahead, ready to tackle any obstacles that dare cross my path[18]– but not before indulging in my sacred morning espresso routine. In a flash, Lucy appears, wearing a shy smile as she presents me with my signature coffee concoction:[19] a unique blend of decaf and regular beans[20] swirled together with creamy almond milk. As I luxuriate in the bold flavours dancing on my tongue, a wave of appreciation washes over me[21] for Lucy's meticulous attention to detail. Like so many others vying for success in this cutthroat industry, she sees our partnership as a stepping stone towards her lofty career aspirations.[22]

Sitting back with my coffee, the liquid courage for my public persona,[23] I can't help but drown in a sea of doubt.[24] All those years of grinding to reach the pinnacle of success[25] seem futile as the ratings take a nosedive,[26] hitting me like a ton of bricks[27] à la Marie

---

17. This is her seeing herself from the outside and judging the expression in her eyes, but this is an unnatural way to have a character describe themselves in first-person POV (see the Recurring Notes chapter).
18. "brace myself" is very different from "ready to tackle." Is she having doubts or isn't she? This paragraph clashes with the previous one.
19. If she's not making the coffee and Lucy is, is this really "indulging in *my* … routine" (emphasis mine)?
20. It's a blend of the pressing of those beans, not the beans themselves. This phrasing is a bit imprecise.
21. Avoid naming emotions (see the Recurring Notes chapter).
22. This seems to go into Lucy's POV, though we can't know what she's thinking in someone else's first-person POV unless Lucy has specifically said something to this effect. The character seems to draw a causal relationship between Lucy's attention to detail and her using the protagonist as a stepping stone, but the two don't seem obviously related. Lucy could be a coffee snob, so why assume this is her motive?
23. Explaining the theme here. We've already seen the character getting ready for her day and assuming a bold face.
24. This restates what has already been established without adding any more context. Instead of repeating, try to add layers of meaning. What kind of self-doubt? Why is it triggered today? This leads to the bigger question of "Why does the story start today, of all days?" (see the Recurring Notes chapter).
25. Success is subjective and means different things to different people (and characters). This is a missed opportunity to specify this character's goal.
26. How long has this been going on? The present tense makes it tough to get oriented.
27. A cliché image, I'm afraid.

Antoinette dealing with unrest at Versailles.[28] I take a deep breath, channeling every ounce of resilience within me, and give myself a stern pep talk: "[*Sam Preston, pull yourself together.*]"[29] The path to fame has been paved with **hurdles and very public stumbles**, yet today's uncertainties threaten to eclipse all past victories.[30]

Struggling against the weight of imposter syndrome exacerbated by lingering hangover symptoms and Xanax-induced haze,[31] I approach the crew with a façade of confidence[32] ... [and] vague dread.[33] I emit a delightful, expensive, and alluring aroma. An injection of fabulosity.[34] But look closer. My face naturally settles into a scowl that could scare off puppies.[35] I've mastered the art of flashing a fake grin when needed, **though I guard against laughter to avoid creases**.[36]

The bags under my eyes could rival designer handbags[37] at a high-end fashion show, proof of my exhaustion and weariness.[38]

---

28. Same. This keeps hitting the same information: Things are bad. But other than ratings and imposter syndrome (mentioned in the following paragraph), we don't get specific.
29. This is internal dialogue, not spoken (at least I don't think, if Preston is bent on keeping up appearances). It needs to be formatted in italics, not quotation marks.
30. Ratings tank over time. Did something more specific and sudden happen recently?
31. I'd move on in the present moment and get into plot, rather than continuing to ruminate on her overall state. Whether she's hung over or not, her general mood is very clear.
32. Well established.
33. Same. She's already interfaced with Nick and Lucy, though, so is she only "approaching the crew" now?
34. This restates the idea of the façade.
35. She's seeing herself from the outside, but in first person POV, we tend to have characters see themselves from the inside out.
36. Same idea restated.
37. This gives us a hint about her world, but I'm not entirely sure about comparing bags to ... other kinds of bags.
38. Need to explain what under-eye bags signify, especially given the surrounding context?

Oh, and let's not forget my talent for deception[39]—I've assured Molly, our producer, that I'm steering clear of alcohol for now.[40]

Here I am, fifty-two years old … acting like Snow White, feeding all the fucking birds[41] … I shudder to think what will happen if the boss brings in a co-host, a bubble head[42] millennium,[43] dumb, useless, twat just because the of the figures dropping these past months.[44]

There can be just one star. There's no place for a small, twenty-year-old bottle blonde with a botched nose job in spike heels and full breasts[45] that require no visible means of support turning up on set in a leather mini dress. I can sense the soles of my feet itch with envy[46] and grip my fists. How do I persuade Marcus, the big boss, it would be a massive mistake to bring on a co-host?[47]

---

39. This is established earlier, including in the previous paragraph.

40. If her drinking is an issue and she drank last night, maybe mention this sooner or have Molly corner her in scene and ask if she's been drinking. This will put these ideas into action and raise the stakes.

41. The crew? The fans? Her own expectations? This is a bit of a leap, so I'm not sure I follow.

42. "bobblehead"?

43. "Millenial"?

44. The idea of bad ratings has already been established. I'm looking for something more concrete that might trigger her bad day *today*. Maybe they're having an all-cast meeting and won't tell her what it's about, etc.

45. This isn't parallel. It'd need to be "in spike heels and with full breasts" or the list would need to be reorganized. (I suggest three items per list anyway, especially since Preston's take on a potential new co-anchor was already established in the previous paragraph.)

46. I really like the fresh image of her soles itching, though do we also need to name "envy" here?

47. The writer has introduced quite a few named characters, but we've only really seen Nick and Lucy, and not in action. They've entered and departed rather silently. Molly and Marcus have been alluded to, but consider making them more present. Instead of simply arriving on set and thinking about her life, Preston should be heading to a meeting where she strongly suspects she'll have to plead her case.

SAMPLE 12 OVERVIEW

The character's vibe is very clear, and we're immediately thrust into tension on set. Both of these are good starting points! That said, I'd love to have more set-up for the present moment's conflict. It seems like ratings have been sliding for a while, and Preston has earned her reputation with some bad behavior. We are, therefore, presented with the status quo, so it's unclear why today is different. First, consider getting deeper into why Preston feels such inner struggle. Sure, we can throw a label on it, like imposter syndrome, but this is an ongoing complication. Was she sober for her longest stretch yet before she relapsed the night before? Why this level of self-loathing *today*? The writer could add some urgency to her arrival on-set by having her head to a meeting with the producer and director. She knows she's in bad shape, has been dreading this, and worries she's about to get fired. A concrete reason for her to feel the way she does —paired with some plot momentum and a looming ominous event —would add high stakes, conflict, and tension to the setting flyover. Consider balancing Preston out with a bit of spark, too. Not everyone immediately wants to root for an anti-hero, especially since some of her problems seem self-inflicted. What's an aspirational angle to play up here? Backstage intrigue? A "save the cat" moment? Preston's earnest attempt to turn her life around still managing to slip through her fingers? Let's balance her tortured inner self with something that'll make her a hero worthy of the journey and hint at potential character development.

ACTION

REVISING YOUR OPENING

Revision and self-editing are huge topics in the writing craft world, and there are many guides devoted exclusively to teaching them. Since our focus is on first pages and chapters, I'll keep this section brief and relevant.

Now that you've had a chance to imbibe real work and see my feedback on it, what are your impressions? Did you find any surprising takeaways? Were any of your existing instincts or approaches validated? Have you changed your mind about your opening or a specific craft skill? What might you apply to your own work?

Throughout this guide, I've prepared you for the idea of doing a complete rewrite of your beginning. If you find you don't have to, you're definitely in the minority and can count yourself lucky. It might also be that you haven't yet developed the ability to think critically about your own writing, which is okay.

Revision and self-editing are some of the last skills to fall into place, even in an experienced creator's process. Below, I'll broadly outline what happens once you finish a first draft, then offer some action items as you go back to the page.

Immediate Next Steps

The first thing you must to before your revise your beginning is to finish the manuscript. One of my favorite quotes about drafting and revision is:

"The first draft is just you telling yourself the story."

TERRY PRATCHETT

I'm totally fine with you skipping the opening in your initial drafting process because you're not going to know all of the ingredients yet—and likely won't until you finish *and* revise the entire manuscript at least once. Your theme or the character's arc might shift around the midpoint, and you could find you're bringing your story in for a landing at a very different airport than the one you originally intended to fly into. That's completely normal. Stories evolve all the time, regardless of a writer's intentions or best-laid plans.

Once a draft exists, you'll want to reread the project and see how you perceive it. I often suffer from writing amnesia and forget what I've done the second it leaves my fingertips. The first time you read a manuscript might be a surprise—good, bad, or both. You might please yourself in certain sections, or find yourself disappointed. That's fine. Take it all in and try not to react too much.

After that, I strongly recommend putting the project away for at least two weeks. This gives you the benefit of developing a "new set of eyes" for the work. It's tough to see your storytelling objectively. Time and distance allow you to disengage and become more analytical. Read it again after a break—or once you've begun work on another project, if you can juggle more than one piece of writing simultaneously. What are your impressions now?

Once you feel more confident about the full scope of the manuscript and the meaning you want to leave readers with, you can reverse engineer a much more relevant beginning. Your current opening might be geared toward the theme of finding one's voice. But maybe your protagonist came to you with such a clear and insistent sense of self that this starting point no longer makes sense for their growth arc.

You can still play with this theme if it's relevant—maybe your character has found their voice but is using it without thinking and hurting those closest to them in the opening scene. Or you can scratch your first idea and start over. Show us the protagonist grappling with something that's more in line with who they end up becoming over the course of the story.

Another issue you might face is an opening conflict that's either too on the nose or irrelevant. You had no idea you were going to add a romance subplot to the story until you were compelled to do so. If the opening tension centers on the character bemoaning their love life, that might be too obvious—maybe even verging on philosophizing or throat-clearing. Conversely, you might have a character's monologue about love kicking off a story that no longer has romance at its heart. Neither example scene feels in alignment with the rest of the project. Tune down the thematic element, change the conflict, or go in a different direction altogether.

One very telling—but also extremely vulnerable—exercise would be to give your story opening to someone who doesn't know what the book is about. Have them read it, then ask: "What do you think will happen in this story?"

Listen to their answer and try to divorce your insecurity, nausea, or immediate emotional reaction from the exchange. Did they guess something that actually aligns with the broader narrative? Or are they completely off base? If the latter, that's not on them—it's on you. Something's wrong with the information and action you're presenting in your beginning, or the way you've characterized your protagonist. You're either sending weak or misleading signals. Scrap the first chapter and start again.

Highlighting Your Craft Elements

It might help to go through your first few pages and use different highlighter colors to track theme/premise details, character context, plot/conflict elements, and world/setting information. Is your opening a meditation on your theme? All about character? Moving quickly into tension and plot? Full of setting data?

Your first few pages should be densely highlighted to show what you're choosing to establish, when, and why. Once you see your beginning in another format or coded visually, you might want to make adjustments.

Here are two examples from the Published First Lines chapter with three highlight colors each. With *The God of the Woods* by Liz Moore, I identified elements of Character, Setting, and Action/Conflict:

> *God of the Woods* by Liz Moore
>
> *Louise / August 1975:*
>
> The bed is empty.
>
> Louise, the counselor—twenty-three, short-limbed, rasp-voiced, jolly— stands barefoot on the warm rough planks of the cabin called Balsam and processes the absence of a body in the lower bunk by the door
>
> **Key:**
>
> Character
> Setting
> Action/Conflict

Several craft elements come together in these first two sentences, and readers are immediately grounded in time, scene, and conflict. We even get a pretty comprehensive picture of Louise, the counselor character.

With the opening to *Shred Sisters* by Betsey Lerner, I highlighted elements of Premise/Theme, Voice/Vibe, and Intrigue:

Shred Sisters by Betsy Lerner

Prologue:

Here are the ways I could start this story:

Olivia was breathtaking.

For a long time, I was convinced that she was responsible for everything that went wrong.

No one will love you more or hurt you more than a sister.

Key:

Premise/Theme
Voice/Vibe
Intrigue

Try doing the same with your opening paragraphs and check whether they're in balance. If not, how can you zero in on fewer craft elements to start or sprinkle various pieces of information more evenly? Put these ideas on your self-editing to-do list.

After generating some revision ideas of your own, enlist the help of a trusted third party, whether that's a passionate reader who'll be able to offer a qualified reaction, a writing group or critique partner, or a paid freelance editor. (More on this in the following section.)

Once you have notes, it's time to parse through them and figure out a revision plan. Which feedback do you resonate with? Why might you feel drawn to one note over another? Which changes will you actually enact? What are you most excited to try?

Revision is an iterative process, and there is no "correct" number of times you'll find yourself going back over the project. You might try ironing out the plot with one pass, then focus on character. Only once the bigger structural pieces are in place and unlikely to change, should you turn your attention to the sentence-level writing. Sometimes a revision of the beginning will mean you'll have to make adjustments downstream. Be prepared.

After some revision, writers run up against the very common question of "How do I know when it's done?" Sometimes, a project feels "done" when you can't stand to look at it again, but this is an emotional reaction, rather than a craft-based consideration.

Oftentimes, it's actually approaching done when several trusted readers or paid editorial professionals have chimed in with notes which seem doable, rather than big-picture changes which seem impossible to pull off.

To test whether you're truly feeling finished (instead of simply running out of ideas), put the project away and return to it with fresh eyes one last time, if possible. Only then might you consider going on submission.

The Role of Third-Party Feedback

If you read my author bio, you might've noticed that I provide paid editorial services. However, please know that I'm not making a sneaky sales pitch when I tell you to get third-party feedback. Yes, I may be biased, but I make this recommendation in good faith because it's that important.

Basically, writers are notorious for taking it easy on themselves and for developing emotional attachments to their creative work. I get it. It's only natural to be invested in your own creation. However, this level of investment tends to make all of us slightly blind. It also makes us take it easy on ourselves during self-editing. I'm always surprised by how reluctant writers are to do a blank-page revision and start from scratch with a scene, chapter, or act. (Or the whole enchilada!)

I get it—those words already exist! They were hard-won! But they might not be the right words or story ingredients, and it's okay to be open-minded about making big changes. After all, "revision" means "to see again," and not "retain as much material as possible and move commas around." The bigger the risk you take in truly re-envisioning your manuscript, the bigger the potential reward.

Getting another person's advice is going to be instrumental in correcting for any unintended biases or blind spots you might have. Of course, writing notes are only as good as the person giving them, which is why I always recommend finding a critique partner who's experienced in your genre and category, or at least a non-writer who's very well read in the same. Matching with the right writing partner can be time-consuming, as it's often a process of trial and error. Hiring someone is going to raise your odds of getting relevant and actionable feedback, but it can be expensive. All of these options are available to you, and I have a list of resources and ideas for finding critique partners and editing professionals in Appendix A.

The best kind of feedback is actionable and resonates with your powerful existing intuition. "It's great!" from an unqualified reader —or one who's related to you and therefore incentivized to be kind —might feel good at first, but it won't challenge you. Similarly, "This sucks!" doesn't give you much to work with and might crush your spirit, to boot. If a reader is doing their job and expressing *why* they're giving a piece of advice, you'll be able to consider the note and whether to take action.

That's right—not every writing critique requires obedience. I always tell my clients to take the wisdom and leave the rest. Measure the feedback against your own intentions, impressions, and goals. This is a skill honed over time. At first, you might find most critiques hard to take. If you catch yourself rejecting every single note, and if every critique partner or editor you seek out is an idiot who doesn't understand your genius, you might need a reality check. As you gain experience, you'll be better able to curate the offered ideas and make intentional changes.

There are many ways to adjust a piece of writing to achieve a certain effect, and your ideas—as the project's creator—are going to be the most relevant. You know your story best and will find the right solution to any problem. My goal in offering notes is to communicate my read on the project and explain why I'm giving a certain piece of feedback. Very rarely do I offer an explicit prescriptive idea as a fix. It's the writer's job to decide if and how to implement revision. All I can do is show them how I'm perceiving their work. If someone else tells you *exactly what to do*, take it with a grain of salt. But if they identify an issue and you can see the logic behind the note, put your thinking cap on.

Conference Polish Syndrome

A word of warning about revising your story beginning—and *only* your story beginning. I call it Conference Polish Syndrome because writers often go to conferences, get round after round of feedback on their opening pages, revise the heck out of them … and the manuscript's quality noticeably falls off a sharp cliff after page 11. This is a very real issue.

I get it. Revision is hard to do well, and it's grueling to pull off consistently for 300 pages. Especially since you know the beginning is incredibly important. It's only natural to devote the most focus and energy there. It's also natural to get impatient when revising for the fifth time or when you find yourself in the home stretch of a revision. Thoughts like, "They're agents and editors. Won't they, you know, *edit* this for me?" creep in. You're tempted to let the project ride and convince yourself those issues niggling in the back of your mind aren't really all that bad.

And maybe it *is* good enough, and the things you're worried about *aren't* actually problems. Understandably, you want to showcase that you *can* write like hell by pulling out all the stops with your opening. You assume you'll get the gatekeeper on the hook and make your case for revising the rest of the manuscript *together*. Preferably after a contract and paycheck.

Well, tough stuff. This isn't generally how it works. An agent or publisher won't sign you on the strength of ten pages, no matter how amazing they are. Novels and even memoirs (which used to sell on a proposal and handful of sample chapters) sell as complete manuscripts these days. The reason is simple: Gatekeepers want concrete proof that you can craft a narrative, execute a character arc, weave plots and subplots together, follow a structure, and bring the whole thing to a satisfying resolution.

In general, you only get one shot at submitting your manuscript (well, okay, maybe two shots at most, per the discussion of resubmission in my book, *Irresistible Query Letters: 40+ Real World*

Query Letters With Literary Agent Feedback). You want to put your strongest, most polished, most fully realized foot forward. A consistently stellar submission will make you look dedicated as a writer and offer gatekeepers an easy and enjoyable reading experience. It's rare to find one in the slush pile.

Patiently revising page by page from the beginning to the bitter end is the best thing you can do to raise your chances of an offer of representation or a publishing contract. (You'll likely do more editing with the literary agent and acquisitions editor once the book sells. It's only over when the last round of copy edits is turned in.) The worst thing you can do for your odds is to spend all of your revision energy on the first ten pages, then phone in the rest.

Does this suck? Yes. Does this mean you could be sinking months or years into writing and revising a manuscript that ends up going nowhere, even if it represents your best effort at the time? Also yes. Why can't you just squeak by on your good looks, beautiful brains, and first ten pages? Because one of the inherent parts of getting a book deal is that *it's hard*. You can always publish independently if you don't want anyone else's stamp of approval. But there, you're still competing for reader eyeballs and dollars against all the other people who've recently self-published. Quality and the ability to tell a good story are a requirement in the indie space as well.

The product—a published book—shouldn't be your ultimate goal, anyway. If you're only focused on the output of your efforts and hate the craft, revision, learning, and growth involved in being a writer, you're going to have a bad time. Writing and storytelling are incredibly labor-intensive. The potential reward is the privilege of publishing a book every year (if you're very lucky to get on this kind of schedule with a dedicated house or two), or, more likely, a book every few years, as you'll probably still be working a day job and juggling other responsibilities. This kind of rhythm takes time and, yes, hard work to establish.

The art and craft of writing and revision are daily practices. They must be their own reward or you won't be happy with the occasional contract, good review, or in-person appearance. The sweaty reality of being a writer—both the good and the bad of it—should be the stuff that gasses up your tank. But if you want it enough, you're on the right track by investing in your skills and your creative self.

CONCLUSION

The first pages of your story aren't just the beginning of the fiction or memoir journey your characters take. They're also the opening play you'll make to introduce yourself and your writing to literary agents, acquisition editors, and, eventually, readers. In this competitive modern publishing landscape, where there are millions of options for entertainment and escape, you have to grab your opportunity to win over gatekeepers and audiences. This is why first pages matter.

Now that you know what's expected and what your marching orders are, remember that you'll likely revise your beginning many times. Sometimes a great new strategy will come to you easily. Other times, you'll need to wait until a brainstorm strikes. Be ready to listen to your intuition, leverage feedback, and do the hard work of revision. Not only will you be homing in on the project at hand, you'll be learning about and developing your own signature style as a creative writer. Storytelling is a calling for many people, and it all starts with your first line.

I'm honored to have played a small supporting role in your mission to learn, grow, and challenge yourself. There's nothing I love more than a dedicated writer with high standards and the desire to continually level up. I hope I've demystified the subject of novel and memoir beginnings for you, and that, when you get back to the page, you're braver and more confident than ever. Keep reading, keep inspiring yourself with successful story openings from published and unpublished works, and keep putting your creativity out there. By writing compelling first pages, you are also writing the beginning of your own creative journey. Here's to a good story ... opening.

APPENDIX A

Articles and resources mentioned or alluded to in this guide are collected below.

Craft Articles

- "Emotional Writing: How to Write Feelings": https://kidlit. com/emotional-writing/
- "Describing Emotions in Writing": https://kidlit.com/ describing-emotions-in-writing/
- "Writing Character Growth: Characters in Denial": https:// kidlit.com/character-growth/
- "Using the Rhetorical Question in Fiction Writing": https:// kidlit.com/using-the-rhetorical-question-in-fiction-writing/
- "The Inciting Incident and Character Buy-In": https:// kidlit.com/inciting-incident/
- "Writing Character Description in First Person POV": https://kidlit.com/third-person-style-narration-in-first-person/
- "Writing Dialogue in Fiction: The Blurt": https://kidlit. com/writing-dialogue-in-fiction/

- "Directing Reader Attention with Descriptive Prose": https://kidlit.com/descriptive-prose/
- "How to Start a Chapter: Ground the Reader": https://kidlit.com/how-to-start-a-chapter/
- "Expository Dialogue": https://kidlit.com/obvious-telling-in-dialogue/
- "Dangling Modifiers and How to Correct Them": https://bit.ly/dangling-modifier
- "Redundant Writing and the Law of Diminishing Returns": https://kidlit.com/the-law-of-diminishing-returns/
- Story Mastermind Novel Outline Framework: https://bit.ly/novel-outline

Query and Submission Resources

- "Comp Titles in a Query and Other Questions About Book Comps": https://kidlit.com/comp-titles-in-a-query-book-comps
- "Finding Comp Titles": https://goodstorycompany.com/blog/finding-comp-titles
- Manuscript Wish List: https://manuscriptwishlist.com
- Association of American Literary Agents: https://aalitagents.org
- Literary Rambles: https://literaryrambles.com
- Agent Query: https://agentquery.com
- Writer's Digest: https://writersdigest.com
- Duotrope: https://duotrope.com
- Publishers Marketplace: https://publishersmarketplace.com
- ChillSubs: https://chillsubs.com
- Submission Tracker Spreadsheet: https://bit.ly/subspreadsheet (Go to "File" and then "Make a copy …" to repurpose it for yourself on your own Google Drive.)

Resources for Finding Editors and Other Collaborators

- "Finding Critique Partners": https://www.goodstorycompany.com/blog/critique-partners
- "How to be a Good Critique Partner": https://www.goodstorycompany.com/blog/how-to-be-a-good-critique-partner
- Reedsy: https://reedsy.com
- Upwork: https://www.upwork.com/
- Fiverr: https://www.fiverr.com/
- Good Story Editing: https://goodstoryediting.com
- Mary Kole Editorial: https://marykole.com

RESOURCES FOR WRITERS

I've spent almost two decades creating educational materials for writers and designing courses, books, and services focused on craft and industry topics. Please check out my resources and offerings.

Webinars

I regularly teach free webinars about query letters, character, interiority, plot, and first pages. Some webinars offer the opportunity for live feedback. Please check out a current list of my upcoming presentations and workshops here:

https://goodstorycompany.com/workshops

I can also Zoom in to your critique group or design a bespoke talk for a writing retreat or conference on any number of industry and craft subjects.

Editorial Services, Ghostwriting, and Writing Workshops

If you enjoyed this book, consider getting personalized one-on-one feedback from me. My specialty is deep developmental editing with a character focus. Alternatively, I am happy to step in as a discreet ghostwriter or offer direct ghost revision to execute changes directly. We can also work together in a small group writing workshop intensive setting.

Developmental Editing Services:

https://marykole.com

Ghost Revision and Ghostwriting Services:

https://manuscriptstudio.com

Story Mastermind Small Group Writing Workshops:

https://storymastermind.com

Free Story Mastermind Outline Framework:

https://bit.ly/novel-outline

Courses

It is my (perhaps manic) goal to create as many writing resources in as many formats as possible. I hope you find these courses useful. I'm always grateful when a written or recorded version of me can be of service.

Writing Mastery Academy Character Class:

With Jessica Brody, of *Save the Cat Writes a Novel* fame!

https://www.writingmastery.com

Writing Blueprints Submission Resource:

If a deep dive into the submission process sounds helpful, this self-paced course contains over ten hours of instruction. You'll get access to agent interviews, over thirty handouts, and a comprehensive step-by-step submission guide.

https://bit.ly/kolesub

LinkedIn Learning:

My popular Crafting Dynamic Characters class is also available on this platform.

https://www.linkedin.com/learning/crafting-dynamic-characters/

Udemy:

These budget-friendly classes cover assorted writing and publishing topics in an easy-to-digest format.

https://www.udemy.com/user/mary-kole/

Good Story Company

In 2019, I founded Good Story Company as an umbrella brand so my amazing team and I could collaborate in the service of writing and writers. GSC is where you'll find our most comprehensive library of resources and services. You can also sign up for our email newsletter and follow us on social media to get our most current updates.

Good Story Company:

https://goodstorycompany.com

Good Story Podcast:

https://goodstorypodcast.com

Good Story YouTube Channel:

https://youtube.com/goodstory

Writing Craft Workshop Membership:

https://goodstorycompany.com/membership

Good Story Marketing:

https://goodstorycompany.com/marketing

Workshops and Events:

https://goodstorycompany.com/workshops

The Insider's Guide to Publishing Your Book Substack:

https://goodstoryco.substack.com/

WAIT! BEFORE YOU GO!

If you enjoyed this book, there are **three small things** you can do to make a big difference to me and Good Story Company. Thank you so much for your time, kind attention, and consideration!

Subscribe to Our Newsletter

Our respectful, short, and non-spammy newsletter features all of our latest and greatest free resources, workshops, events, and critique opportunities. Go here to sign up:

https://bit.ly/hellogsc

Leave an Honest Review

Please also consider leaving a review for this title with your retailer of choice, as well as Goodreads. I love getting feedback of my own, and testimonials help our discoverability and marketing efforts, allowing us to reach more writers.

Reach Out

Finally, I'd love to hear your experience and celebrate your accomplishments. If you run into some trouble in the writing and publishing worlds, don't be a stranger, either. Drop me a line:

mary@goodstorycompany.com

ACKNOWLEDGMENTS

With this book, I followed the same model as I did in *Irresistible Query Letters: 40+ Real World Query Letters With Literary Agent Feedback*, which features over forty real-life queries submitted by writers. It took a while, but I finally gave *Query Letters* a sibling. Together, they cover the two most crucial components of a creative writer's submission package.

This guide literally wouldn't have been possible without the twenty-six writers who contributed to the Workshop (some credited, some using a pen name, some anonymous). I'm so grateful to each and every one of you for courageously and selflessly sharing your creative work, first with me, and now with the larger community. It's so rare to get a glimpse of works-in-progress at various stages, at least in any kind of quantity. You might see your critique partner's pages or join a class or forum, but that's about it. I loved editing these samples and I really hope seeing the drafts and feedback is helpful not only to the individuals being workshopped but to anyone peeking in.

As always, my team at Good Story Company allows me to do the work I love. Thank you Kristen Overman, Amy Wilson, Rhiannon Richardson, Jenna Van Rooy, Kaylee Pereyra, and Kate London. Thank you also to the editorial clients who've trusted me over the years.

Love, love, love to John Cusick, Julie Murphy, my Westie Besties, Lauren Burris and Scott Marasigan, Todd, Theo, Finn, Ella, Gertie, Olive, and Luna.

ALSO BY MARY KOLE

Writing Irresistible Kidlit: The Ultimate Guide to Crafting Fiction for Young Adult and Middle Grade Readers

———

Writing Irresistible Picture Books: Insider Insights Into Crafting Compelling Modern Stories for Young Readers

Writing Irresistible Picture Books Workbook

———

Irresistible Query Letters: 40+ Real World Query Letters With Literary Agent Feedback

Irresistible Query Letters Workbook

———

How to Write a Book Now: Craft Concepts, Mindset Shifts, and Encouragement to Inspire Your Creative Writing

———

Writing Interiority: Crafting Irresistible Characters

Writing Interiority Workbook

———

Writing Irresistible First Pages: How to Craft Compelling Story Openings That Will Hook Gatekeepers and Readers

www.ingramcontent.com/pod-product-compliance
Lightning Source LLC
Chambersburg PA
CBHW062130040426
42335CB00039B/1873